sicilian grand prix attack

by James Plaskett

EVERYMAN CHESS

Published by Everyman Publishers plc London

First published in 2000 by Gloucester Publishers plc, (formerly Everyman Publishers plc), Northburgh House, 10 Northburgh Street, London, EC1V 0AT

British Library Cataloguing-in-Publication Data
A catalogue record for this book is available from the British Library.

ISBN 1 85744 291 1
ISBN 13: 978 1 85744 291 5

Distributed in North America by The Globe Pequot Press, P.O Box 480, 246 Goose Lane, Guilford, CT 06437-0480.

All other sales enquiries should be directed to Gloucester Publishers plc, Northburgh House, 10 Northburgh Street, London, EC1V 0AT
tel: 020 7253 7887 fax: 020 7490 3708
email: info@everymanchess.com
website: www.everymanchess.com

EVERYMAN CHESS SERIES (formerly Cadogan Chess)

Chief Advisor: Garry Kasparov
Commissioning Editor: Byron Jacobs
General Editor: John Emms

Typeset and edited by First Rank Publishing, Brighton.
Production by Navigator Guides.
Cover Design by Horacio Monteverde.

Printed and bound in the UK

CONTENTS

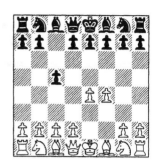

1 e4 c5

BIBLIOGRAPHY

Books
The Grand Prix Attack, Gary Lane (Batsford 1997)
Beating the Anti-Sicilians, Joe Gallagher (Batsford 1994)
Encyclopaedia of Chess Openings Volume B (Sahovski Informator 1997)
Nunn's Chess Openings, John Nunn, Graham Burgess, John Emms and Joe Gallagher (Everyman 1999)

Periodicals
Informator
New in Chess Yearbook
British Chess Magazine
CHESS Monthly

INTRODUCTION

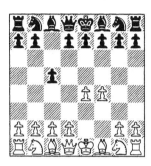

The idea of meeting the Sicilian with an early f2-f4 has acquired various names over the years including the Larsen-Santasiere and the Grand Prix Attack. Statistically it remains one of the most successful methods of combating the Sicilian, other than the main lines involving d2-d4 and ♘xd4, with many of the world's top players prepared to try it out.

This book is concerned with set-ups where White develops his king's bishop in a way other than on g2 because that development will most probably take us into a standard Closed Sicilian formation. Broadly speaking when White plays ♗c4 it is more likely to lead to middlegames where he engages in attack than in those which derive from his playing ♗b5.

1 e4 c5 2 f4 is a natural continuation and has the advantage of avoiding the thickets of main line Sicilian theory. However, unlike some theory avoidance systems it is actually quite a good move! Early on White already signals that he has kingside aspirations, and you will be seeing many examples of attacks against the black king amongst these pages.

Move Orders
In this book we will examine two differents ways by which White attempts to implement an f2-f4 strategy. He can push forward with 2 f4, or he can first develop with 2 ♘c3, intending to continue with 3 f4 next move. Each method has its advantages and disadvantages and a knowledge of these will be a useful aid to understanding the following material.

As White it is a tricky decision as to whether you should start off with 2 f4 or 2 ♘c3 and your choice may well depend on which systems you feel most comfortable with, or which move orders are most likely to confuse your opponent. Since Black has, principally, two main methods of countering the Grand Prix Attack – systems with ...g7-g6 and systems with ...e7-e6 and ...d7-d5 – we will consider each in turn.

Fianchetto Systems against 2 f4
Many Black players meet all sorts of Closed Sicilian systems with an automatic fianchetto of the king's bishop. If White opens 1 e4 c5 2 f4 and Black is

determined upon a fianchetto then he can either play 2...g6 or 2...♘c6 3 ♘f3 g6. If he plays 2...g6 then White can of course play 3 ♘f3 but after 3...♗g7 he has little better then 4 ♘c3, which rather defeats the object of avoiding 2 ♘c3 in the first place. So White may well opt for 3 d4!? – a complex move which is examined in detail in Chapter 8. If Black is concerned about this then he may choose instead 2 f4 ♘c6 3 ♘f3 g6, but now White can play 4 ♗b5 and there is no simple way to meet the threat of capturing on c6.

Fianchetto Systems against 2 ♘c3

After 1 e4 c5 2 ♘c3 whether Black fianchettoes immediately or not is of little consequence. The most common sequence is 2...♘c6 3 f4 g6 4 ♘f3 ♗g7. However, if Black tries to be subtle and play 2...g6 3 f4 ♗g7 he does not really get anywhere after 4 ♘f3 as he now has little better than 4...♘c6. For example, 4...e6 is well met by 5 d4 while 4...d6 allows both 5 ♗c4 and 5 ♗b5+. However, the sequence 1 e4 c5 2 ♘c3 ♘c6 3 f4 g6 4 ♘f3 ♗g7 is not a problem for Black. 5 ♗c4 is well met by 5...e6 (see Chapter 2), while 5 ♗b5 can be countered by 5...♘d4 (see Chapter 1). This last variation shows why White does not really want his knight on c3. After 6 ♘xd4 cxd4, he has to waste time moving his knight again. Compare this with 1 e4 c5 2 f4 ♘c6 3 ♘f3 ♗g7 4 ♗b5. Now 4...♘d4 lacks some point as 5 ♘xd4 cxd4 does not hit a white knight on c3.

Other Systems against 2 f4

When the Grand Prix Attack was being moulded into a potent weapon in the late 70s and early 80s, the most popular way to start out was with 2 f4. However, over a period of time, the gambit lines with 2...d5 3 exd5 ♘f6 (see Chapter 5) were shown to be, at the very least, fine for Black. Even if Black is loathe to sacrifice a pawn in such a fashion then the simple continuation 2...e6 3 ♘f3 d5 leaves Black, theoretically at least, with a perfectly reasonable game. White's only real opportunity to maintain a complex position without being worse is to meet 2...d5 with 3 ♘c3 (see Chapter 7). All in all 2...d5 is a nuisance for 2 f4 players.

Other Systems against 2 ♘c3

If Black is not going to meet the Grand Prix Attack with a fianchetto, then 2 ♘c3 has a lot going for it. It is possible for Black to play 2...e6, intending the simple equalising manoeuvre with ...d7-d5, but many Black players would be reluctant to do so. The reason is that White might suddenly change tack after 2 ♘c3 e6 and play 3 ♘f3 or 3 ♘ge2, intending to continue with 4 d4, steering the game into an Open Sicilian where Black is committed to ...e7-e6. For players specialising in, say, the Scheveningen or Taimanov this would not be a problem, but Najdorf or Dragon experts may well find themselves in unfamiliar surroundings if they continue along Open Sicilian lines. White's potential switch with 3 ♘ge2 is also an occasional deterrent to 2...♘c6. For example, Najdorf players who lack another string to their bow pretty much have to play 2...d6 in reply to 2 ♘c3 and this usually helps White. The point is that ...d7-d5 is often the break Black is angling for and, having already gone ...d7-d6, he is losing time.

CHAPTER ONE

1 e4 c5 2 ♘c3 ♘c6 3 f4 g6 4 ♘f3 ♗g7 5 ♗b5

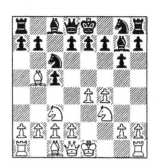

1 e4 c5 2 ♘c3 ♘c6 3 f4 g6 4 ♘f3 ♗g7 5 ♗b5

In this chapter we deal with lines in which Black fianchettoes and White places his bishop on b5. The b5-square is very probably the best square for the bishop if White does not fianchetto. We shall be seeing ♗c4 set-ups running into some difficulties in the next chapter, but the positional sense of doubling Black's c-pawns cannot be argued with.

Games 1-3 see Black allowing the doubling of the c-pawns, while Games 4-6 concentrate on the sequence 5...♘d4 6 0-0 ♘xb5. Games 7 witnesses Polagr trying the unusual 6 ♗d3. Another way for Black to avoid doubled pawns is to arrange to meet ♗b5 with ...♗d7 and we see examples of this plan in Games 8-11.

Game 1
Plaskett-J.Polgar
Hastings 1988

1 e4 c5 2 ♘c3 ♘c6 3 f4 g6 4 ♘f3 ♗g7 5 ♗b5 e6?!

Certainly unwise. 5...d6 also allows

White the opportunity to take on c6 (see Games 2 and 3) so Black's most well regarded move is 5...♘d4, as in Games 4-7. One relatively unexplored alternative that will suit Dragon players is 5...♘a5!?, when after 6 d4 a6 7 ♗e2 cxd4 8 ♘xd4 d6 9 ♗e3 ♘f6 10 0-0 0-0 Black had reached a very satisfactory Classical Dragon-type position in Pinto-Gufeld, US open 1998.

6 ♗xc6! bxc6

The alternative recapture 6...dxc6 was tried in Moutosis-Erdogan, Turkey 1992, but White was better after 7 ♕e2 ♘e7 8 0-0 0-0 9 d3 b6 10 ♘d1 ♗a6 11 ♘f2.

7 e5!

The d6-square looks inviting already. Black committed the same structural lapse in Sveshnikov-Remis, Oviedo (rapidplay) 1992, where White had played f2-f4 at move two and substituted 0-0 for ♘c3. That game went 7 c4!? ♘e7 8 d3 0-0 9 ♘c3 d5 10 ♕e2 ♖b8 11 ♕f2 when Black had a grotty position.

7...d5

Ridding herself of that weakness but isolating the twin c-pawns.

8 exd6

In Hebbinghaus-Kraenzle, German Bundesliga 1995, White passed over this golden opportunity and played 8 d3?, going on to only draw the game. Serves him right.

8...♛xd6 9 d3 ♞f6

Black attempted to offload the weakling in Honfi-Czebe, Budapest 1995, with 9...c4. However, Honfi kept the bishops quiet with 10 d4 and held a big strategical superiority after 10...♞e7 11 ♛e2 0-0 12 ♞e4 ♛d5 13 c3.

10 0-0 ♝a6

11 b3 0-0 12 ♛e1

Structurally Black is up the creek and there is no natural strategy for her to pursue (note the moribund bishop on a6). White has only to stop any tactical tricks to ensure victory.

12...♞d5 13 ♝d2 ♜ad8 14 ♞e4 ♛c7 15 ♞e5 ♝b7

On 15...♝xe5 16 fxe5 ♛xe5? 17 ♞f6+ wins.

16 ♛f2 f6 17 ♞c4 e5

17...f5 does not help either because of 18 ♞xc5 ♝xa1 19 ♞xe6 and 20 ♞xd8.

18 fxe5 fxe5 19 ♛xc5

Now the black cause has become hopeless.

19...♛d7 20 ♝g5 ♜b8 21 ♛xa7 ♞f4 22 ♛c5 ♛f5 23 ♞e3 ♛d7 24 g3 h6 25 gxf4 hxg5 26 fxg5 1-0

Game 2
Hebden-Fedorowicz
Lewisham 1981

---

1 e4 c5 2 ♞c3 ♞c6 3 f4 g6 4 ♞f3 ♝g7 5 ♝b5 d6 6 ♝xc6+ bxc6 7 d3

The actual move order of the game was 2 f4 ♞c6 3 ♞f3 g6 4 ♝b5 ♝g7 5 ♝xc6 bxc6 6 d3 d6 7 ♞c3.

7...♞h6

7...♞f6 is probably a better move and would take us into the next example.

8 0-0 f5

Black must blockade on the kingside or he is in danger of being overrun, e.g. 8...0-0 9 0-0 ♝g4?! 10 f5 ♝xf3 11 ♜xf3 e6 12 f6 and White picked up a piece in Weeramantry-Bolden, US open 1994.

9 ♛e1 0-0 10 e5!

see following diagram

10...♛c7 11 ♛g3 ♜b8 12 ♜e1 ♞f7 13 b3 ♞d8 14 ♞a4! ♞e6

Transferring the knight to its most active place, an idea we shall see again later. But the truth is that in this structure

Black's bishops have no scope and he is stuck for anything to do.

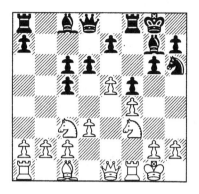

15 ♗b2 d5?! 16 c4!

The Nimzowitschian clamp goes up and the c5-pawn is targeted.

16...♖d8 17 ♖ad1 ♗a6 18 ♗c1 ♕a5 19 ♗d2 ♕c7 20 ♕f2

20 ♘g5 was also crushing as it removes the c-pawn's defender.

20...d4 21 ♕h4 ♗f8 22 h3 ♕d7

He can only wait for the end.

23 ♗a5 ♖dc8 24 ♘g5 1-0

> ### Game 3
> ## Plaskett-Tiviakov
> *Dhaka 1997*

1 e4 c5 2 ♘c3 ♘c6 3 ♗b5 g6

Afterwards Sergei Tiviakov stated that he already disliked this move. 3...♘d4 is the standard response.

4 ♗xc6 bxc6 5 f4 ♗g7 6 ♘f3 ♘f6 7 d3 d6

Through an unusual move order we have reached a position that would usually arise after 2 ♘c3 ♘c6 3 f4 g6 4 ♘f3 ♗g7 5 ♗b5 d6 6 ♗xc6+ bxc6 7 d3 ♘f6.

8 0-0 0-0 9 ♕e1 ♘e8

A standard re-routing. A few yards away Iudalchev-Nguyen Anh Dung was going 9...♖b8 10 b3 ♘e8 11 ♗d2 ♘c7 12 ♕h4 ♘b5 13 e5! ♘d4 14 ♘xd4 cxd4 15 ♘e4 and White went on to win.

10 ♗d2

I was unsure just where I wanted my pieces, so for the time being I carried on developing.

10...f5

The immediate 10...♘e6 invites f4-f5 in reply.

11 e5 ♘c7

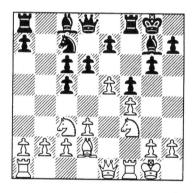

Over dinner that same evening Grandmasters Tiviakov and Malisauskas stated that Black is strategically lost here! My reluctance to accept that stemmed partly from comparisons with lines of the English Opening where Black plays ...e7-e5, ...♗b4 and ...♗x(♘)c3. If those are alright for White then why should Black be in trouble here? Still, if we look at how stymied Fedorowicz became in the last game then it is clear that we are dealing with a very similar structure; the bishop pair have nothing to do. Tiviakov proposed 12 ♘a4!? and then to clamp up the queenside with stuff like c2-c4, b2-b3 and ♗a5. Although this is not as bad for Black as when he has played ...d6-d5, after which the c5-pawn falls off, it is still pretty dismal.

12 ♕e2?!

An inaccuracy prompted by a wrong assessment of the position which we will reach at move 17. Instead Hodgson-De Firmian, Wijk aan Zee 1986, went 12 ♕h4 ♘e6 13 ♖ae1 ♘d4 14 ♘xd4 cxd4 15 exd6 exd6 16 ♕xd8 ♖xd8 17 ♘a4 ♔f7 when Black had done pretty well for himself, but he still went on to lose. Tiviakov now grabs his chance to get some play.

12...♘e6 13 ♖ae1 c4!

Of course Black does not hesitate to get this one in.

14 d4

There are some tricks White can look at after 14 dxc4 ♕b6+ 15 ♔h1 ♕xb2 16 ♖b1 ♕a3 17 ♖b3 ♕a5 but they do not favour him.

14...d5 15 ♘a4 ♗a6

Black hastens to contest the queenside.

16 ♘c5 ♘xc5 17 dxc5 d4

If not this then 18 ♗c3 will establish a winning bind.

18 c3 d3 19 ♕f2

It emerged in the post-mortem that each side thought that he had a strategically won game here! This is very unusual occurrence in a game between grandmas-

ters. Later we concluded that we were both wrong.

19...♖b8 20 ♗e3 e6 21 ♖d1 ♕d5 22 h3 ♖f7 23 ♖d2 ♗f8 24 ♔h2 ♖b5

Here I started to crack up as I saw that it is certainly not just a case of White opening the game up on the kingside to reveal that Black's awful light-squared bishop renders him in effect a piece down.

25 ♘d4?

We analysed 25 ♘g5! as the best. Any ...h7-h6 will leave the black king position severely weakened after a later g2-g4 advance and meantime the loss of the c5-pawn is not so serious. Indeed, for the moment it would not be en prise since the e6-pawn hangs.

25...♖a5!? 26 b3 ♗xc5!? 27 bxc4

Time pressure did not help either. White's position rapidly deteriorates, but I spotted a trick.

27...♗xc4 28 ♖b1 ♖xa2?

Falling for it!

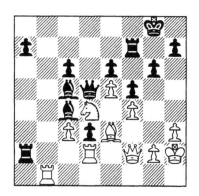

29 ♘xe6! ♖xd2 30 ♗xd2??

Crazy! When taking on c4 I had seen that here I have 30 ♗xc5!, but I then persuaded myself not to play it in the belief that the text could prove better still! After 30 ♗xc5! best play would be

30...♗b5! 31 ♕xd2 ♕xe6 32 ♕e3 with White retaining good compensation for a pawn. 30...♕xg2+? is not so good for Black because after 31 ♔xg2 ♖xf2+ 32 ♔xf2 ♗xe6 33 ♔e3 ♗c4 34 ♔d4 and 35 c4 the d-pawn falls.

30...♖b7!

Cooking White's goose.

31 ♘xc5 ♖xb1 32 ♗e3 d2 0-1

| *Game 4* |
| **Hodgson-Rowson** |
| *Rotherham (2nd match game) 1997* |

1 e4 c5 2 f4 g6 3 ♘f3 ♗g7 4 ♘c3 ♘c6 5 ♗b5 ♘d4

This move, avoiding doubled pawns, looks like the smartest idea, and the theoretical status of Black's position here is very good. The three previous games ought to have communicated what can befall Black if his opponent gets in ♗xc6.

6 0-0

After 6 ♗a4 ♕a5 7 ♗b3 b5 or 6 ♘xd4 cxd4 7 ♘e2 ♕b6 8 ♗d3 d5! 9 e5 f6! White is struggling to even equalise. However, 6 a4!? has been tried by Michael Adams (among others). Black normally plays 6...e6 (there is nothing wrong with 6...♘xb5 7 axb5 d6 8 0-0 ♘f6 either) and then:

a) 7 0-0 ♘e7 8 e5 (if White intends to play this way then the immediate 7 e5 was surely preferable) 8...a6 9 ♗c4 (after 9 ♗d3 ♘xf3+ 10 ♕xf3 d5! White was all tangled up in Adams-Morovic, Las Palmas 1993) 9...d5 10 exd6 and now both 10...♕xd6 and 10...♘ef5 followed by ...♘xd6 are perfectly satisfactory for Black.

b) 7 e5!? a6 8 ♗c4 d5 9 exd6 ♕xd6 10

d3 ♘e7 11 ♘e4 ♕c7 12 c3 with a complicated game in prospect in Ekebjaerg-Jezek, correspondence 1992-94.

For 6 ♗d3 see Game 7.

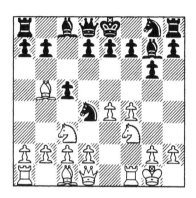

6...♘xb5

After 6...a6 7 ♗d3 White has a superior version of Game 7 in which Black has expended a tempo on the not terribly useful ...a7-a6. However, Black still managed to equalise in Adams-Anand, Groningen 1997, after 7...d6 8 ♘xd4 cxd4 9 ♘e2 ♘f6 10 ♔h1 (10 c3 dxc3 11 bxc3 0-0 12 ♗c2 b5 is also nothing for White) 10...♘d7 11 b4 0-0 12 ♗b2 ♕b6.

7 ♘xb5 d5

The most critical move. The quieter 7...d6 is the subject of the next two main games.

8 e5!?

White hopes to suppress the bishop pair. This looks like a better try for the advantage than 8 exd5 a6 9 ♘c3 ♘f6 where the influence of his fianchettoed bishop is of some significance for Black, e.g. 10 d4 c4! (10...♘xd5 11 dxc5! ♘xc3 12 ♕xd8+ ♔xd8 13 bxc3 ♗xc3 14 ♖b1 offers White good attacking chances in the endgame) 11 ♘e5 ♘d5 12 ♕f3 e6! with an unclear position in Hodgson-Rowson Rotherham (4th match game)

1997. 8 d3 has also been tried but Black ought not to lose sleep over it, e.g. 8...♗d7 9 ♘c3 ♗xc3 10 dxc3 dxe4 11 dxe4 ♗b5 12 ♕xd8+ ♖xd8 13 ♖e1 ♘f6 with a promising ending for Black in H.Hunt-Rowson, Varsity match 1999.

8...a6

Both 8...d4!? and 8...b6!? are also worth exploring for Black.

9 ♘c3 ♗g4

Here too 9...d4 is playable, e.g. 10 ♘e4 ♕d5 11 d3 ♘h6 12 ♕e1 0-0 13 a4, as in Reinderman-Alterman, Wijk aan Zee 1998, and now Alterman recommends 13...a5 with equality.

10 d4 cxd4

In Hebden-Koshy, Dhaka 1995, Black tried 10...c4?!, but after 11 b3! ♖c8 12 ♘a4 White was able to make use of his lead in development.

11 ♕xd4 e6 12 ♕b4!? ♗xf3?!

In O.Jackson-Gallagher, British Championship, Scarborough 1999, Black improved with 12...b5!, when after 13 ♗e3 ♗f8 14 ♗c5 ♗xc5 15 ♕xc5 ♖c8 16 ♕a7 ♖a8 Black had equalised.

13 ♖xf3 ♕e7?

13...b5 was still playable, though not quite as good as on the previous move.

14 ♕a4+ ♕d7 15 ♕xd7+ ♔xd7

This all looks safe enough, but Hodgson whips up an attack from nowhere.

16 ♘a4! ♖b8 17 ♗e3 ♘e7 18 ♗a7!

This is remarkably hard to counter.

18...♖be8 19 ♖b3 b5

Or 19...♔c8 20 ♘c5 b5 21 a4 and it all falls down.

20 ♘c5+ ♔c8 21 ♖a3

And clearly Black is quite lost.

21...g5 22 ♖xa6 gxf4 23 a4 bxa4 24 ♘d3 ♔b7 25 ♖1xa4 ♖a8 26 ♖d6 ♘f5 27 ♘c5+ ♔c7 28 ♗b6+ ♔b8 29 ♖xa8+ ♔xa8 30 ♖d7 ♔b8 31 ♖c7 1-0

It is mate in two.

Game 5
Hebden-Ftacnik
Hastings 1983/84

---

1 e4 c5 2 f4 g6 3 ♘f3 ♗g7 4 ♘c3 ♘c6 5 ♗b5 ♘d4 6 0-0 ♘xb5 7 ♘xb5 d6

This move indicates that Black is planning a quieter treatment than 7...d5. Black aims to gradually make something of his bishop pair and meanwhile retains a very solid position. However, he must be careful not to let White build up a powerful kingside attack.

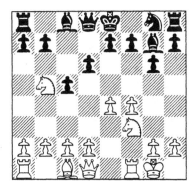 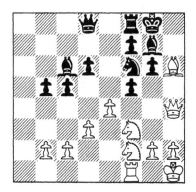

8 a4

To stop Black expanding on the queenside with ...a7-a6 and ...b7-b5. 8 d3 is considered in the next main game.

8...a6

Black can also delay this move, e.g. 8...♘f6 9 d3 0-0 10 ♕e1 e6!? 11 ♕h4 and now 11...a6 was met by 12 ♘xd6!? ♕xd6 13 e5 ♕d8 14 f5 with a very messy position in Hracek-Alterman, European Team Championship, Pula 1997.

9 ♘c3 ♘f6 10 ♕e1 0-0 11 d3 e6 12 ♔h1

White opts for a slow build-up, but 12 e5!? was also possible.

12...b6 13 ♗d2 ♗d7 14 ♘d1 b5 15 axb5 axb5 16 ♖xa8 ♕xa8

Richard Réti once said that this was the best square for the queen, but maybe he was not being attacked at the time.

17 ♕h4 ♗c6 18 ♘f2 ♕d8!

Anticipating 19 f5.

19 f5? exf5 20 ♗g5 h6! 21 ♗xh6

see following diagram

21...♘xe4!

This simple but clever combination quite refutes Hebden's play.

22 ♗g5 ♘xf2+ 23 ♕xf2 ♕d7

Ftacnik now only needs to show a little care to score the point.

24 b3 ♖e8 25 h4 ♖e6 26 ♗f4 ♕e7 27 ♕g3 ♗xf3 28 gxf3 ♗f6 29 h5 ♗h4 30 ♕h3 g5 31 ♗g3 ♗xg3 32 ♕xg3 ♔g7 33 d4 cxd4 34 ♖d1 f4 35 ♕f2

35...♔h6 36 ♖f1 ♖e3 37 ♕d2 ♕f6 38 ♕a5 g4 39 ♕a8 gxf3 0-1

Game 6
Plaskett-Schmidt
Trnava 1984

---

1 e4 c5 2 f4 g6 3 ♘f3 ♗g7 4 ♘c3 ♘c6 5 ♗b5 ♘d4 6 0-0 ♘xb5 7 ♘xb5 d6 8 d3 ♘f6

Black can also try 8...a6 9 ♘c3 b5!?

here, seizing space on the queenside, although his lack of kingside development is a worry.

9 e5!?

An interesting alternative the routine 9 a4 or 9 ♕e1.

9...dxe5 10 fxe5 ♘d5

At home I had looked at 10...♘g4 11 ♗f4 a6 12 ♘c3 ♘xe5 13 ♘xe5 ♕d4+ 14 ♔h1 ♗xe5 15 ♗xe5 ♕xe5 16 ♕f3 0-0 17 ♖ae1 and remember convincing myself that White had good play for the pawn, e.g. 17...♕d6 18 ♕e3 threatening to regain it on e7 or c5 (19 ♘e4), but I suppose that objectively it is doubtful that Black could be worse here.

11 ♕e1 0-0 12 ♕h4 ♕d7 13 ♘c3 ♘b4?!

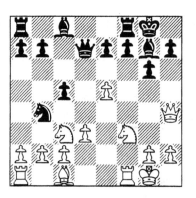

Wandering away from the king does not look apposite.

14 ♘e4

I am not certain what I was thinking about here, and if I had this position again I would play the simple 14 ♖f2.

14...♘xc2

Inflicting some structural damage.

15 ♗h6 f6

On 15...♘xa1? 16 ♗xg7 ♔xg7 17 ♘f6! exf6 18 exf6+ ♔h8 19 ♕h6 ♖g8 20 ♘g5 wins, and the reply to 15...♕g4 is 16 ♕xe7! ♘xa1? 17 ♘f6+ and wins.

16 ♖ac1 ♘d4 17 ♗xg7 ♔xg7 18 ♖xc5 ♘e6 19 ♖c4 b6 20 exf6+ exf6

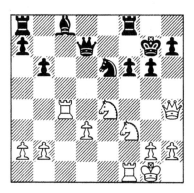

21 ♘d4!

Introducing utter chaos.

21...♘xd4 22 ♘xf6 ♘e2+ 23 ♔h1 h6 24 ♖e4 ♗b7 25 ♖xe2 ♕d6 26 ♖ef2!

Concentrating force like this makes life very hard for Black, particularly in view of his time shortage.

26...♕xd3 27 ♘h5+ ♔g8 28 ♘f6+ ♔g7 29 ♘h5+ ♔g8 30 ♘f4!

Winning an important pawn.

30...♕e4 31 ♕xh6 ♖ad8 32 ♔g1 ♖f6 33 ♘h5 ♖f7 34 ♘g3 ♕c6

Here Black lost on time. A most scrappy game.


```
Game 7
J.Polgar-Topalov
Dortmund 1996
```

1 e4 c5 2 ♘c3 ♘c6 3 f4 g6 4 ♘f3 ♗g7 5 ♗b5 ♘d4 6 ♗d3!?

This tricky move has not been so highly regarded by theory.

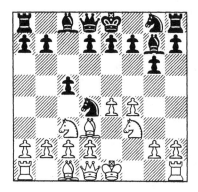

6...d6

6...e6 allows White the opportunity of 7 ♘xd4 cxd4 8 ♘b5 d6 9 c3! and if 9...dxc3 10 dxc3, when Black will have problems with his vulnerable d-pawn, e.g. 10...♘e7 11 ♘xd6+! or 10...a6 11 ♕a4.

7 ♘xd4 cxd4 8 ♘e2 ♘f6

In Dzhindzihasvili-Hübner, Tilburg 1985, Black kept a closer eye on his d4-pawn by developing the knight with 8...♘h6!? and play was equal after 9 c3 dxc3 10 dxc3 0-0 11 0-0 d5 12 e5 ♕b6+ 13 ♔h1 ♘f5.

9 0-0 0-0 10 ♕e1!?

10 c3 was a usual move (but not 10 ♘xd4? ♕b6 11 c3 e5) when Basman-Adorjan, London 1975, was not a great success for White: 10...e5!? 11 cxd4 exd4 12 b3 ♖e8 13 ♘g3 h5! 14 f5 h4 15 ♘e2 ♘xe4 16 ♗xe4 ♖xe4 17 d3 ♖e5 18 fxg6

0-1. Black has also done well with 10...dxc3 11 bxc3 (hoping to make something of his central pawns; 11 dxc3 promises nothing) 11...b6, as in, e.g. Hodgson-Petursson, Reykjavik 1989. The impression is that after 10 c3 White has some difficulties in rearranging his/her minor pieces and that Black's is the more comfortable development, so Polgar tries a different arrangement.

10...♘d7 11 ♗c4

Intending d2-d3, etc. 11 ♕f2 would have avoided the fracas that follows, but after Topalov's 11...♘c5 12 ♘xd4 ♘xd3 13 cxd3 ♗d7 14 b3 ♗b5 Black has excellent compensation for the pawn.

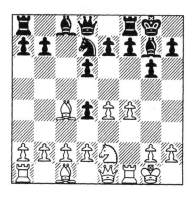

11...d5!?

Wow! 11...♕c7 12 d3 ♘b6 13 ♗b3 ♗e6!? was well worth a go, e.g. 14 f5 ♗xb3 15 cxb3 ♕c2.

12 exd5

12 ♗xd5 is met by 12...♘f6.

12...♘b6 13 d3 ♘xc4!?

One surprise after another. 13...♘xd5 was okay but Topalov stirs things up further.

14 dxc4 b5 15 ♕f2

Returning the pawn. On 15 cxb5 ♕xd5 16 ♘g3 ♗b7 Black has a splendid initiative for it.

15...bxc4 16 ♘xd4 ♕xd5 17 ♗e3 a5!? 18 c3

White crafts her game around the knight at d4.

18...♖d8 19 ♕c2 e6 20 ♖ad1 ♕h5?

This is purposeless. He should just have played 20...♗b7.

21 ♘c6 ♖xd1 22 ♖xd1 ♗b7 23 ♘e7+ ♔h8 24 ♖d7 ♕b5 25 ♕d2

Black's inaccuracy has allowed Judit to seize the d-line and thereby cause problems.

25...♗d5 26 ♖c7 ♗e4

A better chance might have been the ending after 26...♖d8 27 ♘xd5 ♕xd5 28 ♕xd5 exd5 29 ♖xf7 ♖b8.

27 ♘c8!

A nasty knight.

27...♕d5 28 ♘d6 ♔g8 29 ♘xc4 ♖b8 30 ♕xd5 exd5 31 ♗a7! ♖a8 32 ♘d6

White has a pawn more and the more active pieces. This is an exceptional position where the bishop pair has little scope.

32...♗b1 33 ♘xf7 ♗xa2 34 ♘g5 ♖e8 35 ♗d4 ♗h6??

A gross blunder in a bad position, but 35...♗xd4+ 36 cxd4 h5 37 ♖a7 would have left White well on top.

36 ♘xh7 1-0

An imaginative game, but not one that alters the excellent theoretical status that 5...♘d4 enjoys.

Game 8
Rogers-Smyslov
Manila Interzonal 1990

1 e4 c5 2 ♘c3 ♘c6 3 f4 g6 4 ♘f3 d6 5 ♗b5 ♗d7

The actual move order of the game was 1 e4 d6 2 f4 c5 3 ♘f3 ♘c6 4 ♘c3 g6 5 ♗b5 ♗d7.

6 d3 ♗g7 7 0-0 a6!

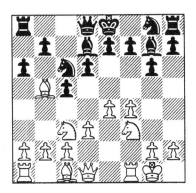

In fact it seems that this was the first significant occasion on which this natural and good move was played. The problem is that 7...e6 can be met by 8 f5! exf5 9 exf5 ♗xf5 10 ♗g5 with a strong attack, as in Sutovsky-Kempinski, Polanica Zdroj 1999, while 7...♘f6 8 ♔h1 0-0 9 ♗xc6 ♗xc6 was also promising for White in Epishin-A.Petrosian, Groningen open 1990.

8 ♗xc6 ♗xc6 9 ♕e1

See Game 11 for the alternative development scheme involving the sequence 9 ♔h1 ♕d7 10 ♕e2!?

9...♕d7!

The most flexible.

10 ♔h1

If 10 ♕h4 then 10...f5! is a good reply. 10 a4 is seen in Games 9 and 10.

10...♘h6!?

Black thus reserves the option of ...f7-f5, but there is probably not a great deal wrong with 10...♘f6 either, so long as Black does not rush headlong into a kingside attack by castling too quickly.

11 ♗d2

Rogers thought this a little too passive (he likes to keep busy) and suggested the gambit 11 f5!? instead, meeting 11...gxf5 with 12 ♘h4 fxe4 13 ♘xe4. Maybe.

11...b5!

In Baker-King, 4NCL 1997, Black rushed to block on the kingside with 11...f5, but after 12 ♘d5!? fxe4 13 ♕xe4 ♘f7 14 ♖ae1 White quickly established a grip on the position.

12 ♖b1 b4 13 ♘d1 f5! 14 ♘g5 ♘f7! 15 exf5 gxf5 16 ♘f3

On 16 ♘e6 ♗f6 Black already prepares the eviction with 17...♗d5.

16...0-0 17 ♘e3 ♖ae8 18 ♕g3 ♔h8 19 ♕h3 e6 20 ♘c4 ♖g8

Black has similar assets to Game 9, Ljubojevic-Kasparov, with the significant difference that his king is not as secure. This makes opening up the game a little trickier.

21 ♘g5 ♘xg5 22 fxg5 ♗f8 23 c3 ♖g6 24 cxb4 cxb4 25 ♖bc1

25 ♗xb4 ♖xg5 would be a trade very much to Black's liking.

25...♗e7 26 ♕h5 e5 27 h4 f4 28 ♖f2! ♖b8

Or 28...♕h3+ 29 ♔g1 ♕xd3 30 ♗xb4 and White is alright.

29 ♔h2 ♗f8?

The bishop re-routes to g7, but it was far better to shift it to c7 with 29...♗c7, when Black is doing very well. Smyslov starts to lose the thread.

30 b3 ♗g7 31 d4!

If you are not making a nice centre work for you then it can just become a liability. Rogers fights back.

31...♖e6 32 ♖d1 ♕e8?

Black should have kept the queens on with 32...♕c7! (33 d5 ♗e8) when he is more apt to make something of his piece activity.

33 ♕xe8+ ♗xe8 34 d5 ♖g6 35 g3! fxg3+ 36 ♔xg3 h5 37 ♗e3

Now only White has any winning chances, and he tacks around looking for them.

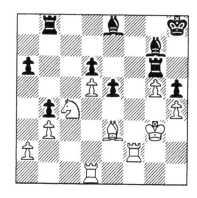

37...♔g8 38 ♗b6 ♖b7 39 ♗e3 ♗f7 40 ♘a5 ♖c7 41 ♘c4 ♗f8 42 ♖df1

♖g7 43 ♗d2 ♖b7 44 ♘e3 a5 45 ♔h2 ♖b8 46 ♘f5 ♖g6 47 ♘e3 ♖g7 48 ♘f5 ♖g6 49 ♘h6+

Smyslov has stayed alert so Rogers exchanges off a pair of minor pieces and gets a rook to the seventh.

49...♗xh6 50 ♖xf7 ♖f8 51 ♖xf8+ ♗xf8 52 ♔g2

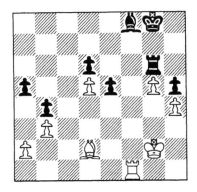

52...♖g7 53 ♗e3 e4!

He must go active to have any hope. The bishop ending after 53...♖c7 54 ♖c1 is dead lost.

54 ♗f4?

Rogers later preferred 54 ♔f2.

54...♖f7 55 ♗g3 ♖b7 56 ♖f6 ♖b5! 57 ♗xd6 ♗g7 58 ♖f5 ♔h7 59 g6+!

A necessary trick since the line 59 ♗c7 ♔g6 60 d6 ♔xf5 61 d7 ♖d5 62 d8♕ ♖xd8 63 ♗xd8 ♔g4 produces a drawn ending because the black king is so active.

59...♔xg6 60 ♖g5+ ♔f7 61 ♖xh5?

Missing a pretty coup. 61 ♗e7!! wins as 61...♔xe7 62 d6+ picks up the rook.

61...♗f6 62 ♗f4 ♔g6?

Blundering back; 62...♖c5! 63 ♔g3 a4! would have drawn. Now, with a series of accurate moves, Rogers clinches victory.

63 ♖h6+ ♔f5 64 ♔g3! ♖c5

The bishop ending after 64...♖xd5 65

♖h5+ ♔e6 66 ♖xd5 ♔xd5 67 ♗e3 is lost.

65 ♖h5+ ♔g6 66 ♔g4 ♗d4 67 ♖g5+ ♔f7 68 ♖f5+ ♔e8 69 d6 1-0

A tremendous struggle.

Game 9
Ljubojevic-Kasparov
Linares 1991

1 e4 c5 2 ♘c3 d6 3 f4 ♘c6 4 ♘f3 g6 5 ♗b5 ♗d7 6 0-0 ♗g7 7 d3 a6 8 ♗xc6 ♗xc6 9 ♕e1 ♕d7!? 10 a4!?

This was new, previous games having seen 10 ♔h1.

10...b6

Black often castles long in this line, but in Hebden-Summerscale, British Championship, Norwich 1994, where ♔h1 had been substituted for a2-a4, he took a radically different path of hitting the white centre straight away with ...f7-f5 and no subsequent ...0-0-0, i.e. 10...♘f6 11 ♗d2 ♘h5!? 12 ♖b1 f5!? 13 ♘d5 fxe4 14 dxe4 ♖b8 and the game was later drawn.

11 b3

Two other early ...f7-f5s came in Jansa-Stohl, Prague 1992: 11 h3 f5!? 12 ♗d2 ♘f6 13 e5 ♘h5 14 exd6 ♕xd6 15

♘e5 ♗b7 16 ♔h2 0-0 17 ♕e2 ♖ae8 18 ♖ae1 ½-½, and when the same players met again three years later with 11 ♗d2 ♘h6!? 12 h3 f5!? 13 ♘d5 fxe4 14 dxe4 ♗xd5 15 exd5 ♗xb2 16 ♖b1 ♗f6 17 ♖xb6 ♘f5 18 c3 h5!? with an unclear situation which Black ended up winning at move 32.

11...♘f6 12 h3 ♘h5 13 ♗d2 f5

Hence Black takes the sting out of any white build-up on the kingside...

14 exf5 gxf5 15 ♕h4 ♘f6 16 ♖ae1 0-0-0

...and then makes a home for his majesty elsewhere.

17 a5 b5 18 b4 cxb4 19 ♘a2 ♘d5 20 ♘xb4 ♗f6 21 ♕f2 ♘xb4 22 ♗xb4 ♖hg8 23 ♖e2 ♖g6 24 ♕e1 ♖dg8

Simple chess. Kasparov doubles along the g-file and then opens things up for his bishops. In this opposite-side castling scenario White is under by far the greater pressure.

25 ♔h2 e5 26 fxe5 ♗xe5+ 27 ♔h1 ♕b7

27...♕g7! (Kasparov) would have been simpler.

28 d4!

A terrible blunder. Instead 28...♕g7 29 ♕f2 ♗f4 would maintained a strong attack according to Kasparov.

29 ♖xg2 ♖xg2

Kasparov must have missed that 29...♗xf3 30 ♖xf3 ♕xf3 is met by 31 ♕c3+! ♕xc3 32 ♖xg8+ and Black can resign.

30 ♔xg2 ♕g7+ 31 ♔h1

Now it should be all over.

31...♗f4 32 ♕e6+

32 d5 ♗xd5 33 ♕c3+ would have forced instant resignation.

32...♗d7 33 ♕d5 ♕g3 34 ♕a8+?!

Whilst not throwing away the win, this is a decentralisation that will necessitate further exact play to ensure victory. 34 ♖e1! was simpler.

34...♔c7 35 ♖e1?

But this costs half a point. White could have threaded his way to a win with the sequence 35 ♕a7+ ♔d8 36 ♕b8+ ♔e7 37 ♖e1+ ♔f7 38 ♕b7 ♕xh3+ 39 ♔g1 (Kasparov).

35...♕xh3+ 36 ♔g1 ♕g3+ 37 ♔f1 ♕h3+ 38 ♔e2

38 ♔g1 ♕g3+ would have been a perpetual.

38...♗c6 39 ♕a7+ ♔c8

28...♖xg2??

40 ♖f1??

As is so often the case, it is the last move of the time control that is the decisive error. One of many ways to draw was 40 ♘d2 ♕g4+ 41 ♔d3 ♕g3+ etc.

40...♕g2+ 41 ♔e1 ♗g3+ 42 ♔d1 ♕xf1+ 43 ♘e1 ♗xe1 0-1

On two other occasions Kasparov has succeeded in salvaging a draw against a world-class opponent when a rook down for next to nothing: against Timman at Bugojno 1982 and versus Korchnoi at Brussels 1986. Here he actually won such a game. As Hungarian IM Tibor Karolyi observed of the world's greatest talents: 'They are also lucky.'

Game 10
Ljubojevic-Portisch
Reykjavik 1991

---

1 e4 c5 2 ♘c3 d6 3 f4 ♘c6 4 ♘f3 g6 5 ♗b5 ♗d7 6 0-0 ♗g7 7 d3 a6 8 ♗xc6 ♗xc6 9 ♕e1 ♕d7 10 a4 b6 11 h3

Attempting to profit from his experience in the previous game. He will now react to ...♘h5 with an immediate g2-g4.

11...♘f6 12 ♗d2 h5

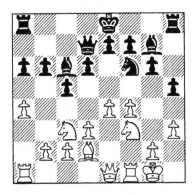

Such a classical player as Portisch cannot have been happy with a weakening

move like this. 12...b5 is to be considered.

13 e5 ♘h7

On 13...♘d5 14 ♘g5 is strong.

14 exd6 ♕xd6

Also after 14...♗xf3 15 ♖xf3 ♕xd6 16 f5 the weakening of the black kingside gives White the edge.

15 ♘e5 ♗xe5?!

A better defence was 15...♗b7 16 a5 b5 17 ♘e4 ♕c7 18 ♗e3 ♗xe5 19 fxe5 ♗xe4 20 dxe4 ♕xe5 21 ♕f2 ♘f6 22 ♗xc5 ♘f6.

16 fxe5 ♕d4+ 17 ♕f2! ♕xf2+ 18 ♖xf2 ♘f8 19 ♖af1 ♖h7 20 a5!

Queenside softening operations now commence.

20...b5

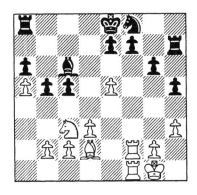

21 b4! cxb4 22 ♘a2 b3

Even though this splits up White's pawns, it creates serious problems down the newly opened c-line. Better was 22...♗b7.

23 ♘b4 ♗b7 24 cxb3 ♘e6 25 ♖c1 ♖d8

On 25...♖c8 26 ♖xc8+ ♗xc8 27 ♗e3 Black's queenside problems persist.

26 ♗e3 ♖d7 27 ♖d2 f6?

Overlooking something. 27...♘d4 was a tougher defence when 28 ♗xd4 ♖xd4

29 ♘c6 keeps an edge, or White could pursue a more tactical line with 29 ♖c7!? ♖xb4 30 ♖xb7 ♖xb3 31 ♖c2 ♔d8 32 ♖c6 ♖xd3 33 ♖xa6 with a probably decisive advantage because of the dead rook on h7. But Black might be a spoilsport and simply retreat with 29...♖d7.

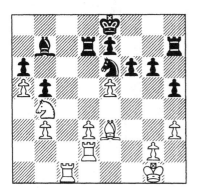

28 ♘xa6!

Ljubo rarely misses a trick.

28...fxe5

Or 28...♗xa6 29 ♖c6 and White is always going to be better because he is essentially playing with an extra rook, e.g. 29...♘c7 30 e6 ♘xe6 31 ♖xe6 ♗c8 32 a6! ♖xd3? 33 a7 etc.

29 ♘c5 ♘xc5 30 ♖xc5 ♗a6 31 ♖xe5 ♖f7 32 ♗c5 ♖f5 33 ♖de2 ♖xe5 34 ♖xe5 ♔f7

Or 34...♖xd3 35 ♖xe7+ ♔d8 36 b4 ♗c8 37 ♖g7 and the combination of White's aggressively placed pieces and passed a-pawn give Black, with his king stranded on the back rank, no chance to survive, e.g. 37...♗f5 38 a6 ♗e4 39 a7 ♖a3 40 ♗b6+ ♔e8 41 ♗a5 and wins.

35 d4 e6 36 ♖e3 ♖d5 37 b4 ♖f5 38 ♗d6 ♖d5 39 ♖f3+ ♔e8 40 ♖f8+ ♔d7 41 ♗e5

Black resigned, as the advance of the passed a-pawn will prove decisive.

Game 11
Plaskett-Shipov
Hastings 1998/99

1 e4 c5 2 ♘c3 d6 3 f4 ♘c6 4 ♘f3 g6 5 ♗b5 ♗d7 6 0-0 ♗g7 7 d3 a6 8 ♗xc6 ♗xc6 9 ♔h1 ♕d7 10 ♕e2

A new move, attempting to improve upon the usual 10 ♕e1. However, in many ways 10 ♕e2 is a more logical move. As Black players become more clued in, White is increasingly unlikely to get away with a crude mating attack based on ♕e1-h4 and f4-f5. Therefore the idea of placing the queen on a different colour complex to the dark-squared bishop, is logical and constitutes good positional play.

10...f5?

This is often a good method of blunting the power of a white kingside attack, but here the move is inappropriate. Black weakens the light squares in general and the e6-square in particular and does nothing for his development.

11 ♘d5

With the threat of ♘b6.

11...♖d8?

After this Black is almost lost. The

best try was 11...fxe4 12 dxe4 ♗xd5 13 exd5 ♘f6 but after 14 c4 White has a clear advantage.

12 ♘g5!

Now the white knights run riot.

12...♘f6 13 ♘b6

White's knights are fantastic pieces and he is not about to trade them in for modest material gains. 13 ♘e6 ♘xd5 14 exd5 ♗xd5 15 ♘xd8 gives White a clear advantage, but I wanted to play for the attack.

13...♕c7 14 ♘c4 fxe4 15 ♘e6 ♕c8 16 f5!

Opening further lines against the stranded black king.

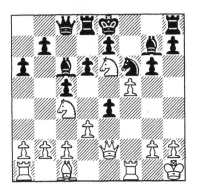

16...♖g8 17 ♘b6 exd3 18 cxd3 ♕b8

19 fxg6 ♗h8 20 g7 ♗xg7 21 ♗g5

Neatly combining attack and defence. White shields the g2-square whilst bringing his remaining pieces into play.

21...♗h8 22 ♖ae1 ♖d7 23 ♖xf6!

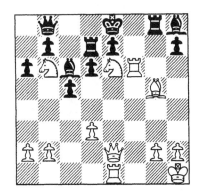

It is rather ironic that White has been declining to accept the advantage of the exchange over the past few moves and now chooses to sacrifice rook for knight himself.

23...exf6

Or 23...♗xf6 24 ♕h5+ ♖g6 25 ♘f4 ♗xg5 26 ♘xg6 hxg6 27 ♕h8+ ♔f7 28 ♕xb8 and White has a winning material advantage.

24 ♘xc5+ ♔d8 25 ♘cxd7 ♗xd7 26 ♕e7+ ♔c7 27 ♘d5+ 1-0

Summary

The main lesson from this chapter is that Black should not allow his c-pawns to be doubled (see Games 1-3). The resulting positions are almost always bad and, even when they are playable, they are very difficult to handle. Meanwhile White's game plays itself. Arranging to meet ♗b5 with ...♗d7 (Games 8-11) is perfectly okay for Black and leads to balanced positions. The lines with 5 ♗b5 ♘d4 should also be fine for Black and 7...d5 8 e5 is quite playable for the second player despite the outcome of Game 4.

1 e4 c5 2 ♘c3

2...♘c6

      2...d6 3 f4 ♘c6 4 ♘f3 g6 5 ♗b5 ♗d7 6 d3 ♗g7 7 0-0 a6 8 ♗xc6 ♗xc6 *(D)*
         9 ♕e1 ♕d7
            10 ♔h1 – *Game 8*
            10 a4 b6
               11 b3 – *Game 9*
               11 h3 – *Game 10*
         9 ♕e2 – *Game 11*

3 f4 g6 4 ♘f3 ♗g7 5 ♗b5 *(D)* **♘d4**

      5...e6 – *Game 1*
      5...d6 6 ♗xc6 bxc6 7 d3
         7...♘h6 – *Game 2*
         7...♘f6 – *Game 3*

6 0-0

      6 ♗d3 – *Game 7*

6...♘xb5 7 ♘xb5 *(D)* **d5**

      7...d6
         8 a4 – *Game 5*
         8 d3 – *Game 6*

8 e5 – *Game 4*

6...♗xc6   *5 ♗b5*   *7 ♘xb5*

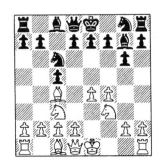

CHAPTER TWO

1 e4 c5 2 ♘c3 ♘c6 3 f4 g6 4 ♘f3 ♗g7 5 ♗c4

1 e4 c5 2 ♘c3 ♘c6 3 f4 g6 4 ♘f3 ♗g7 5 ♗c4

In the 1970s there were few published works on this line and several professional or semi-professionals in England were able to exploit this to rack up a series of victories on the UK tournament circuit. Since then though the theoreticians have moved in to give the ground a thorough reconnaissance and hence the system is now no longer so feared, at least not at grandmaster level.

By contrast with ♗b5 systems, where White may consider playing a middle-game with positional aspirations, perhaps against weakened black pawns, in this line it is rare for him not to pursue direct attacking play, and often with the aid of sacrifices. One of the problems though is that these motifs are limited and thus easier to anticipate, hence the assimilation of black antidotes. More successful modern exponents of ♗c4 are tending to hang back on sacrificing with f4-f5.

Paradoxically one of the earliest games to draw attention to this set-up, especially in conjunction with the gambit of the f-pawn, was not a Sicilian but an English Opening: Saidy-Fischer, USA 1969, went 1 c4 e5 2 ♘c3 ♘c6 3 g3 f5 4 ♗g2 ♘f6 5 d3 ♗c5 6 e3 f4!? 7 exf4 0-0 8 ♘ge2 ♕e8 9 0-0 d6 10 ♘a4 ♗d4! 11 ♘xd4 exd4 12 h3 h5 13 a3 a5 14 b3 ♕g6 15 ♘b2 ♗f5 16 ♕c2 ♘d7 17 ♖e1 ♘c5 18 ♗f1 ♖a6! 19 ♗d2 ♖b6 20 ♗xa5 ♖xb3 21 ♗d2 ♖a8 22 a4 ♖a6 23 a5 ♔h7 24 ♖ed1 b6 25 ♗e1 bxa5 26 ♘a4 ♖xd3! 27 ♗xd3 ♗xd3 28 ♕a2 ♘b4 29 ♕a3 ♘c2 30 ♕b2 ♘xa1 31 ♖xa1 ♘xa4 32 ♖xa4 ♕e4 33 ♗xa5 ♖xa5 34 ♖xa5 ♕e1+ 35 ♔h2 ♕xa5 0-1. Splendid stuff, and notable particularly for Fischer's prosecution of a strategical plus and not, as so often in this line, a kingside attack.

These lines are much more attractive for White when Black is already committed to ...d7-d6. If he can play ...d7-d5 in one go, as seen in Games 12-13, White has less than nothing.

Black has various ways to combat White's intended adverntues on the kingside:

a) Accepting White's gambit with ...g6xf5 (Game 14).

b) Accepting White's gambit with ...e6xf5 (Games 15-17).

c) Countering in the centre with ...d6-d5 (Games 18-19).

d) Countering in the centre with ...♘d4 (Games 20-21).

Game 12
Wedberg-Kharlov
Haninge 1992

---

1 e4 c5 2 ♘c3 ♘c6 3 f4 g6 4 ♘f3 ♗g7 5 ♗c4 e6 6 f5

After 6 e5 d6 7 exd6 ♘f6, as in Barle-Ribli, Bled 1979, Black is fine. If White wishes to play an early e4-e5 he can also try 6 0-0 ♘ge7 and now 7 e5 (7 d3 d5 8 ♗b3 0-0 is unpromising for White, since he is basically just a whole tempo down on Games 19-22) when the safest route to equality is 7...d6! 8 exd6 ♕xd6 9 ♘e4 ♕c7 10 d3 b6, and here Black followed up with ....♗b7 and ...0-0-0!? in Perez-Tukmakov, Cordoba 1991.

6...♘ge7

After 6...exf5?! 7 d3 ♘ge7 8 0-0 0-0 9 ♕e1 White develops a ferocious kingside initiative, and although 6...gxf5 and

6...♘e5 are playable, the text move has been so successful for Black in practice that there is no need to be greedy.

7 fxe6 fxe6

The other recapture is perfectly feasible and has often been seen. Here we consider the more critical consequences of recapturing towards the centre as we were taught in our first chess lessons.

8 d3

After 8 0-0 d5 9 ♗b5 (or 9 ♗b3 c4) 9...0-0 Black has at least equalised.

8...d5 9 ♗b3

9 exd5 exd5 10 ♗b3 b5! transposes to the main game, while 9 ♗b5 0-0 is similar to the previous game.

9...b5!

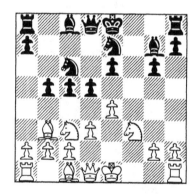

Natural enough. Black will swamp the bishop.

10 exd5

After 10 0-0 ♕b6! 11 exd5 c4+ 12 ♔h1 cxb3 13 dxc6 dxc2 14 ♕xc2 0-0 Black was able to take advantage of the two bishops in Anjuhin-Yudasin, Finland 1997. Instead White can guarantee the bishop's preservation with 10 a3 (10 a4?! is probably inferior and Black quickly got the upper hand in A.Stein-Liberzon, Israel 1978, after 10...b4 11 ♘e2 ♘a5), but, as you might imagine, taking time out for such a measure in such a sharp position does not trouble Black at all. Minasian-Tiviakov, Kherson 1991, continued 10...c4 11 ♗a2 a6 12 0-0 0-0 13 ♗g5 ♖f7 14 ♕d2 ♗b7 with equal chances. The current theoretical evaluation is that that may be White's only objective route to equality from here, because the romantic sacrificial lines have been refuted.

10...exd5 11 0-0

This had been thought the better way to give up the piece. 11 ♘xb5 ♕a5+ 12 ♘c3 is refuted by 12...c4! (this move, giving up another pawn, is best because it stifles the bishop on b3) 13 dxc4 d4 14 0-0 dxc3 and White does not have enough, e.g. Weinzettl-Züger, Vienna open 1986, went 15 c5 cxb2 16 ♘g5 bxa1♕ 17 ♗f7+ ♔f8 18 ♗b3+ ♗f6 19 ♘e4 ♕d4+ and Black won in a few more moves.

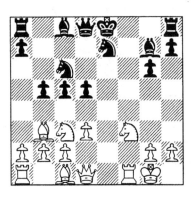

11...c4! 12 dxc4 dxc4 13 ♕xd8+ ♘xd8!

Strangely enough, this obvious recapture was a novelty. On 13...♔xd8 14 ♖d1+ White can make an awful mess.

14 ♘xb5 cxb3 15 ♘c7+

White goes for it. After 15 axb3 0-0 16 ♖xa7 ♖xa7 17 ♘xa7 ♗b7 he did not

have enough for the piece in Rossen-Coleman, Copenhagen 1996.

15...♔d7 16 ♘xa8 bxc2

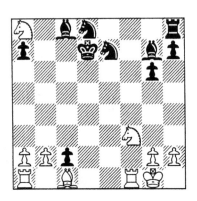

17 ♗f4?

This is the decisive mistake. 17 ♖f2 ♗b7 18 ♖xc2 ♗xa8 19 ♗e3 was better, and not too far from equal.

17...♖f8! 18 ♘e5+ ♗xe5 19 ♗xe5 ♖xf1+ 20 ♖xf1 ♘dc6 21 ♗c3 ♗a6!

The knight's corpse can be collected later. First Kharlov ensures that he will keep his decisive asset on c2.

22 ♖c1 ♗d3 23 ♔f2 ♘d5 24 ♗d2 ♘cb4!? 25 a3 ♘c6

Now there is a weakness at b3. Subtle guys, these Russians.

26 ♖e1 ♗f5 27 h3 h5 28 ♔g3 ♘d4 29 ♔h4 ♘b3 30 ♗g5 ♗d3 31 ♔g3 ♘c5 32 ♔f3 ♘e6 33 ♗c1 h4 34 ♔f2 ♗f5 35 g3

Or 35 ♖e5 ♘df4.

35...♘c5 36 ♔f3 ♘d3 37 ♖g1 ♘xc1 38 ♖xc1 hxg3 39 ♔xg3 ♘e3 0-1

Game 13
Hebden-Speelman
British Ch, Torquay 1982

1 e4 c5 2 f4 g6 3 ♘f3 ♗g7 4 ♘c3 ♘c6 5 ♗c4 e6 6 f5 ♘ge7 7 fxe6

fxe6 8 d3 0-0

More restrained than 8...d5.

9 ♗g5

After 9 0-0 d5 Black has again equalised.

9...h6 10 ♗h4

Now Black bursts out all over. 10 ♗xe7 would avoid that, but with his bishop pair and central control Black is still doing very nicely.

10...g5 11 ♗f2 d5 12 ♗b3 g4!?

Black handled it quite differently in Veltkamp-Gorbatov, Decin 1996, with 12...d4 13 ♘e2 ♘a5 14 0-0 ♘xb3 15 axb3 ♘g6 and stood comfortably, whereas in Knezevic-Smejkal, Smederevska Palanka 1971, play became complex after 12...♘d4 13 ♗xd4 cxd4 14 ♘e2 ♕b6 15 0-0 dxe4 16 ♘d2 ♖xf1+ 17 ♕xf1 e3 18 ♘e4 ♘d5 19 h4 gxh4 20 ♘f4, though Black emerged the winner in the end. Jonathan had a brainstorm.

13 ♘d2 c4!? 14 dxc4 d4 15 ♘a4

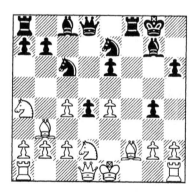

15...♖xf2!?

The Speelman cometh!

16 ♔xf2 ♕a5

White has the exchange and a pawn more, but his game is all over the place and Black has terrific activity.

17 ♖f1 ♗d7 18 ♔g1 ♘e5 19 c3

♗xa4 **20 cxd4**

Or 20 ♗xa4 dxc3 and ...♖d8 when White is under terrific pressure.

20...♘d3

21 ♕xg4??

Now Speelman quickly puts him away. 21 ♗xa4 was far more testing.

21...♕xd2 22 ♕xe6+ ♔h8 23 ♗xa4 ♕xb2 24 ♖ad1 ♕xd4+ 25 ♔h1 ♘c6 26 ♖d2 ♕e3 27 ♗xc6 ♕xd2 0-1

Highly original play by Black.

The problem with ♗c4 in the preceding two games is that Black has not yet committed himself to ...d7-d6 and can therefore make the ...d7-d5 break in one move. In the remaining games of this chapter White delays committing his bishop until Black has played ...d7-d6 and this makes the whole ♗c4 idea far more viable.

Game 14
Chandler-Arnason
Moscow 1990

---

1 e4 c5 2 ♘c3 d6 3 f4 ♘c6 4 ♘f3 g6 5 ♗c4 ♗g7 6 0-0 e6

Recent practice has seen a great preference for this move over 6...♘f6 and now:

a) Plaskett-Byrne, London 1990, continued 7 d3 0-0 8 ♕e1 e6 9 e5!? ♘e8 9 ♗b5!? ♗d7 11 ♘e4 ♕c7 12 ♕h4 f5 13 ♗xc6 ♕xc6 14 ♘eg5 h6 15 ♗d2! with the advantage.

b) White managed a standard kingside hack in Sorokin-Baburin, Voronezh 1988, with 8 f5!? gxf5 (Weinzettl-Szalanczy, Oberwart 1991, varied with 8...♘a5 9 ♕e1 ♘xc4 10 dxc4 e6 11 ♕h4 ♘d7 12 ♗g5 f6 13 fxg6 hxg6 14 ♗e3 ♕e7 and the game was swiftly drawn) 9 ♕e1 fxe4 10 dxe4 ♗g4 11 ♗f4 ♗xf3 12 ♖xf3 ♘h5 13 ♗g5 ♘e5 14 ♖h3 ♘xc4 15 ♕h4 ♗d4+ 16 ♔h1 f6 17 ♕xh5 ♖f7 18 ♗h6 ♘e5 19 ♘d5 c4 20 c3 ♗c5 21 ♖f1 ♔h8 22 ♖f5 e6 23 ♗g5! 1-0.

7 f5

7 d3 is the subject of Games 18-22.

7...gxf5

Here Black is obliged to accept the pawn sacrifice with either 7...gxf5 or 7...exf5 (Games 15-17) as 7...♘ge7?! 8 fxe6 fxe6 (or 8...♗xe6 9 ♗xe6 fxe6 10 ♘g5) 9 ♘g5 is troublesome and 7...♘f6 8 d3 0-0 9 fxe6 fxe6 10 ♗g5 gives White the kind of attacking position on the kingside that he is striving for.

8 d3 ♘f6 9 exf5 0-0

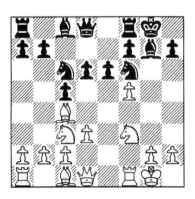

10 a3

Chandler settles back into a middlegame where he is happy enough to have parted with his f-pawn in order to smash up the black kingside.

10...d5 11 ♗a2 exf5 12 ♗g5 ♗e6 13 ♕d2 ♘e7

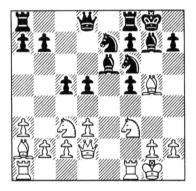

Extra padding for his king.

14 ♘e2

An extra attacker for the opponent's king.

14...♘g6 15 ♘g3 ♕d6 16 ♗xf6 ♗xf6 17 ♘h5

Thus the knight arrives at its most menacing post, but to get it there White has had to give up his excellent dark-squared bishop.

17...♗h8 18 ♕h6 f6 19 ♖ae1 ♖ae8

20 c3 ♖f7 21 d4 c4 22 ♗b1 ♕f8 23 ♕d2 ♗g7 24 ♕f2 ½-½

This game is perhaps not unrepresentative of the state of the gambit lines with ♗c4 against the fianchetto in that Black, with accurate play, is not too seriously troubled.

Game 15
Abramovic-Kozul
Yugoslavia 1985

1 e4 c5 2 ♘c3 ♘c6 3 f4 d6 4 ♘f3 g6 5 ♗c4 ♗g7 6 0-0 e6 7 f5 exf5 8 ♕e1 ♘ge7 9 d3 h6

Castling lines his king up into the crossfire of the rook along the f-file, the queen, soon to arrive at h4, the one bishop down the a2-g8 diagonal and the other poised to join the attack at g5 or h6. Considering that the knight may also be arriving at d5 in some variations, one can understand Black's reluctance to go that way, but not connecting your rooks has its problems too. One example of the perils of 9...0-0?! is Tarjan-Rattinger, Mayaguez 1971: 10 ♕h4 ♕d7 11 ♗h6 fxe4 12 ♘g5 ♕g4?? 13 ♖xf7 ♕xh4 14 ♖xg7+ ♔h8 15 ♖xh7 mate.

10 ♕g3

10 exf5 is seen in Game 17.

10...♘e5 11 ♗b5+?

11 ♘xe5 was better, as in the next main game.

11...♗d7 12 ♗f4

Kozul now hits upon an exchanging sequence that more than solves any problems he has.

12...♘xf3+ 13 ♖xf3 ♗xc3 14 ♗xd7+ ♕xd7 15 bxc3 g5! 16 ♗d2 f4 17 ♕e1 0-0-0

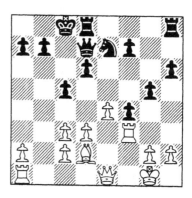

Of course this is by far the safest spot for the black king.

18 g3 fxg3 19 hxg3 ♘c6 20 ♖f5 ♘e5 21 ♕e2 ♖de8 22 d4 ♘c6 23 ♕d3 ♖e7 24 dxc5 dxc5 25 ♖xc5 ♕g4 26 ♖f1 ♕xe4 27 ♕xe4 ♖xe4 28 ♖xf7 ♖d8

Nominally White has material equality but structurally he is very badly off indeed.

29 ♖f2 ♔c7 30 c4 b6 31 ♖cf5 ♘e5 32 c5 ♘g4 33 cxb6+ axb6 34 ♖g2 ♖ed4 35 ♖f7+ ♔c6 36 ♗e1 ♖e8 0-1

Game 16
Hodgson-Malisauskas
St Petersburg 1984

1 e4 c5 2 ♘c3 ♘c6 3 f4 g6 4 ♘f3

♗g7 5 ♗c4 d6 6 d3 e6 7 f5 exf5 8 0-0 ♘ge7 9 ♕e1 h6 10 ♕g3 ♘e5 11 ♘xe5!?

Another interesting idea.

11...♗xe5 12 ♗f4 ♗xf4 13 ♖xf4 g5

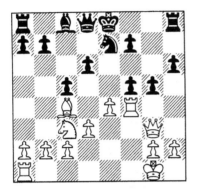

14 ♖xf5!? ♘xf5 15 exf5 0-0 16 ♖f1

Black has major, and possibly insuperable problems.

16...♕f6 17 ♘e4 ♕e5 18 ♕h3 ♔g7 19 f6+ ♔h7 20 ♕h5 ♗e6 21 ♗xe6 fxe6 22 f7 ♕d4+ 23 ♔h1 ♔g7

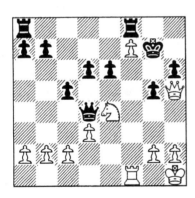

24 ♘f6

Now the attack will be decisive.

24...♕h4 25 ♘e8+ ♔h7 26 ♕e2 e5 27 g4 d5 28 ♕xe5 ♖axe8 29 ♕f5+ 1-0

A game very much in the Hodgson style.

1 e4 c5 2 ♘c3 d6 3 f4 ♘c6 4 ♘f3 g6 5 ♗c4 ♗g7 6 0-0 e6 7 f5 exf5 8 d3 ♘ge7 9 ♕e1 h6 10 exf5

Another weapon in the white arsenal, though not one that has enjoyed much success.

10...♗xf5 11 g4 ♗xg4! 12 ♗xf7+ ♔xf7 13 ♘e5+ ♔g8 14 ♘xg4

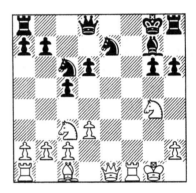

14...♘d4!

A stomping move! 14...♘f5? is obviously met by 15 ♖xf5! gxf5 16 ♕e6+ ♔h7 17 ♕xf5+ ♔g8 18 ♘d5 ♘d4 19 ♕g6 with a vicious attack. However, 14...♘e5!? might also be worth a go.

15 ♕f2

15 ♕e4 ♕d7 16 ♘d5 ♘xd5 17 ♕xd5+ ♕e6 is no use.

15...♘df5

Another minor piece nearer to the king is always a help when the opponent has a glimmer of attacking play.

16 ♕g2 ♕d7 17 ♘e4

On 17 ♗f4 Black might try 17...h5!?

17...♖f8 18 c3 b6 19 ♗f4 d5 20 ♘d2 d4 21 ♘e4 g5 22 ♗e5 ♗xe5

23 ♘xe5 ♕e6 24 ♘g4 dxc3

Despite his extra pawn Gelfand strives not for simplicity but for the very sharpest lines almost every time.

25 ♖ae1 ♕c6 26 bxc3 ♔g7

Gelfand carefully sidesteps any potentially embarrassing knight checks on the f6-square.

27 d4 ♘g6 28 dxc5 bxc5 29 ♕f2 ♘d4 30 ♘ef6

Both 30 ♕e3 ♘c2 and 30 ♘gf6 ♘f4 are decisive.

30...h5!

Wrapping it up.

31 cxd4

Alternatively, 31 ♖e7+ ♘xe7 32 ♘xh5+ ♔g6 33 ♘e5+ ♔xh5 and wins, or 31 ♘xh5+ ♖xh5 32 ♖e7+ ♔g8 33 ♕xf8+ ♘xf8 34 ♘f6+ ♔h8 wins, or in this line if 33 ♘f6+ ♔h8 34 cxd4 ♘f4 wins.

31...hxg4 32 ♘e8+ ♕xe8 0-1

Theoretically this was an important game and the imaginative manner of Black's victory also tells you why Kasparov predicted before the 1991-1993 World Championship cycle that Gelfand would be his challenger. But Nigel Short eliminated him, in part due to the Grand Prix Attack (see Game 20)!

> ## Game 18
> ## Spangenberg-Ftacnik
> *Moscow Olympiad 1994*

1 e4 c5 2 ♘c3 d6

Ftacnik readies his standard Najdorf. Preparing for him is simple because you can always be sure what he is going to do.

3 f4 g6 4 ♘f3 ♗g7 5 ♗c4 e6 6 0-0 ♘e7 7 d3 ♘bc6 8 f5 d5

8...exf5 9 ♕e1 transposes back to Games 15-17 and 8...gxf5 is risky because of 9 ♘g5, while in the recent rapidplay game Rogers-Ftacnik, Znojmo 1999, Black experimented with 8...0-0 9 fxe6 (perhaps 9 fxg6!?) 9...♗xe6 10 ♗xe6 fxe6 and was ultimately victorious.

9 ♗b3 dxe4

9...gxf5 10 exd5 ♗xc3 11 bxc3 ♘xd5 12 ♕e1 yields White fine play and in Kraus-Pick, Dortmund 1993, he went on to win after 12...h6 13 ♘e5 ♘xe5 14 ♕xe5 ♕f6 15 ♖xf5! ♕xe5 16 ♖xe5 f6 17 ♖h5 ♘xc3 18 ♔f2 ♗d7 19 ♖xc5 etc.

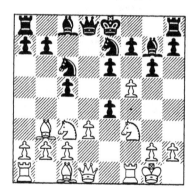

10 fxg6!?

A startling novelty! 10 f6 ♗xf6 11 ♘xe4 ♗g7 12 ♗g5 f5 13 ♘f2 0-0 14 ♕e1, as in Silva-Har Zvi, Barcelona

1993, should be good for Black.

10...exf3 11 gxf7+ ♔f8 12 ♕xf3 ♕d4+

After 12...♘d4 13 ♕h5 ♘ef5 14 ♘e4 White has good compensation. Ftacnik sends the queen off to sort things out via recurrent exchanging opportunities.

13 ♔h1 ♘e5 14 ♕e2

On 14 ♕h5 ♕g4 is irritating.

14...♕g4

Or 14...♘f5 15 ♘b5 and the band plays on.

15 ♕f2 b6 16 h3 ♕g6 17 ♗f4 ♗b7

Sensibly developing another piece (17...♘xf7?? loses to 18 ♕f3!).

18 ♖ae1 c4

Yet another example of this blocking sacrifice against the bishop on b3.

19 dxc4

I am intrigued by 19 ♖xe5!? when 19...♗xe5? 20 ♗xe5 picks up the rook at h8. Ftacnik gave reams of analysis hereabouts and suggested 19...cxb3 20 axb3 ♘f5, but I would then like to follow up with 21 ♘e4!? with great complications.

19...♘xf7

Black must have been very glad to see the back of that guy.

20 ♘b5?!

A mistaken escapade, but that is ob-served very much in retrospect. On 20 c5!? the defence 20...♗d4!? 21 ♗h6+! (a very useful finesse for it makes the king occupy the g8-square and thus prevents the rook from going there) 21...♔g8 22 ♗e3 ♗xc3 23 bxc3 ♘f5 24 ♗f4 ♖e8 was proposed, but I am far from con-vinced that White is worse were he to substitute 24 cxb6!? in this line.

20...♘f5!!

Whilst organising his defences, Ftac-nik cunningly weaves a counterattack.

21 ♘c7 ♖e8!

I should think that this came as a sur-prise.

22 ♘xe8

Too late to back out. On 22 c3 ♖e7 23 ♗f4 e5 wins.

22...♗d4!

Suddenly it becomes clear who is the attacker.

23 ♕d2

On 23 ♕e2 ♖g8 the attack on g2 will decide, viz. 24 ♘c7 ♗xg2+ 25 ♔h2 e5! 26 c5 ♗xf1 27 ♖xf1 ♗e3! 28 ♗xe5 ♘xe5 and Black wins.

23...♖g8 24 ♖e2 ♕g3!! 0-1

Now 25 ♗xg3 ♘xg3+ 26 ♔h2 ♘xf1+ 27 ♔h1 ♘xd2 28 ♖xd2 ♖xg2! 29 ♖xg2 ♔xe8; or 25 ♕b4+ ♗c5 26

♕xc5+ bxc5 27 ♗xg3 ♘xg3+ 28 ♔h2 ♘xf1+ 29 ♔g1 ♔xe8; or 25 ♕xd4 ♕xh3+ 26 ♗h2 ♗xg2+; or 25 ♗h6+ ♔xe8 26 ♗a4+ ♔e7 all win for Black. A stunning finale.

Game 19
Short-Oll
Tallinn/Parnu 1998

1 e4 c5 2 ♘c3 d6 3 f4 ♘c6 4 ♘f3 g6 5 ♗c4 ♗g7 6 0-0 e6 7 d3 ♘ge7 8 ♕e1 0-0?!

It is risky for Black to castle too early in this line. For 8...♘d4 see Game 20 and for 8...h6 see Games 21 and 22.

9 f5 d5

9...exf5? 10 ♕h4 is suicidal.

10 ♗b3 c4

After 10...dxe4 11 dxe4 gxf5 12 ♕h4 White gets his standard kingside attack.

11 dxc4

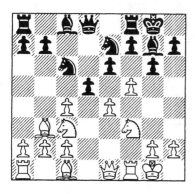

11...d4

Or 11...dxc4 dxe4 12 f6 ♗xf6 13 ♘xe4 ♗g7 14 c5 ♕c7 15 ♕h4 f6 16 ♗f4 ♕a5 17 ♗d2 with a very active position for White in Hracek-Wahls, German Bundesliga 1996.

12 f6 ♗xf6 13 e5

White clears the e4-square with gain

of tempo and now has a very dangerous attack.

13...♗g7

Understandably, Black wishes to keep the dark-squared bishop. 13...♗xe5 leaves White with all the chances. He has good attacking chances against Black's weakened kingside and if that doesn't come off, he has a back-up plan of using the bishop pair in the endgame. Practice has seen 14 ♘xe5 dxc3 15 ♕xc3 ♘xe5 16 ♕xe5 ♘f5 17 c3 (this move, preventing the exchange of queens with ...♕d4+, seems best) 17...f6 and now:

a) 18 ♕e2 e5 19 c5+ ♔g7 20 ♕f2 ♕c7 21 h3 b6 22 g4 ♘e7

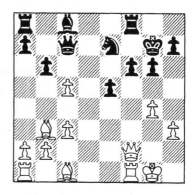

White now found a beautiful finish: 23 ♗h6+!! ♔xh6 24 g5+ ♔xg5 (24...♔g7 25 gxf6+ ♔h8 26 fxe7 wins and so the black king is lured to its doom) 25 ♕e3+ ♔h4 26 ♕h6+ ♔g3 27 ♖ae1 1-0 Berzinsh-Jaracz, Swidnica 1999. 27...♘f5 is met by 28 ♖xf5 and mate quickly follows.

b) 18 ♕e4 ♕b6+ 19 ♖f2 ♔g7 20 g4 ♘d6 21 ♕e3 ♕c6 22 g5 f5 23 ♕e5+ ♔g8 24 ♗e3 ♘f7 25 ♕b5 and White had all the chances in Macieja-Ftacnik, Krynica 1998.

14 ♘e4 ♘xe5 15 ♘xe5 ♗xe5 16

♗g5

White has a terrifying attack.

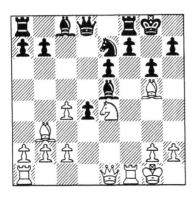

16...f5 17 ♕h4 ♖f7 18 ♘f6+

This leads to a clear plus for White but in his notes to this game Short indicates that 18 c5!? was also very promising.

18...♗xf6

Black must eliminate one of White's attacking units. 18...♔h8 turned out badly in the encounter Mitkov-Stefansson, Hartberg 1991, e.g. 19 ♖ae1 ♕a5? (this loses a piece; Black had to try 19...♗d6) 20 ♘g4! ♗g7 21 ♗xe7 ♕c7 22 ♗d8 ♕c5 23 ♘f6 h6 24 ♘e4 ♕f8 25 ♘g5 ♖f6 26 c5 ♗d7 27 ♗c7 ♕xc5 28 ♗e5 1-0.

19 ♗xf6 ♕f8 20 ♗xd4 ♘c6 21 ♗e3 ♕e7 22 ♕xe7 ♖xe7

Thanks to his accurate defence Black has avoided immediate loss but still has a very poor endgame in which White's bishop pair and active position give him all the play.

23 c5?

see following diagram

As Short points out, White's best plan was 23 ♗g5 ♖e8 24 ♖ad1 e5 25 c5+ ♗e6 26 ♖d7.

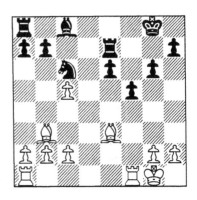

23...♔g7?

Oll misses his chance. With 23...♘a5, eliminating White's bishop pair, he would have obtained good drawing chances, e.g. 24 ♖ad1 ♘xb3 25 ♖d8+ ♔f7 26 cxb3 ♖d7 27 ♖d1 ♖xd1+ 28 ♖xd1 ♔e8 and White's initiative is fizzling out.

24 ♗g5 ♖e8 25 ♖ad1 h6 26 ♗d2 e5 27 ♗c3

Now White is back on track.

27...♗e6 28 ♗xe6 ♖xe6 29 ♖d7+ ♖e7 30 ♖xe7+ ♘xe7 31 ♗xe5+ ♔f7 32 ♖d1 ♘c6 33 ♗c7

White is a good pawn up and Short does not allow his opponent any further chances.

33...♖e8 34 ♔f2 ♖e7 35 ♖d6 ♖e4

36 c3 a5 37 b3 a4 38 ♗c7 ♖e7 39 ♗b6 axb3 40 axb3 f4 41 b4 ♘e5 42 ♗d8 ♖e8 43 ♗c7 ♔f6 44 ♗xe5+ ♖xe5 45 ♖d7 ♖e3 46 c4 ♖c3 47 ♖xb7 ♖xc4 48 ♔e2 ♖c2+ 49 ♔d3 ♖xg2 50 c6 ♔e6 51 b5 f3 52 c7 ♔d7 53 b6 1-0

In the remaining games of this chapter we see White refraining from an early f4-f5 gambit, preferring a slower build-up.

> ### Game 20
> ### Short-Gelfand
> *Brussels Candidates Quarter-Final 1991*

1 e4 c5 2 ♘c3 d6 3 f4 ♘c6 4 ♘f3 g6 5 ♗c4

Never before seen in such a high-level event.

5...♗g7 6 0-0 e6 7 d3 ♘ge7 8 ♕e1 ♘d4

This treatment has become quite popular.

9 ♘xd4 cxd4 10 ♘e2

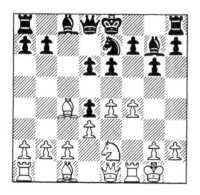

10...0-0

Now it is safe for Black to castle. Note that 10...d5?! is premature because of 11 ♗b5+, as after 11...♗d7 12 ♗xd7+ ♕xd7 13 e5 ♘c6 14 b4! Black cannot

hang on to the advanced d-pawn for long.

11 ♗b3

So that ...d6-d5 does not arrive with tempo and can thus be met by e4-e5.

11...♘c6

Aiming to knock out the bishop from a5. In his notes Short suggests 11...f5!? with similar play to Game 22.

12 ♗d2 d5

12...♗d7 13 ♔h1 also slightly favours White, while after 12...a5 13 a4 ♕b6 14 ♕h4 White can prepare the usual assault.

13 e5! f6 14 exf6 ♗xf6

15 ♔h1!

Vacating g1 so that the knight can head for e5.

15...a5

An annoying little move which demands an accurate response.

16 a4

Precise. On 16 a3 a4 17 ♗a2 ♕b6! 18 ♖b1 ♕c5 19 ♖c1 ♕b6, so you see the problem.

16...♕d6

The latent dangers for Black are revealed in a line like 16...♕b6 (a bit further away from the king) 17 f5! when either 17...gxf5 18 ♘f4 or 17...exf5 18 ♕g3 exposes him to a powerful white initiative. Boris sensibly stays more central.

17 ♘g1! ♗d7 18 ♘f3 ♘b4

Gelfand banks on a queenside counter demonstration, as per usual in the Sicilian, but he would probably have done better to try to challenge in the centre with 18...♖ae8. After the game move Short manoeuvres adroitly to defend the queen's flank whilst building up for an attacking breakthrough.

19 ♕f2! ♕c5 20 ♗c3! ♘c6 21 ♖ae1 b6 22 ♗d2 ♘b4?

Quite wrong. Black underestimates the threats and takes away an important defender. 22...♖ae8 was called for.

23 ♕g3!

Gelfand's idea is perhaps revealed in the line 23 ♘e5? ♗xe5 24 ♖xe5 ♘xc2! 25 ♖c1 ♕d6, threatening to take on e5.

23...b5

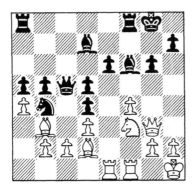

24 f5! exf5

Or 24...bxa4 25 fxg6 axb3 26 gxh7+ and the attack is decisive after either 26...♔h8 27 ♘e5 or 26...♔xh7 27 ♘g5+ ♗xg5 28 ♕xg5.

25 ♘e5 ♗e8

On 25...♗xe5 26 ♕xe5 ♖ae8 White knocks the props out of Black's game with 27 ♗xb4, but the best defence was

25...♖a7! when White would retain a big plus with 26 ♘xd7 ♖xd7 27 ♖xf5.

26 axb5 ♕xb5 27 ♖xf5 ♔h8 28 ♖xf6!

Smashing his way in.

28...♖xf6 29 ♘g4 ♖f5 30 ♘h6 ♖h5 31 ♕f4 1-0

A very fine game by Short.

Game 21
Anand-Gelfand
Reggio Emilia 1991/92

---

1 e4 c5 2 ♘c3 d6 3 f4 ♘c6 4 ♘f3 g6 5 ♗c4 ♗g7 6 0-0 e6 7 d3 ♘ge7 8 ♕e1 h6!?

A novelty. One glance at the white formation reveals where he has ambitions, so Gelfand does not castle yet. But the question now arises as to how safe his short castled king could ever be!?

9 ♗b3

The following year at Wijk aan Zee Sax chose 9 ♕g3 against Gelfand but after 9...d5 10 ♗b3 0-0 he was too precipitate in throwing in 11 f5 (11 ♕h4 f5 would have been about equal) and after 11...dxe4 12 dxe4 exf5 13 ♕h4 fxe4 14 ♘xe4 ♘f5 Black came out on top. Soon afterwards, at Linares 1992, Short tried 9 ♗d2 0-0 10 ♗b3 d5 11 ♖d1 f5 12 exf5 exf5 13 ♔h1 a6 14 ♘e2, but he did not obtain much from the opening either. Boris obviously believes in this formation for Black.

9...a6!

see following diagram

9...0-0 would allow the usual 10 f5! exf5 11 ♕h4 with strong attack, while 9...♘d4 is considered in the next main game.

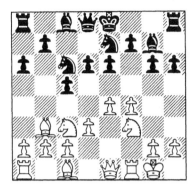

10 a4!?

It is a moot point whether White should take time out to clamp down on Black's queenside aspirations or just get on with it on the kingside. There are two ways for White to attack:

a) 10 e5!? ♘f5 (it is risky to accept the pawn sacrifice with 10...dxe5 11 fxe5 ♘xe5 12 ♘xe5 ♕d4+ 13 ♔h1 ♕xe5 because of Anand's 14 ♕f2!) 11 ♔h1 and now the safest way for Black to play is to close the position with 11...d5 (after 11...♘fd4 12 ♘e4 ♘xf3+ 13 ♖xf3 dxe5 14 fxe5 ♘xe5 15 ♖f1 White had good attacking chances for the pawn in An-and-Gelfand, Wijk aan Zee 1996) 12 ♘e2 h5 13 c3 b6 with equality in Khalifman-Van Wely, European Club Cup 1999.

b) 10 ♗d2 b5 11 f5!? gxf5 12 ♘h4 and now the game Sutovsky-Psakhis, Tel Aviv 1999, went 12...f4 13 ♗xf4 ♘e5 14 ♕g3 ♖g8 15 ♔h1 ♕c7 16 ♘f3 ♗h8 17 ♕h3 with a promising position for White. Perhaps either 12...fxe4 or 12...b4 would have been more of a test of White's idea. Shortly after that game Sutovsky varied with 11 ♘h4 b4 12 ♘d1 against Gelfand at Tel Aviv, but this encounter does not tell us much as the

players agreed a draw here!

10...♖b8 11 ♕g3

After 11 ♘d1 b5 12 axb5 axb5 13 ♘f2 0-0 14 c3 b4 Black quickly got going on the queenside in J.Polgar-Gelfand, Pamplona 1999/2000.

11...♘d4

Structurally this does compromise Black a little. The immediate 11...b5! was probably better and this idea received a practical test in the game Belotti-Novikov, St Vincent open 1998, which continued 12 axb5 axb5 13 f5?! exf5 14 ♗f4 c4! and Black quickly assumed the initiative.

12 ♘xd4 cxd4 13 ♘e2 b5 14 axb5 axb5 15 ♕f2

Some restraint is required. 15 f5?! is over the top and the line 15...exf5 16 ♗f4 ♖b6 17 e5 only blows up in White's face after 17...g5! 18 h4 ♘g6 19 hxg5 dxe5.

15...♕b6 16 f5

Now he kicks off.

16...exf5 17 exf5 gxf5 18 ♘g3?!

Anand seems unsure of which specific targets he is going after over the next few moves. 18 ♘f4 was better.

18...♗e5 19 ♗f4 ♗e6 20 ♖ae1 ♕c7 21 ♘h5?

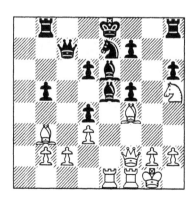

Probably missing the efficacy of the reply. 22 ♕e2! was simpler and stronger with Black having dismal prospects whichever way he chooses to give back the central pawn, e.g. 21...♔d7 22 ♗xe5 dxe5 23 ♕xe5 ♕xe5 24 ♖xe5 and he still has lots of weaknesses.

21...♔d7!

Necessity is the mother of invention! At any rate the knight on h5 is not at its most dangerous post, so Black at least has a prayer.

22 ♖e2 ♖bf8!

On 22...♘g6?! 23 ♕g3 is awkward.

23 ♗xe6+?!

But this is not the right way to pursue the advantage. 23 ♖fe1! was correct after which Black cannot reach equality, e.g. 23...♘c6 24 ♘g3 with a powerful attack, or 23...♘g6 24 ♕g3 ♘xf4 25 ♘xf4 ♖hg8 26 ♕h4! ♖g4 27 ♕xh6 ♖h8 28 ♗xe6+ ♔d8 29 ♕xh8+ ♗xh8 30 ♗xf5 ♖g8 31 ♘d5 with pressure.

23...fxe6 24 c3 ♗xf4 25 ♘xf4 e5!

Gelfand fights him off with fierce ingenuity.

26 ♖fe1 ♖f7 27 ♘h5 dxc3 28 d4 ♕b6! 29 bxc3 ♖c8 30 dxe5 ♕xf2+ 31 ♔xf2 dxe5 32 ♖d1+ ♔e6 33 ♘f4+ ♔f6 34 ♖d6+ ♔g7 35 ♖xe5

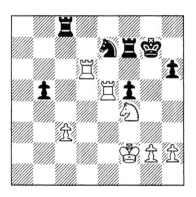

35...♘g8!

One final moment of accuracy secures the draw. Instead 35...♖xc3? would have lost to 36 ♘h5+, e.g. 36...♔g8 37 ♖d8+ ♖f8 38 ♘f6+ ♔f7 39 ♖xf8+ ♔xf8 40 ♖xe7! or 36...♔h7 37 ♖d7 ♔g6 38 ♘f4+ ♔g5 39 ♘d5! ♖c2+ 40 ♔g3 ♘c6 41 ♖xf7 ♘xe5 42 ♖g7+ ♔h5 43 ♘f6 mate.

36 ♖xb5 ♘f6 37 ♔f1 ♖xc3 38 ♖xf5 ♖c1+ 39 ♔e2 ♖e7+ 40 ♘e6+ ♔g6

Not 40...♔f7? 41 ♔d2 winning.

41 ♖e5 ♖c8 42 ♖e3 ♖ce8 43 ♔d3 ♖d7 44 ♖g3+ ♔h7 ½-½

Game 22
Topalov-Van Wely
Wijk aan Zee 1996

---

1 e4 c5 2 ♘c3 d6 3 f4 ♘c6 4 ♘f3 g6 5 ♗c4 ♗g7 6 0-0 e6 7 d3 ♘ge7 8 ♕e1 h6 9 ♗b3 ♘d4

Something of a blend of the last two examples.

10 ♘xd4 cxd4 11 ♘e2 0-0 12 ♔h1

Amongst other purposes this move vacates g1 for the knight.

12...f5

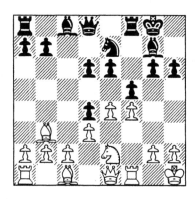

This is by no means forced, and indeed constitutes a weakening, but it does have the virtue of holding things up for a while on the kingside. The alternative 12...d5 13 e5 leads to very similar play to Game 20.

13 ♘g1 ♔h8 14 ♘f3 ♗d7 15 ♗d2 ♖c8 16 ♕g3 fxe4 17 dxe4 d5

Had he not played the earlier ...f7-f5 then some such resolution of the central tension might have worked out, but as it is Van Wely's position is soon riddled with vulnerable points.

18 exd5 exd5 19 ♘h4 ♖f6 20 ♘f3 ♘f5 21 ♕f2 ♗b5 22 ♖fe1 ♗c4 23 ♘xd4 ♕b6 24 c3 ♘xd4 25 ♗e3 ♖f7 26 ♗xc4 dxc4 27 ♖ad1 ♖e8 28 ♗xd4 ♖xe1+ 29 ♕xe1 ♗xd4 30 ♖xd4

---

see following diagram

As mentioned, the weak spots in Black's camp prevent him from reaching equality, and even in this simplified setting his king is not safe.

30...♕xb2 31 h3

Luft.

31...♕b5 32 ♕e6 ♔g7 33 ♖xc4 h5 34 a4 ♕b1+ 35 ♔h2 ♕c1 36 ♕e5+ ♔h7 37 ♕d5 ♖e7 38 ♕d4 ♖f7 39 ♕xa7! ♕e1 40 ♕g1 ♕e2 41 ♕d4 ♕f1 42 ♖b4 ♖e7 43 ♕f6 ♖g7 44 ♖e4 ♕f2 45 ♕d4 ♕c2 46 ♖e5 ♕a2 47 ♕e4 ♔h6 48 ♖e8 ♔h7 49 ♖f8 ♖f7 50 ♖b8 1-0

Summary

White's rather crude attack based on ♗c4 has been causing problems for Black for many years. Although this plan is frowned upon at the highest levels there are numerous examples of Black being obliterated on the kingside in under 30 moves. Even players as strong as Boris Gelfand have succumbed to White's onslaught. Having said that, the most promising version of this attack by far is when Black commits himself to ...d6 at an early stage (this is something that diehard Najdorf players often do when meeting 2 ♘c3, as 2...♘c6 3 ♘f3 – intending 3 d4 – can embarrass them). The lines where Black plays ...e7-e6, and then ...d7-d5 in one go (Games 12-13) are more than satisfactory for the second player.

1 e4 c5 2 ♘c3

2...d6

      2...♘c6 3 f4 g6 4 ♘f3 ♗g7 5 ♗c4 e6 6 f5 ♘ge7 7 fxe6 fxe6 8 d3 *(D)*
          8...d5 – *Game 12*; 8...0-0 – *Game 13*

3 f4 ♘c6 4 ♘f3 g6 5 ♗c4 ♗g7 6 0-0 e6 7 d3

      7 f5 *(D)*
          7...gxf5 – *Game 14*
          7...exf5 8 ♕e1 ♘ge7 9 d3 h6
               10 ♕g3 ♘e5
                    11 ♗b5+ – *Game 15*; 11 ♘xe5 – *Game 16*
               10 exf5 – *Game 17*

7...♘ge7 8 ♕e1 *(D)*

      8 f5 – *Game 18*

8...h6

      8...0-0 – *Game 19*
      8...♘d4 – *Game 20*

9 ♗b3 a6

      9...♘d4 – *Game 22*

10 a4 – *Game 21*

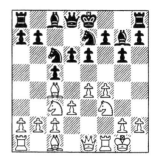

        8 d3   *7 f5*   *8 ♕e1*

CHAPTER THREE

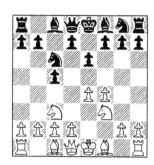

1 e4 c5 2 ♘c3 ♘c6
3 f4 e6 4 ♘f3

---

1 e4 c5 2 ♘c3 ♘c6 3 f4 e6 4 ♘f3

If as Black you are happy with White taking play into a Sicilian Taimanov via an early d2-d4, then this is a quite reputable response to the Grand Prix Attack. Most obviously if Black springloads his d-pawn with ...e7-e6 then there is a natural deterrence to White developing his bishop on one of its most threatening squares, c4, because of being straightaway hit with ...d7-d5 in response.

The material in this chapter breaks down as follows: 4...d5 5 ♗b5 and now 5...♘f6 is seen in Games 23-26 while 5...♘e7 is the subject of Games 27-31. The more circumspect 4...♘ge7 is seen in Games 32-36 and, finally, the unusual 4...♘f6 is tried in Game 37.

Game 23
Plaskett-Velimirovic
Belgrade 1988

1 e4 c5 2 ♘c3 ♘c6 3 f4 e6 4 ♘f3 d5

4...♘ge7 is seen in Games 32-36, while 4...♘f6 is Game 37. After 4...a6

White's best choice is probably to transpose to a Closed Sicilian in which the move ...a7-a6 is not particularly useful for Black with 5 g3 as 5 a4 d5 is harmless.

4...♕c7!? is rarely seen, but White would probably have nothing better than transposition to an Open Sicilian with 5 d4.

5 ♗b5 ♘f6

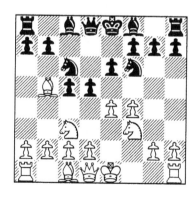

5...♘e7 is the subject of Games 27-31. The alternatives are:

a) 5...a6 provokes a move White wants to play anyway and Black fell well short of equality in Portisch-Pomar, Malaga

---

1961, after 6 ♗xc6+ bxc6 7 d3 ♘f6 8 0-0 ♗e7 9 ♕e1 0-0 10 b3 ♕c7 11 ♘a4.

b) 5...dxe4 6 ♗xc6+ bxc6 7 ♘xe4 ♘f6 8 ♕e2, as in Maahs-Bach, Hamburg 1994, is better for White.

c) 5...d4 6 ♗xc6+ bxc6 7 ♘b1 ♗a6 8 d3 c4 9 0-0 ♘f6, as in G.Ginsburg-V.Baklan, Cappelle la Grande 1997, when White could have maintained a slight edge with 10 b3 c3 11 ♖e1 according to Baklan.

6 ♕e2

White has a wide choice here between the game move, 6 ♘e5 (Game 24), 6 d3 (Game 25) and 6 e5 (Game 26). Finally, in Sarapu-Helmers, from the New Zealand-Norway match of the 1984 Olympiad, White took straightaway on c6 and after 6 ♗xc6+ bxc6 7 ♕e2 ♗e7 8 0-0 0-0 9 ♔h1 (9 d3 is more natural) 9...c4 10 e5 ♘d7 11 b3 ♘b6!? 12 ♕f2 c5 13 ♗a3 ♗a6 14 bxc4 ♖c8 they split the point.

6...♗e7 7 0-0

White has two main alternatives here:

a) Things rapidly came to the boil in Storm-Bern, Biel open 1989, after 7 ♗xc6+ bxc6 8 d3 ♗a6 9 e5 ♘d7 10 0-0 ♕c7 11 f5!? exf5 12 e6 fxe6 13 ♕xe6 ♘f8 14 ♕xf5 ♗c8 15 ♕h5+ g6 16 ♕h6, but Black scrambled out to an eventual draw.

b) In Hebden-Franco, Calella open 1985, White did not time things quite right and he was repulsed after 7 ♘e5 ♕c7 8 ♗xc6+ bxc6 9 b3 c4! 10 0-0 ♗a6 11 bxc4 ♗b4! 12 ♖f3? (12 exd5 was better, but Black is doing fine) 12...0-0 13 ♖b1 and here 13...♗xc3 was good. Franco chose 13...♖ab8 instead, but won at move 33.

7...0-0 8 ♗xc6 bxc6 9 d3

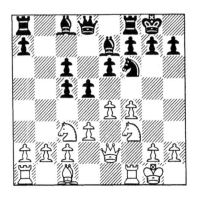

9...a5!?

A novelty – and an interesting one too. In Bilek-Stein, Kecskemet 1968, Black flicked in 9...c4! and soon stood better after 10 d4 ♘xe4 11 ♘xe4 dxe4 12 ♕xe4 ♕d5. Since 10 dxc4 ♗a6 11 b3 ♗b4 is also satisfactory, this is probably Black's best line.

10 ♗d2 a4 11 ♘e5 ♕c7 12 ♖f3 ♘e8!? 13 ♖e1 ♘d6

A noteworthy regrouping.

14 ♖h3 g6

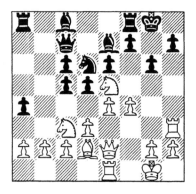

I had assumed that this sort of middlegame was just worse for Black with his cumbersome c-pawns, but Velimirovic changed my mind that afternoon as I realised that Black might have a completely viable game. Eventually I hit upon a retreat of the well placed knight at e5 as the best way forward.

15 ⦰g4!? f5!?

I was under the impression that my last move had prevented this.

16 ⦰h6+ ♔g7 17 exd5 ♗f6!?

By unpinning the e-pawn he now threatens to take back on d5, and I realised how the knight on h6 is a bit out of it.

18 dxe6 ♗xe6!? 19 ♕xe6 ♖ae8 20 ⦰d5

No choice. I was still bewildered as to what he was up to.

20...♗d4+

On 20...♕d8 White bails out with 21 ⦰xf6! ♖xf6 22 ♗c3.

21 ♔f1

21...♕d8??

So this was his idea. There is a rather large hole in it. However, after 21...cxd5 22 ♕xd5 ♗xb2 he would have had some compensation due to the awkward knight at h6.

22 ⦰e7

There was a notable change in my opponent's demeanour after this move appeared on the board, since now he is clearly busted.

22...♖f6 23 ♕e2 ♗xb2 24 c3 c4 25

♕e5 ⦰e4 26 ♖xe4 fxe4 27 ⦰g4 ♕xe7 28 ♖xh7+ 1-0

Game 24
Watson-Kupreichik
Hastings 1984/85

---

1 e4 c5 2 ⦰c3 e6 3 f4 d5 4 ⦰f3 ⦰c6 5 ♗b5 ⦰f6 6 ⦰e5

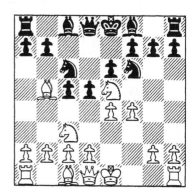

6...♕c7

6...♗d7 was played in Nun-Morawietz, Oberwart open 1992, when after 7 ♗xc6 ♗xc6 8 ⦰xc6 bxc6 9 d3 ♕b6 10 ♕e2 ♗e7 11 b3 0-0 12 ⦰a4 ♕c7 White ought to have kept a small edge with 13 c4.

7 ♕f3

Or 7 ♕e2 ♗e7 8 0-0 0-0 9 ♗xc6 bxc6 and now:

a) 10 d3 and:

a1) 10...♗a6 occurred in Villareal-Miola, Lucerne Olympiad 1982, and Black ingeniously liquidated his weak pawns after 11 b3 ♗d6 12 ♗a3 ♖fd8 13 ⦰g4 ⦰xe4! 14 ⦰xe4 dxe4 15 ♕xe4 c4! with approximate equality, since 16 ♗xd6 ♖xd6 threatens 17...f5 and hence White has no time to take on c4.

a2) In Safranska-Kruppa, Berlin 1994, Black varied by starting the transfer of his knight, 10...♘e8 11 ♗d2 ♘d6 12 ♖ae1 f6 13 ♘f3 ♗d7 14 b3 ♘b5 15 ♘a4 ♘d4 16 ♕d1 ♖ad8 with chances for both sides.

b) In Watson-Spraggett, Commonwealth Championship 1995, White played 10 b3 but Kevin Spraggett turned in a marvellous performance to extract the maximum from the latent potential of his pieces: 10...c4!? 11 bxc4 ♗b4 12 exd5 cxd5 13 cxd5 exd5 14 ♗b2 ♖e8 15 ♔h1 ♗b7 16 a3 ♗c5 17 ♕d3 ♖ad8 18 ♖ab1 ♕c8!? 19 ♘b5 d4!? 20 ♘xd4 ♕a8 and Black went on to win.

7...a6 8 ♗xc6+ bxc6 9 0-0 ♗d6

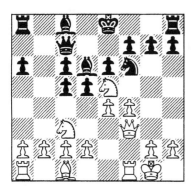

10 d3!?

In Tseshkovsky-Sveshnikov, Sochi 1980, White chose the quite unnatural 10 ♘d3?! and after 10...c4 11 ♘e1 0-0 12 d3 cxd3 13 cxd3 ♗e7 Black's problems were behind him. But to avoid such a positionally undesirable retreat White has to allow, for a couple of moves, a gambit. In my opinion Kupreichik ought to have grabbed it and tried to weather the storm of his queen being kicked around, but ceding the opponent the initiative is not to his taste.

10...0-0 11 ♔h1 a5 12 ♗d2 ♗a6 13 ♖fe1

Now the pawn is no longer there for the winning.

13...♖ad8 14 ♖ad1 c4

Trying to do something.

15 dxc4 dxc4 16 ♕g3

Watson, whose style of play was once described by Spassky as that of 'a drunk machine gunner', lines up an attack.

16...♔h8 17 ♘f3!

An excellent stratagem, made all the more admirable because it involves the retreat of a well-placed piece.

17...♗b4

Grabbing a pawn here fails to 17...♘h5? 18 ♕h4 ♘xf4? 19 ♘g5 h6 20 ♗xf4 ♗xf4 21 ♘xf7+.

18 ♘g5 ♖d4

Kupreichik flails around in search of active play, but the long-term strategical factors are against him, and, as so often in these lines, his queen bishop is dreadful.

19 e5 ♘g8 20 ♕f2 ♖d7

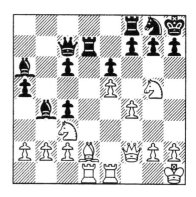

21 f5

Here we go.

21...h6 22 f6! g6

On 22...hxg5 23 ♗xg5 the attack crashes through. Kupreichik does his best to keep White's pieces away from his king for as long as possible, but William gets it in the end.

23 ♕h4 ♖fd8 24 ♘f3 ♗f8

In addition to his space advantage and attack White also has a big strategical plus.

25 ♘e4 c3

The only hope is to get the light-squared bishop working.

26 bxc3 c5 27 ♖b1! ♗b7

It will enjoy only a brief influence upon events.

28 ♖xb7! ♕xb7 29 ♘xc5! ♕d5

On 29...♗xc5 30 ♗xh6 does him in.

30 ♘xd7 ♖xd7 31 c4

Now Watson makes no mistake in winning this won game.

31...♕c5 32 a4 h5 33 ♖b1 ♗h6 34 ♗xh6 ♘xh6 35 ♕f4 ♘g8 36 h3 ♕f8 37 c5 ♖c7 38 ♘g5 ♘h6 39 ♘e4 ♔g8 40 g4 ♕a8 41 ♔h2 ♔h7 42 ♘g5+ ♔g8 43 ♘e4 ♔h7 44 gxh5 ♘f5 45 hxg6+ fxg6 46 ♘g5+ ♔h8 47 ♘xe6 ♖c6 48 ♕e4 ♕c8 49 ♕xc6! ♕xc6 50 ♖b8+ 1-0

Game 25
Adams-Lautier
Chalkidiki 1992

---

1 e4 c5 2 ♘c3 e6 3 f4 d5 4 ♘f3

♘f6 **5 ♗b5+ ♘c6 6 d3**

A relatively rare move.

6...♗e7

In Langner-Polasek, Czech Championship 1995, Black replied 6...♗d7!? and after 7 0-0 d4!? 8 ♘e2 ♗e7 had interesting prospects.

7 ♗xc6+ bxc6 8 0-0 ♗a6

Lautier attempts a finesse to assist with the dissolution of his two c-pawns. After 8...0-0 9 b3 White stands well. Instead he played 9 ♗d2 in Hug-Gligoric, Skopje 1972, and after 9...♗a6 10 e5 ♘d7 11 ♕e1 d4 12 ♘e4 c4 13 ♗a5 ♘b6 14 dxc4 ♗xc4 Black was better. In Narciso-Ochoa de Echaguen, Spanish Championship 1993, 9 ♘e5 was played and following 9...♕c7 10 ♕e1 ♘e8! 11

♖f3 f6 12 ♘g4 c4!? 13 ♖h3 f5 14 ♘e5 cxd3 15 cxd3 ♗f6 play was obscure, but White delivered later mate on g7.

9 e5

9 ♕e2 is another approach.

9...♘d7 10 b3 c4 11 dxc4 dxc4 12 ♖e1

The doubled pawns have gone, but not all of Black's headaches have gone with them. He still has a number of weak squares in his camp.

12...♘b6 13 ♘e4 0-0 14 ♗e3 ♘d5 15 ♕d2 ♘xe3 16 ♕xe3 ♕b6 17 ♖ad1

The d6-square is weak.

17...♖fd8 18 ♘d6 cxb3 19 axb3 h6 20 ♖d2 c5

Electing to pursue equality in a middlegame.

21 ♖ed1 ♗b7 22 ♔h1

With his monster knight at d6 White is always going to be better.

22...♗c6 23 ♖d3 ♗b5

Forcing a slight weakening of b3, but this does not matter much.

24 c4 ♗a6

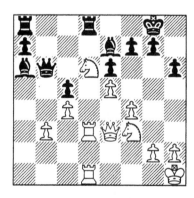

25 f5!

Michael gets on with it.

25...exf5 26 ♘xf5 ♕e6

On 26...♗f8 27 ♖xd8 ♖xd8 28 ♖xd8

♕xd8 29 e6 White's domination and absence of pawn weaknesses cede him the advantage.

27 ♘d6 ♗e7

Or 27...♗xd6 28 ♖xd6 ♖xd6 29 ♖xd6 ♕c8 30 ♖d5 and the weak c-pawn falls anyway.

28 ♕xc5 ♗b7 29 ♕f2 ♖ad8 30 ♘d4!

This tactic is decisive.

30...♕xe5

Or 30...♕g6 31 ♕xf7+! ♕xf7 32 ♘xf7 ♔xf7 33 e6+ and wins.

31 ♘xf7 ♗xg2+

Desperation.

32 ♕xg2 ♔xf7 33 ♘c6 ♕e6 34 ♘xd8+ ♖xd8 35 ♕f2+ 1-0

Game 26
Bangiev-Tukmakov
Ukraine 1979

---

1 e4 c5 2 f4 ♘c6 3 ♘f3 e6 4 ♘c3 d5 5 ♗b5 ♘f6 6 e5

Also not so common although, naturally, viable.

6...♘d7

Or 6...♘g8 7 ♗xc6+ bxc6 and now:

a) Play became very sharp in Kosten-Gurgenidze, Palma 1989, 8 d3 ♘h6 9 0-0 ♘f5 10 ♘e2 c4 11 g4 cxd3 12 cxd3 ♘h4 13 ♘g3 ♕b6+ 14 ♔h1 ♘xf3 15 ♕xh3 h5!? 16 gxh5 c5 but Kosten weathered the storm to emerge victorious in the end.

b) Mitkov-Velimirovic, Vrnjacka Banja 1991, varied with 8 b3 ♗a6 9 d3 ♘h6 10 0-0 c4 and was later drawn. The game Horvath-Jovanovic, Budapest 1996, might have thrown more light on this line had the players not agreed to a draw here.

7 ♗xc6

This has to be the most consequent move. In Rumens-Denman, British Championship 1980, White castled and went on to stand a little better after 7 0-0 ♗e7 8 ♕e1 (not 8 ♘e2?! ♕b6 9 ♗xc6 c4+! 10 ♔h1 bxc6 and Black stood fine in Lindberg-Karlsson, Stockholm 1992) 8...0-0 9 ♕g3 ♔h8 (9...♘b4!?) 10 d3 ♘b4 11 ♖f2 a6 12 ♗xd7 ♗xd7 13 b3, but since he parted with the bishop anyway it must make more sense for the bishop to double Black's pawns as it goes. But in J.Martin-Lobron, Gran Canaria 1990, Black avoided the doubling of his pawns and started active operations immediately with 7...♘d4 8 ♗a4 ♕a5. After 9 ♗xd7+ ♗xd7 10 ♔h1 ♘f5 11 d3 h5 12 ♘e2 h4 13 c3 ♗b5 14 ♕c2 ♕a6 15 ♖d1 d4! 16 cxd4 ♗c6!? 17 dxc5 0-0-0!? he had seized the initiative.

7...bxc6 8 0-0!?

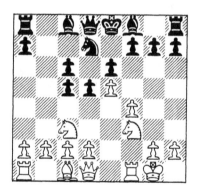

Interesting. White permits the undoubling of the pawns by ...c5-c4 but hopes to make something of a general looseness in the black camp, plus the space advantage that the e5-pawn confers, to generate attacking play. In Nordstrom-L.A.Schneider, Stockholm 1988, the game was unclear after 8 d3 ♗e7 9 b3 0-0 10 0-0 f6 11 ♗b2 fxe5 12 fxe5 ♕e8!?

13 ♕d2 ♗a6 14 ♔h1 ♕h5 15 ♘e2 ♖ab8. Campora-Sahovic, Panchevo 1985, varied with 10...f5 when Sahovic manoeuvred skilfully in the middlegame, advancing his a-pawn to exchange it off at b3 and also swivelling his bishop via e8 to h5, as in a Dutch Defence. But the rigidity of the structure meant that the man with the knight pair was always likely to stand better and White won in the end. Something similar occurred in Keitlinghaus-Pekarek, Prague 1992, with 9 0-0 0-0 10 ♕e1 ♖b8 11 b3 f5 12 ♗a3 ♖f7 13 ♘a4 h6 14 c4 g5, but that time Black managed to draw.

8...c4 9 b3 ♗a6 10 bxc4 ♗xc4 11 d3 ♗a6 12 ♘e2 g6 13 ♗e3 ♕a5 14 h3 h5 15 ♔h2 ♗e7 16 ♗f2 h4

Thus Tukmakov not only suppresses the g2-g4 break but also stops a swap of dark-squared bishops via ♗h4.

17 ♘ed4 ♖c8 18 ♘b3 ♕a4 19 ♕d2 c5 20 c3 c4 21 dxc4 ♖xc4 22 ♗d4!

Superficially one might have thought it more natural for one of the knights to occupy this spot, but Bangiev sees that this is the right minor piece to sit here.

22...0-0?

Now Bangiev takes his chance to exploit the weaknesses around the black king created by the advance of the h-pawn. 22...♖c6 would have been better.

23 f5! exf5

On 23...gxf5 24 ♕h6 is hard to deal with.

24 ♖fe1!

There is not much that Black can do about the projected advance of the e-pawn, since 24...♕c6 runs into a fork at a5.

24...♖e8 25 e6 ♗d6+ 26 ♔h1 ♘f8

There is no satisfactory defence against the combined white pieces.

27 ♕h6 ♖xd4 28 exf7+ ♔xf7 29 ♘bxd4 ♗g3 30 ♘g5+ ♔g8 31 ♘de6 ♕d7 32 ♘xf8 1-0

A well-conducted attack against a strong opponent.

Game 27
Rumens-Franklin
London 1976

---

1 e4 c5 2 ♘c3 ♘c6 3 f4 e6 4 ♘f3 d5 5 ♗b5 ♘e7

This development of the knight has been generally preferred to 5...♘f6.

6 exd5

The main alternative, 6 ♘e5, is considered in Game 31. Instead 6 ♕e2 worked out well in Rossolimo-Zuckerman, US Championship 1966/67, after 6...dxe4 7 ♘xe4 a6 8 ♗xc6+ ♘xc6 9 b3 ♗e7 10 ♗b2 0-0 11 0-0 (11 ♘eg5!?) 11...b6 12 ♘eg5!? (12 ♖ad1 ♗b7 13 d4 cxd4 14 ♘xd4 ♕c8 was equal in Niko-lac-Hakki, Bahrain 1990) 12...h6?! 13 ♘e5! with the initiative. 6...a6?! is also not very good and in Hickl-A.Yousif, Thessaloniki Olympiad 1988, after 7 ♗xc6+ bxc6 8 d3 g6 9 0-0 ♗g7 10 ♕f2 d4? 11 ♘a4 ♕a5 12 b3 0-0 13 ♗a3

Black threw in the towel. However, 6...d4, as in Bangiev-Novikov, Kiev 1978, looks a good enough answer to me. I would also advocate 6...d4 as the best response to 6 0-0, a continuation quite often chosen by handlers of the white pieces.

6...exd5?!

Although this might seem the correct move according to the classical precepts that advocate the avoidance of isolated doubled pawns, it is the knight recapture which should be made (see Games 29 and 30), for Black has clocked up a dismal score with 6...exd5.

7 ♕e2!

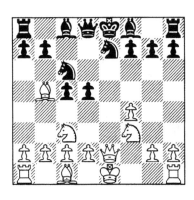

7...♗g4

7...a6 8 ♗xc6+ bxc6 simply falls in with White's plans, while 7...f6?! makes an ugly impression and Black was routed in S.Nikolic-Whitehead, Lone Pine 1979: 8 d4 cxd4 9 ♘xd4 ♔f7 10 ♘f3 ♗e6 11 0-0 ♘f5 12 ♗d3 ♗c5+ 13 ♔h1 ♕d7 14 a3 a6 15 ♗d2 h5 16 ♗e1 ♘e3 17 ♗f2 d4 18 ♘e4 ♗a7 19 ♗xe3 dxe3 20 ♖ad1 ♕c7 21 f5 ♗d7 22 ♗c4+ ♔h8 23 ♘d6 h4 24 ♕d3 ♖h5 25 ♕d5 and Black resigned. 7...♕d6 is considered in the next example.

8 ♗xc6+

In Lazic-Molnar, Szekszard open 1994, White declined the chance to double the c-pawns but just castled and after 8 0-0 ♛d6 9 ♗xc6+ ♛xc6 10 h3 ♗xf3 11 ♛xf3 0-0-0 12 f5 g6 13 fxg6 fxg6 14 d3 play was unclear.

8...bxc6 9 0-0 ♛a5

I find this an unnatural square for the queen. In Zinn-Doda, Lugano 1968, Black preferred 9...♛d6 but was brilliantly defeated after 10 b3 c4 11 dxc4 ♛c5+ (thus Black rids himself of the pawn weakness but he still suffers from weak squares and a lag in development) 12 ♔h1 ♛xc4 13 ♛e1 f6 14 d3 ♛c5 15 ♖b1 ♔f7 16 ♖b3 ♛a5 17 ♘d4 ♗d7 18 ♖b7 ♛d8 19 ♘a4 ♗c8 20 ♘c5! ♛d6 21 ♗a3! ♗xb7 22 ♘xb7

22...♛d7 (22...♛xa3 23 ♛e6+ ♔e8 24 ♘xc6 or 23...♔g6 24 f5+ and the attack continues on either 24...♔h6 25 ♘d6 or 24...♘xf5 25 ♛xf5+ ♔f7 26 ♛e6+ ♔g6 27 ♘xc6) 23 ♘c5 ♛c8 24 f5 ♘g8 25 ♛g3 ♘h6 26 ♘ce6 ♘xf5 27 ♖xf5 g6 28 ♖xf6+! and Black resigned since 28...♔xf6 29 ♛f4 is mate.

Black varied in Rumens-Benjamin, Charlton 1976, with 10...♛e6 but still ended up in big trouble after 11 ♛f2 ♗xf3 12 ♛xf3 ♘f5 13 ♗a3 ♘d4 14

♛d3 ♛f5 15 ♖ae1+ ♔d7 16 ♛a6.

10 d3 0-0-0

Certainly one might imagine that the king would be safer here than on f7.

11 ♗d2 ♛c7

Acknowledging the incorrect stationing and so losing a tempo.

12 h3 ♗xf3 13 ♛xf3 ♘f5 14 ♛f2 h5 15 ♘a4 d4

Forced. If 15...♛d6 then 16 b4!

16 ♖ae1 ♗d6 17 ♖e4! h4

The arrival of the knight at g3 now greatly complicates White's attempts to probe Black's queenside weaknesses.

18 ♛e1 ♛d7

Here 18...♘g3 is met by 19 ♗a5 and each side will 'win' the exchange but the consequences will be that White keeps by the far superior minor piece. Franklin avoids the skewer.

19 ♗a5 ♖de8

19...♖df8 is met by the same nice tactic, 20 ♗b6!, e.g. 20...♘g3 21 ♛a5 ♘xf1 22 ♗xa7 ♗c7 23 ♛a6+ ♔d8 24 ♘xc5 and wins.

20 ♗b6!

An elegant, and necessary, finesse. Without it White has difficulty in prosecuting the attack further.

20...♖xe4

On 20...♘g3 comes 21 ♗xa7! ♖xe4 22 ♕a5! with advantage, so Black swaps rooks first.

21 dxe4 ♘g3 22 ♖f3

Off to the war zone.

22...♕e7

Now the white bishop is under threat, but Rumens maintains the momentum of the attack right through to a pretty finish.

23 e5! axb6 24 ♘xb6+ ♔d8 25 ♕a5 ♗b8

There is no better defence.

26 ♖b3!

Correctly forgoing the regain of material in the line 26 ♘d5+ ♗c7 26 ♘xe7 ♗xa5 27 ♘xc6+ ♔c7 28 ♘xa5 when Black can put up tough resistance with 28...♖a8.

26...♕c7 27 ♕a8!

Threatening 28 ♘d5.

27...♔e7 28 ♘c4 ♕c8

To avoid the pin.

29 ♖b7+ ♔e6 30 ♘b6 ♕d8 31 ♕a6!

The black king cannot escape the insurgents.

31...♖f8

Trying to prevent the capture of the f-pawn after White checks on c4, but it is already too late to come up with a defence.

32 ♕c4+ ♔f5 33 ♘d7! ♕a5

A last hope of counterattack, but White moves first.

34 ♕d3+ ♔xf4

Or 34...♔e6 35 ♘xf8+ ♔d5 36 c4 mate.

35 ♕f3+ ♔g5 36 ♕g4+ ♔h6 37 ♕xh4+ ♘h5 38 ♘xf8 ♗xe5 39 g4 g6 40 ♖xf7 1-0

The king hunt comes to an end.

A splendid game from Rumens who conducted the attack with great imagination and precision.

Game 28
Kosten-Rovid
Budapest 1984

---

1 e4 c5 2 ♘c3 e6 3 f4 ♘c6 4 ♘f3 d5 5 ♗b5 ♘e7 6 exd5 exd5 7 ♕e2 ♕d6 8 ♗xc6+!?

I believe that this was the first time that this move was played. Alternatively:

a) 8 ♘e5 leads to a loss of time by comparison with Zinn-Doda after 8...f6 9 ♗xc6+ bxc6 10 ♘f3, which Black should exploit with 10...♗g4!? Instead in Hebden-Kristensen, Silkeborg 1983, Black played 10...g6?! and soon stood clearly worse after 11 b3 ♔f7 12 ♗a3 ♕xf4 13 ♗xc5 ♘f5 14 ♗xf8 ♖xf8 15 0-0 ♔g8 16 ♖ae1, when Hebden went on to exploit Black's dark-square weaknesses on the queenside to win. Instead of 8...f6, 8...♗d7 left Black in big trouble in Rogoff-Tukmakov, Graz Student Olympiad 1972, after 9 ♗xc6 ♗xc6 10 ♘b5! ♕d8 11 0-0 f6 12 ♘xc6 bxc6 13 ♘c3 ♔f7 14 f5, and Black did not equalise either in King-Podzielny, Germany 1985, with 8...a6 9 ♗xc6+ bxc6 10 b3 f6

11 ♘f3 ♔f7 12 ♗a3 ♘f5 13 g3 a5 14 0-0 ♗a6 15 d3 ♗b5 16 ♖ae1.

b) 8 0-0 ♗g4 9 ♗xc6+ ♕xc6 10 h3 ♗xf3 11 ♕xf3 g6 12 f5! gxf5 13 d4!? cxd4 14 ♘e2 was very obscure in Davies-Suba, Cardiff 1984, but the 8...a6? of West-Booth, Australian open 1993, is a loss of time and after 9 ♗xc6+ bxc6 10 b3!? ♕xf4 11 ♘e5 ♕d4+ 12 ♔h1 ♗e6 13 ♗b2 ♕b4 14 ♖ae1 ♕b7 15 ♘a4 Black was in a very bad way and got mated at move 28.

c) An alternative approach was tried in A. Adamski-Schinzel, Polish Championship 1980: 8 d4!? c4 9 b3 cxb3 10 axb3 ♗g4 11 h3 ♗xf3 12 ♕xf3 0-0-0 13 0-0!? ♘xd4 14 ♕f2 ♕c5 15 ♗d2 ♘ec6 16 b4!? ♕xb4 17 ♖fb1 ♕c5 18 ♘a4 ♕xb5 19 ♖xb5 ♘xb5 20 ♕e2 a6. This is obscure, but White went on to win. In Oratovsky-Bruk, Israeli Championship 1994, Black varied with 10...♕e6!?

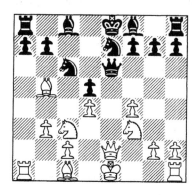

when after 11 ♘e5 ♗d7 12 0-0?! the game quickly burnt itself out and was agreed drawn in five more moves, viz. 12...♘xe5! 13 ♕xe5 ♖c8!? 14 ♗xd7+ ♔xd7 16 ♖ac1 f6 17 ♕xe6+. White should have preferred 12 ♗xc6 with an advantage after either 12...bxc6 13 0-0 f6 14 ♘xd7 ♕xd7 (14...♕xe2 15 ♘xf6+)

15 ♘a4, or 12...♘xc6 13 f5! ♕e7 14 ♘xd5 ♘xd4 15 ♕e4 ♘xc2+ 16 ♔d1 ♗xf5 17 ♕xf5 ♖d8 18 ♔xc2 ♖xd5 19 ♖e1. Frankly, I am surprised that such a natural as move as 8 d4 has not been seen more frequently.

8...♕xc6

In Hebden-Yap, Moscow 1986, Black held the draw after 8...bxc6 9 d3 g6 10 0-0 ♗g7 11 ♖e1 ♗e6 (this move is, of course, the most natural and acceptable way to block the e-file) 12 ♘a4 0-0 13 ♕f2 d4 14 ♘g5 ♗f5 15 b3 ♘d5 16 ♗a3 ♘b4 (this piece also does a blocker's job) 17 ♕d2 ♖ab8 18 ♘e4 ♗xe4 19 ♖xe4 f5 and drawn in 53 moves.

9 ♘e5

Thus White gains some time, but Rovid must have thought that he would be able to boot the knight out without any problems.

9...♕d6 10 0-0 a6 11 d3 f6?!

Far from being repulsed, Kosten has just been presented with the chance to ingeniously get an attack going.

12 ♕h5+! g6 13 ♘xg6! ♘xg6 14 f5 ♕e5 15 ♗d2! ♕d4+ 16 ♖f2 ♕h4 17 ♖e1+ ♔f7

On 17...♔d8 18 ♕f3 White retains a dangerous initiative after either 18...♘e7

19 ♘xd5 or 18...♘e5 19 ♕xd5+. Still, these were certainly better than the text as now he goes down without a fight.

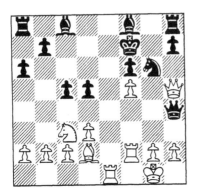

18 fxg6+ hxg6 19 ♕xd5+ ♔g7 20 g3 ♕h3 21 ♘e4 ♖h5 22 ♕d8 1-0

Game 29
Hebden-Hort
London (Lloyds Bank) 1982

---

1 e4 c5 2 f4 e6 3 ♘f3 ♘c6 4 ♘c3 d5 5 ♗b5 ♘e7 6 exd5 ♘xd5!?

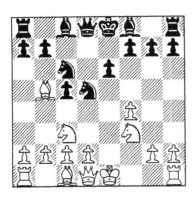

Black allows his queenside to be smashed up in the pursuit of active counterplay.

7 ♘e5

7 0-0!? is considered in the next main game, while 7 ♗xc6+ bxc6 8 ♘e5 ♗d6!

was fine for Black in Minasian-Becerra Rivero, Lucerne 1997.

7...♗d7 8 ♗xc6 ♗xc6 9 ♘xc6 bxc6

All as in Smyslov-F.Olafsson from the 1959 Candidates tournament. The powerfully centralised knight, an active bishop and use of the b- and d-lines constitute good compensation for the doubled and isolated c-pawns.

10 0-0 ♗e7

Black fianchettoed in Kosten-Cvetkovic, Belgrade 1988, and stood about equal after 10...g6!? 11 ♕e2 ♗g7 12 ♘e4 ♕e7 13 d3 0-0 14 c3 f5 15 ♘d2 e5 16 ♘c4 ♖ae8 17 fxe5 ♗xe5.

11 ♕e2 0-0

12 ♘e4

I imagine that Hebden did not want to grant the opportunity of ...♘xc3, hence he sends his knight off on an unlikely tour before starting the development of his queen bishop. I prefer 12 d3.

12...♘b6

In Lazic-Cvetkovic, Yugoslav Championship 1994, play became sharper after 12...f5!? 13 ♘g5!? ♘xf4 14 ♖xf4 ♗xg5 15 ♕xe6+ ♔h8 16 ♖f2 ♖e8 17 ♕c4 ♖e1+ 18 ♖f1 ♖xf1+ 19 ♕xf1 ♗xd2.

13 ♖b1

Preparing the fianchetto without permitting ...♕d4+.

13...♖e8 14 b3 f5 15 ♘g3 ♗f6 16 ♗a3 ♕d6 17 ♔h1 g6 18 ♕f2 ♘d7

19 ♘e2?

Hort recommended 19 ♖ad1 as slightly better for White. Hebden unwisely invites complications which prove unfavourable for him.

19...♕xd2

Not declining the chance.

20 ♕f3 ♕xc2 21 ♕xc6 ♕xa2 22 ♕xd7 ♕xa3 23 ♘g1

Not the sort of move with which to continue a self-initiated attempt to complicate. Now Hort reorganises his game and soon shows a decisive advantage.

23...♕a6 24 ♕d2 ♖ad8 25 ♕c2 ♖d5 26 ♘f3 ♕d6 27 ♕c4 ♖b8 28 ♕a4 ♕d7 29 ♕a2 ♖b4 30 g3 ♖d3 0-1

After this victory Hort dismissed Hebden with the opinion 'He is only an optimist, and that is not good enough.' Still each, with their different styles, was to finish co-winner of that tournament.

Game 30
Korolev-Obukhovsky
USSR 1973

---

1 e4 c5 2 ♘c3 ♘c6 3 f4 e6 4 ♘f3

d5 5 ♗b5 ♘e7 6 exd5 ♘xd5 7 0-0!?

An intriguing gambit.

7...♘xf4!?

Accepted! In Watson-Murey, Brighton 1983, Black captured on c3 and White should have taken back with the b-pawn to keep a small edge. Black declined the gambit in Minasian-Alterman, Manila Olympiad 1992, with 7...♗e7 and play continued 8 ♗xc6+ bxc6 9 ♘e5 ♕c7 10 d3 0-0 11 ♘e4 f6 12 ♘c4 f5 13 ♘g3 (finding a comfortable spot for the queen's knight seems a recurrent problem for White in this line) 13...♗f6 14 ♕e2 ♘b6 with a complex game.

8 d3 ♘g6 9 ♘g5 f6 10 ♗xc6+ bxc6 11 ♕f3 ♘e5 12 ♕g3 ♕d4+

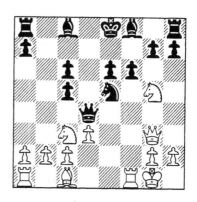

12...♗e7! makes it very tough for

White to justify his gift, for Black will soon be castling away from the flak. The text compels White to sacrifice a piece to keep his initiative running, but he retains a fierce attack for it.

13 ♗e3 ♕g4 14 ♕f2!

Keeping the kettle boiling.

14...fxg5 15 d4 cxd4 16 ♗xd4

A critical moment.

16...♘f3+

This is not quite satisfactory as a way out, but 16...♕f4 runs into problems too after 17 ♗xe5 ♕xe5 18 ♕f7+ ♔d8 19 ♖ad1+ ♗d6 20 ♖xd6+ ♕xd6 21 ♖d1 ♕xd1+ 22 ♘xd1 and Black is nowhere near equality. 17...♕xf2+ 18 ♔xf2 is a better defence, but the development lag means Black is still struggling. It would have called for extraordinary pluck to try 16...♘d7, but it could be the best!?

17 ♕xf3 ♕xd4+ 18 ♔h1 ♕d7 19 ♖ad1 ♕c7 20 ♘e4

Every white piece is pulling its weight and there is no way Black can survive such a pounding.

20...♗a6 21 ♕h5+ g6 22 ♘f6+ ♔f7 23 ♘d5+ ♔g7 24 ♘xc7 gxh5 25 ♖d7+ ♔g6 26 ♘xa6 ♗g7 27 ♖d6 ♖he8?

This blunder of the exchange makes a difficult task hopeless.

28 ♘c7 ♖ad8 29 ♘xe8 ♖xe8 30 ♖e1 ♔f5 31 c3 c5 32 ♖d7 ♗f6 33 ♖xa7 ♖b8 34 ♖f1+ ♔g6 35 ♖a6 ♔f7 36 b3 h4 37 ♖a7+ ♔g6 38 ♖a6 ♖e8 39 ♖c6 ♗xc3 40 ♖xc5 ♗d4 41 ♖c6 ♔h5 42 h3 e5 43 ♖ff6 g4 45 ♖f5 mate

---

Game 31
Short-Topalov
Dos Hermanas 1997

---

1 e4 c5 2 ♘c3 ♘c6 3 f4 e6 4 ♘f3 d5 5 ♗b5 ♘e7 6 ♘e5!?

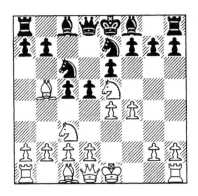

This did not cause Black many problems and I am surprised that Short played it given its poor reputation, the clear route to equality that Black now takes and also the good theoretical standing of 6 exd5.

6...♗d7

Black had already shown that he can take over the initiative with 6...d4!?, as in Figler-Podgaets, USSR 1971, which continued 7 ♗xc6+ ♘xc6 8 ♘xc6 bxc6 9 ♘b1 d3 10 c4 e5! Topalov's move looks good too.

7 ♘xd7

The consequences of the opening

were a lot rosier for White in Fiore-Tatai, Formia open 1995, where he played 7 exd5 ♘xe5 (7...exd5 is simplest) 8 fxe5 ♗xb5 9 ♘xb5 ♘xd5 10 0-0 ♗e7 11 ♕g4 g6 12 d3 ♕d7 13 ♘c3 ♘xc3 14 bxc3 h5 15 ♕g3 h4 16 ♕f3 ♖h7 17 ♖b1 0-0-0 18 c4 and won at move 47.

In a game from the 1995 Yugoslav Championship, Barlov-Abramovic, Black came out of the opening with no problems after 7 ♘xc6 ♗xc6 8 ♕e2 dxe4 9 ♘xe4 ♖c8 10 b3 ♘f5 11 ♗b2 ♗e7 12 ♗xc6+ ♖xc6 13 0-0 0-0 14 ♖ae1 ♘d4.

7...♕xd7 8 exd5 exd5 9 0-0 0-0-0 10 a3

This is an indication of the lack of adequate natural moves for White. The possession of the pair of bishops does not count for much here, but Black's extra central control and space do.

10...♘f5

Very natural, but the alternative development of the bishop with 10...g6 was strong too.

11 ♗e2

An admission that his opening has not worked. On 11 d3 Topalov might well have replied 11...h5, which has the additional point that as well as bolstering the f5-knight, a similar future to the game for the knight and h-pawn is not ruled out. Now Black has several satisfactory moves, e.g. 11...g6, but decides to go for it.

11...c4! 12 ♗f3 ♗c5+ 13 ♔h1

see following diagram

13...h5! 14 ♗xd5 h4 15 h3

What else?

15...♘g3+ 16 ♔h2 ♘xf1+ 17 ♕xf1 ♖he8 18 ♗xc4 ♕d4 19 d3

Grabbing the f-pawn would have left

him exposed to dangerous attacking threats after 19...♖f8 20 ♗e6+ ♔b8. Short seeks sanctuary in an ending, but his inability to generate any activity makes life tough.

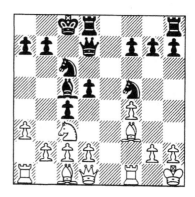

19...♕f2 20 ♕xf2 ♗xf2 21 ♗d2 f5 22 ♗b5 ♖d6 23 ♖f1 ♗g3+

From here the bishop will help to pose recurrent mating threats on White's back rank.

24 ♔g1 a6 25 ♗xc6 ♖xc6 26 ♖c1 b5 27 ♔f1 ♖ce6

Despite nominal equality, White is severely hampered by the imposing black pieces which are limiting his mobility through recurrent back-rank mating threats.

28 ♖d1 ♔b7 29 d4

Trying to do something, but this pawn will require support and it looks lonely for the rest of its brief life.

29...♖d6 30 d5 ♔b6 31 b4 ♔b7 32 ♗c1 ♖d7 33 ♘e2 ♖ed8 34 ♘c3 ♖c8 35 ♖d3 ♖e7 36 ♗e3 ♖ce8 37 ♘d1 ♖e4

Threatening to take the f-pawn.

38 d6 ♔c6!

Topalov prefers to round up this one instead.

39 d7 ♖d8 40 ♘c3 ♖e6 41 ♘e2 ♖xd7 42 ♖c3+ ♔b7 43 ♘xg3 hxg3

The exchange of White's rook greatly assists Black in the exploitation of his material advantage, and Short can hardly prevent that.

44 ♔e2 ♖c7 45 ♖xc7+ ♔xc7 46 ♔f3 ♔d7 47 ♗d4 ♖g6

The rook goes temporarily passive to protect his g-pawns, but it will soon reactivate.

48 ♔e3 ♔e8 49 ♔f3 ♔f7 50 c3 ♔e6 51 ♔e3 ♔d5 52 ♔d3 ♖e6 53 ♗xg7 ♖e1

The penetration by the rook is decisive.

54 ♗d4 ♔e6 55 ♔d2 ♖a1 56 ♔e2 ♖xa3 57 ♗e5 a5 58 bxa5 ♖xa5 59 h4 ♖a3 60 h5 ♔f7 61 ♗d4 ♔g8 62

h6 ♔h7 63 ♗g7 ♔g6 64 ♔d2 ♖a2+ 65 ♔e3 ♖f2 0-1

Game 32
Hebden-Razuvaev
Manchester (Benedictine) 1983

---

1 e4 c5 2 f4 e6 3 ♘f3 ♘c6 4 ♘c3 ♘ge7 5 d4

Thus White invites transposition into a Taimanov Sicilian. 5 ♗b5 is ineffectual, as with the knight already poised to recapture Black can simply play 5...a6 6 ♗xc6 ♘xc6.

5...♘xd4

Another possibility here is the far rarer 5...d5!? In Campora-Rodriguez, Argentine Championship 1989, White obtained the advantage after 6 dxc5 ♕a5 7 ♗e3 dxe4 8 ♘d2 ♘d5 9 ♘xd5 exd5 10 c3 ♗e7 11 ♗e2 ♗h4+ 12 g3 ♗f6 13 0-0 0-0 14 ♘b3 ♕c7 15 ♕xd5, but perhaps Black can try 8...♘f5!? For a consideration of lines stemming from 5...cxd4 6 ♘xd4 a6, see Games 35 and 36. With the text Black takes play into a form of Sicilian that can only be reached via the move order of the early f2-f4.

6 ♘xd4 cxd4 7 ♕xd4 ♘c6 8 ♕f2

By far the most natural square.

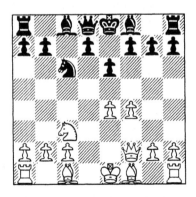

8...b6

Black has a wide choice here. 8...d5 is considered in Games 33 and 34, while he can also try:

a) 8...♗b4 9 ♗d3 and now:

a1) 9...0-0 10 0-0 d6 11 ♗e3 b6 12 ♖ad1 ♗xc3 13 bxc3 ♕e7 14 ♕g3 f5 15 ♖fe1, as in Sigurjonsson-Ciocaltea, Caracas 1970. White stands better as the doubling of the c-pawns is not such a problem here compared to the game. However, in Dishman-Small, London 1988, Black varied successfully with 10...f6 when the play became more characteristic of a standard Taimanov Sicilian after Black declined to take on c3: 11 ♕h4 ♗e7 12 f5 ♘e5 13 ♘e2 ♖f7 14 ♘f4 g5!? 15 fxg6 hxg6 16 ♕g3 ♖g7 17 ♗e2 b5.

a2) In Horvath-Czebe, Budapest 1995, Black played in experimental mode with 9...d6 10 ♕g3 ♕f6 11 0-0 h5?! 12 e5 h4? but he was smashed by 13 ♕g4 dxe5 14 ♘e4 ♕h6 15 fxe5 ♘xe5 16 ♗b5+ ♔e7 17 ♗g5+ f6 18 ♕f4 ♗c5+ 19 ♔h1! ♗e3 20 ♕xe3 1-0.

b) 8...♕a5, when in Gdanski-Twardon from the 1993 Polish Championship, White tried the same ♕g3 idea with equally brutal consequences after 9 ♕g3!? (and not 9 ♗e3? ♗a3!) 9...♘b4 10 ♗d3 ♘xd3+ 11 cxd3 b5 12 0-0 ♗c5+ 13 ♔h1 0-0 14 f5 ♔h8?! 15 f6 gxf6 16 ♖xf6 ♗d4 17 ♖h6 and Black resigned.

c) White adopted standard Open Sicilian moves against 8...d6 in Thormann-Tischbierek, East German Championship 1979, and stood better after 9 ♗c4 ♗e7 10 ♗e3 0-0 11 0-0 ♕c7 12 ♗b3 ♗d7 13 ♖ad1 ♘a5 14 ♕g3 ♘xb3 15 cxb3 ♗f6 16 f5 ♗e5 17 ♕h4.

d) 8...♗e7 and now:

d1) In Lararevic-Levitina, Yugoslavia 1983, White's kingside build-up left her with the better chances after 9 ♗d3 0-0 10 0-0 ♘b4 (10...d6 is more solid) 11 ♗e3 ♘xd3 12 cxd3 b6 13 f5.

d2) White castled on the other wing in Meister-Sorokin, Russian Championship 1990, viz. 9 ♗e3 0-0 10 0-0-0 ♕a5 11 ♔b1 d6 12 g4 ♗d7 13 g5 ♖fc8 14 f5 ♘e5 15 ♖g1 ♖xc3 with obscure complications.

e) Black played 8...a6 in Peterwagner-Schuh, Austrian Bundesliga 1989/90, but had White responded with 9 ♗e3, intending to plant the bishop on b6, he would have held an obvious advantage.

9 ♗e3!? ♗b4 10 ♗d3 0-0 11 0-0 ♗xc3 12 bxc3 ♗b7

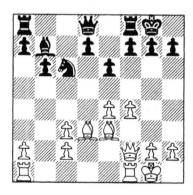

13 ♖ad1 f6 14 ♖d2 ♕e7 15 ♖fd1 ♖ad8

Since Black soon goes to the c-file anyway this looks inaccurate.

16 ♕e2

There are some similarities to a French Defence, but here it is not obvious what Black's strategy ought to be. Hebden pursues a simple policy of opening things up for his bishops, and when the action transfers to the kingside the remote placing of Black's minor pieces tells against Razuvaev.

16...d6 17 ♗f2 ♘a5 18 ♗b5!?

A very difficult sort of move to categorise. 'Probe', as Mark Hebden might say.

18...♗a8

Maybe 18...e5!?

19 e5! fxe5 20 fxe5 ♕g5 21 ♗g3 d5?

He probably overlooked the seriousness of White's reply. 21...dxe5 leads to a situation where White, with his bishop pair, has all the chances, but it was still the best hope.

22 ♖d4!

This is terribly hard to meet.

22...♖c8 23 ♗h4! ♕h6 24 ♗e7 ♖f5 25 ♖h4 ♕g6 26 ♗d3

Black has been strafed by the white bishops, as in so many Fischer games where his opponents played the French Winawer. Razuvaev has had to give up an exchange and his cause is now hopeless.

26...♖xc3 27 ♗xf5 exf5 28 ♗b4 ♖c8 29 ♗xa5 bxa5 30 e6 ♖e8 31 ♖e1 ♕f6 32 ♖xh7! ♕d4+ 33 ♔h1 ♕g4 34 ♕xg4 fxg4 35 ♖h4 ♗b7 36 ♖xg4 ♗c8 37 ♖a4 ♗xe6 38 ♔g1 ♔f7 39 ♖xa5 ♖e7 40 ♖a6 1-0

Game 33
Hebden-Kuligowski
Lewisham 1981

1 e4 c5 2 f4 e6 3 ♘f3 ♘c6 4 ♘c3 ♘ge7 5 d4 ♘xd4 6 ♘xd4 cxd4 7 ♕xd4 ♘c6 8 ♕f2 d5 9 ♗d3

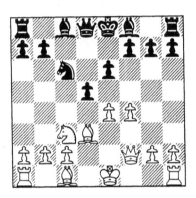

This is the most classical continuation. The alternatives are:

a) In Hug-Smyslov, Petropolis Interzonal 1973, White took on d5 but Black rather more than equalised after 9 exd5 exd5 10 ♗d3 ♗e7 11 ♗d2 0-0 12 0-0-0 d4 13 ♘e4 ♕d5, and went on to win. In Bangiev-Poliantsev, Kiev 1981, White varied with 11 0-0 but could not show that Black's isolated d-pawn was in any way a liability for him after 11...0-0 12 a3 ♗f6 (12...f5!?) 13 ♕f3 ♗e6 (13...d4 is perhaps not as trustworthy since after 14 ♘d5 ♖e8 15 ♗d2 ♗e6 16 c4 dxc3 17 ♘xf6+ ♕xf6 18 ♗xc3 White stood better in Weinzettl-Titz, Austrian Championship 1987).

b) 9 ♗e3 was played in Hodgson-Birnboim, Tel Aviv 1988, when 9...d4 is answered by 10 0-0-0, but after 9...♗b4 10 exd5 Black would have had excellent play with 10...exd5. Instead he took with

---

the queen and went on to lose after 11 ♗d2 ♕d4 12 ♕g3.

c) In Najer-Lugovoi, St Petersburg open 1993, 9 e5 was played with the game continuing in unusual manner: 9...♗e7 (9...♗b4!?) 10 ♗d3 f6 (10...♘b4) 11 ♕h4 f5 12 ♕h5+ g6 13 ♕h6 ♗f8 14 ♕h3 ♗c5 15 ♗d2 a6 16 0-0-0 h5 17 g4!? d4 18 ♘e2 ♕d5 19 c4 ♕d8 20 gxf5 exf5 21 ♖hg1 and White went on to win.

9...♗e7 10 0-0 0-0 11 ♖d1!?

Threatening to capture the d5-pawn. 11...dxe4 12 ♗xe4 and 13 ♗e3 is distinctly more comfortable for White and, perhaps even more significantly, leads to a middlegame where it is difficult for Black to create counterplay. Sicilian players are rarely content with dull equality, and it may well have been the desire to achieve something more active, as much as objective considerations, that prompted Kuligowski to try another move.

11...d4!? 12 ♘e2

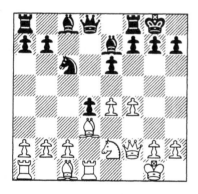

When this position cropped up again in Wahls-Razuvaev, Geneva open 1995, Yuri showed that he had learnt something in the intervening 12 years since his loss to Mark by producing 12...e5!? and the game terminated in a draw after 13 fxe5 ♘xe5 14 ♗f4 ♗f6 15 h3 ♘g6. As

14 ♕xd4 ♗g4 is at least equal for Black the critical line then must be 13 f5. Maybe then 13...♘b4!?

12...♗c5?! 13 a3 a5 14 ♔h1 f6

This is a bit ditherish. Hebden plays simply and purposefully and soon whips up a strong attack.

15 ♘g1! ♕b6 16 ♘f3 ♗d7 17 ♕h4 ♖ad8 18 ♗d2 a4 19 ♖g1! ♘e7 20 g4 ♗b5 21 g5 ♘g6 22 ♕h5 f5 23 ♖g3

It is already looking hard for Black to cope with the white offensive.

23...♗xd3 24 cxd3 ♖fe8 25 ♖h3 ♘f8 26 ♘e5 g6

On 26...♕c7 27 g6 (or even 27 ♖c1!? first) is very powerful.

27 ♘xg6! ♕c7

Or 27...hxg6 28 ♕h8+ ♔f7 29 ♕f6+ ♔g8 30 ♖h8 mate.

28 ♘xf8 ♖xf8 29 g6 ♖d7 30 ♖g1 ♔h8 31 ♖gg3 ♖g7 32 gxh7 ♕f7 33 ♕f3 ♖e8 34 ♖xg7 ♔xg7 35 h8♕+ 1-0

Game 34
Pavlovic-Wilder
Lugano 1989

1 e4 c5 2 ♘c3 ♘c6 3 f4 e6 4 ♘f3

♘ge7 5 d4 cxd4 6 ♘xd4 ♘xd4

6...d5 does not inspire complete confidence. It has been most often countered by 7 ♗e3, as in Hickl-Liberzon, Tel Aviv 1988, which continued 7...dxe4 8 ♘xc6 ♕xd1+ 9 ♖xd1 bxc6 10 ♘xe4 ♘d5 11 ♗c1 ♗b4+ 12 ♔f2 f5 13 ♘g5 ♗c5+ 14 ♔f3 0-0 15 ♗c4 h6 16 ♘h3 ♗d7 17 ♖he1 ♗e8 18 ♔g3 ♖f6 19 ♗xd5 ♖g6+ 20 ♔f3 cxd5 21 g3 ♖c8 22 c3 ♗c6 23 ♔e2 ♗b5+ 24 ♔f3 ♗c6 with a draw, but the impression remains that Black had to struggle for it.

7 ♕xd4 ♘c6 8 ♕f2 d5 9 ♗d3 d4!? 10 ♘b1

White retreats to b1 so as to be able to interpose satisfactorily after a check on b4. However, in Ye Jiangchuan-Li Zunian, Jakarta Zonal 1987, he played 10 ♘e2 ♗b4+ 11 ♔f1, but the experiment looked unimpressive after 11...0-0 12 a3 ♗c5 13 g4 f5 14 gxf5 exf5 15 e5 ♗b6 16 b4 a6 17 ♗b2 ♗e6 18 ♖g1 ♕d7.

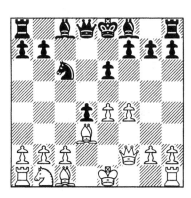

10...♗c5

Black has two main alternatives here:
a) 10...♘b4 was played and now:
a1) In Bangiev-Nasekovsky, USSR correspondence 1986-87, Black took the unusual policy of first developing his queenside. This looks really dodgy, but he somehow got away with it, so perhaps the game is of genuine theoretical importance, although I am suspicious, e.g. 11 ♘d2 ♘xd3+ 12 cxd3

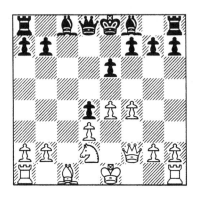

12...b6 (Black was less successful in Hebden-Meulders, Marbella Zonal 1982, with 12...♗d7 13 0-0 ♗b5 14 ♕g3 h5? 15 f5 h4 16 ♕f3 e5 17 b3 f6 18 ♘c4 ♗b4 19 a3 ♗c3 20 ♖a2 a5 21 ♕g4 ♔f7 22 ♘xe5+! fxe5 23 ♕g6+ ♔g8 24 f6 1-0) 13 0-0 ♗a6 14 ♕g3 ♕c7 15 ♖f2 ♖c8 16 ♘b3 g6 17 e5 ♗e7 18 ♘xd4? ♕d8 19 ♗e3 ♗h4 and Black took the rook, ran away with his king and won.

a2) In Spangenberg-Kasparov, Buenos Aires (simultaneous) 1992, White castled at move 11 and Black got on with a more standard pattern of development. After 11 0-0 ♗c5 12 ♘d2 0-0 13 e5 ♘xd3 14 cxd3 ♕d5 15 ♘e4 ♗e7 16 ♕g3 ♔h8 17 ♗d2 ♗d7 18 ♖f3 f5! 19 exf6 gxf6 20 a3 a5!? 21 ♖af1 ♖f7 22 ♕e1 White was able to contain the menace of the activity of the bishop pair and a draw was agreed shortly afterwards.

b) In the 1987 correspondence game Krantz-Zakharov, Black tried 10...♗e7 11 0-0 0-0 12 ♘d2 and only now did he go after the white bishop with 12...♘b4 13 ♘f3 ♘xd3 14 cxd3 ♕b6!? Krantz played 15 b3 and later developed pressure by doubling rooks on the c-file.

11 0-0 0-0 12 a3 f5!?

A more pre-emptive approach to White's kingside build-up than that shown by Kuligowski in Game 33.

13 ♘d2 a5 14 ♔h1 ♔h8 15 ♕e2 ♗d7 16 ♘f3 ♕f6 17 ♗d2 ♖ae8 18 ♖ae1 e5

With this advance the remaining central pawns disappear and it becomes apparent that Wilder's treatment suffices for equality.

19 fxe5 ♘xe5 20 ♘xe5 ♖xe5 21 ♕f2 fxe4 22 ♕xf6 ♖xf6 23 ♖xf6 gxf6 24 ♖xe4 ♖xe4 ½-½

Game 35
Hector-Vandrey
Hamburg Open 1993

---

1 e4 c5 2 ♘c3 ♘c6 3 f4 e6 4 ♘f3 ♘ge7 5 d4 cxd4 6 ♘xd4 a6

The actual move order of the game was 2 ♘f3 e6 3 d4 cxd4 4 ♘xd4 ♘c6 5 ♘c3 a6 6 f4 ♘ge7. The disadvantage of 6...a6 is that White can comfortably retreat his knight to f3.

7 ♘f3 d6

Black had an unhappy time of it in

Svidler-Zapata, New York Open 1995: 7...♘g6 8 ♗e3 ♕c7 9 ♕d2 b5 10 h4! h5 (this is almost certainly a sign that something is seriously amiss) 11 0-0-0 ♗e7 12 e5 ♗b7 13 ♘g5 f5 14 exf6 gxf6 15 f5! and the attack crashed through: 15...♘f8 16 ♘f3 ♖c8 17 ♔b1 ♘a5 18 ♕f2 ♘c4 19 ♗xc4 ♕xc4 20 ♖d4 ♕c6 21 fxe6 dxe6 22 ♖hd1 ♖d8? 23 ♖xd8+ ♗xd8 24 ♖xd8+! ♔xd8 25 ♘d4 1-0. Instead of 8...♕c7, Brendel-Kochiev, Dortmund 1993, went 8...b5 9 f5?! (this does not fit at all) 9...♘ge5 10 ♘xe5 ♘xe5 11 fxe6 dxe6! 12 ♕xd8+ ♔xd8 13 0-0-0+ ♔e8, and with the aid of his splendid knight Black went on to win in 35 moves. 7...b5 is considered in the next main game.

8 ♗e3 ♘g6 9 h4!

Black needs to be very wary of this move after ...♘g6.

9...♗e7 10 h5 ♘f8 11 ♕d2 b5 12 g4 ♗b7 13 g5 ♘d7

The knight has taken four moves to reach a square that normally requires just two, yet White seems curiously unable to exploit this loss of time directly.

14 a4!? b4 15 ♘e2 ♘c5 16 ♘g3 ♕c7 17 ♗h3 0-0-0 18 0-0!?

Hector has handled the early middlegame very creatively. He correctly per-

ceives that his king is safest here behind the advanced pawns, and not, as one might have assumed, on the queenside.
18...g6 19 h6 ♖he8 20 b3 ♔b8 21 ♕f2 ♖c8 22 ♖ad1 ♔a8 23 ♗g2 ♘b8 24 ♖d4 a5 25 ♖fd1

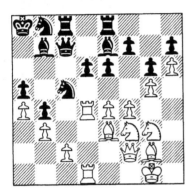

Whilst Black has been trying to make his king as secure as possible (in fact the way he has hidden it in the corner surrounded with a throng of minor pieces reminds me more of the 'bear in the hole' formation from Shogi, Japanese chess, than our own familiar western form of the game) Hector posts his men as dominantly as possible. This is also one of Karpov's favourite methods.
25...e5 26 ♖c4 ♗a6 27 ♗xc5 dxc5 28 ♘xe5 ♗xc4 29 ♘xc4 ♖cd8 30 e5+

Opening up a monster diagonal into the regal chamber.
30...♔a7 31 ♖xd8 ♖xd8 32 ♕f3 ♘a6 33 ♘xa5 ♔b6 34 ♘c6 c4 35 a5+ ♔b5 36 bxc4+ 1-0

Game 36
Gorbatov-Kharitonov
Moscow Open 1995

---

1 e4 c5 2 ♘c3 e6 3 f4 ♘c6 4 ♘f3

a6 5 d4 cxd4 6 ♘xd4 ♘ge7 7 ♘f3 b5 8 ♗d3 ♗b7 9 0-0 ♘c8

We have already seen the problems that Black can run into if he plays an early ...♘g6.
10 a3 ♗e7 11 ♕e2 d6 12 ♗e3 0-0 13 ♖ad1 ♕c7

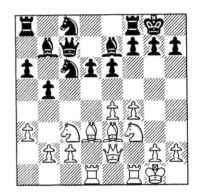

A Sicilian formation which only differs from normalcy in the placing of the king's knights.
14 ♕f2 b4 15 axb4 ♘xb4

From here the knight is poised to knock out the bishop at d3, thereby reducing the threat of a white attack.
16 ♕g3 ♘b6 17 ♗d4 f6 18 ♕h3 ♗c8! 19 e5

Determining the pawn structure.
19...♘xd3 20 ♖xd3 dxe5 21 fxe5 f5! 22 ♕g3 ♗b7 23 b3 ♖ad8 24 ♔h1 ♘d7 25 ♘g5 ♗xg5 26 ♕xg5 ♘c5 27 ♖d2 ♘e4 28 ♘xe4 ♗xe4 29 c3?! a5!

Fixing a soft spot on b3.
30 h4 ♖b8 31 ♖fd1 h6 32 ♕g6 ♕c6 33 ♖a1 f4

see following diagram

In a middlegame with opposite-coloured bishops, the player who gets his threats in first will usually emerge the winner. This time it is Black.

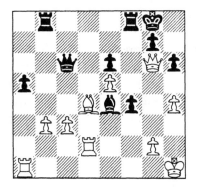

34 ♕g4 f3 35 ♖xa5 fxg2+ 36 ♔h2 ♖f1 37 ♖xg2 ♗xg2 38 ♕xg2 ♖f3 39 ♖a7 ♖b7 40 ♖a8+ ♔h7 41 h5 ♕e4 42 ♕g6+ ♕xg6 43 hxg6+ ♔xg6 44 b4 ♖d3 45 ♖d8 ♔f5 46 ♔g2 ♔e4 47 ♖d6 ♖d2+ 48 ♔g3 ♖f7!

Weaving a mating net.

49 ♖xe6 ♖f3+ 50 ♔h4 ♖h2+ 51 ♔g4 ♖g2+ 52 ♔h4 ♔f5 0-1

Game 37
Hodgson-Nemet
Biel 1983

---

1 e4 c5 2 f4 ♘c6 3 ♘f3 ♘f6 4 ♘c3 e6 5 ♗b5

Black should meet 5 e5 with 5...♘d5.

5...♘d4

Inviting sharp play.

6 e5 ♘xb5 7 ♘xb5 ♘d5

see following diagram

---

8 c4

The game Zhuravliev-Sveshnikov, Riga 1987, saw White gambit a pawn with 8 0-0, but the response was remarkable 8...c4!? 9 d4 ♕b6 10 ♘c3 ♕c6 11 ♘g5 ♘xc3 12 bxc3 b6 13 ♕e2 ♗b7

with balanced chances.

8...♘b4

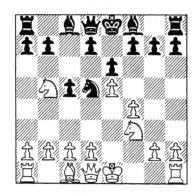

In the game Hodgson-Van Barle, London 1978, Black grabbed the pawn but he was marmalised after 8...♘xf4 9 d4 ♘g6 10 0-0 cxd4 11 ♘g5 f6 12 exf6 gxf6 13 ♘e4 ♗e7 14 ♘bd6+ ♗xd6 15 ♘xd6+ ♔e7 16 ♕xd4 ♕a5 17 c5 e5 18 ♕d5 etc.

9 d4 a6 10 ♘d6+ ♗xd6 11 exd6 cxd4 12 a3 ♘c6 13 0-0 b5!?

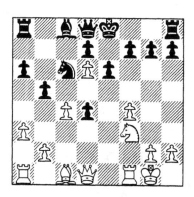

14 c5 ♗b7 15 ♕d3 ♕f6 16 ♗d2 0-0 17 ♖ae1 ♕g6 18 ♕xg6 fxg6 19 ♘e5 ♘xe5 20 fxe5 ♖f5 ½-½

A short draw, but a game with more ideas than most.

Summary

This is a difficult line for Black to handle as he will very likely end up with doubled c-pawns and will have to play dynamically and accurately to demonstrate compensation. The lines with 4...d5 5 ♗b5 ♘f6 (Games 23-26) appear to give White good chances. The alternative 4...d5 5 ♗b5 ♘e7 (Games 27-31) avoiding doubled pawns – temporarily at least – is more problematic. The continuation 6 exd5 exd5 7 ♕e2 leaves Black a little tangled but 6...♘xd5 is more dynamic. Although White can then double the black pawns, his early e4xd5 has freed the black position somewhat.

1 e4 c5 2 ♘c3 ♘c6 3 f4 e6 4 ♘f3

4...d5
> 4...♘ge7 5 d4 ♘xd4 6 ♘xd4 *(D)*
>> 6...cxd4 7 ♕xd4 ♘c6 8 ♕f2
>>> 8...b6 – *Game 32*
>>> 8...d5 9 ♗d3
>>>> 9...♗e7 – *Game 33*; 9...d4 – *Game 34*
>> 6...a6 7 ♘f3
>>> 7...d6 – *Game 35*; 7...b5 – *Game 36*
> 4...♘f6 – *Game 37*

5 ♗b5 ♘e7
> 5...♘f6 *(D)*
>> 6 ♕e2 – *Game 23*; 6 ♘e5 – *Game 24*; 6 d3 – *Game 25*; 6 e5 – *Game 26*

6 exd5 *(D)*
> 6 ♘e5 – *Game 31*

6...♘xd5
> 6...exd5 7 ♕e2
>> 7...♗g4 – *Game 27*; 7...♕d6 – *Game 28*

7 ♘e5
> 7 0-0 – *Game 30*
> 7...♗d7 – *Game 29*

6 ♘xd4

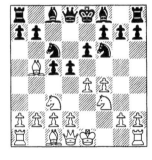

5...♘f6

6 exd5

CHAPTER FOUR

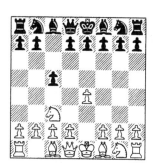

1 e4 c5 2 ♘c3: Other Lines

1 e4 c5 2 ♘c3

This chapter features variations where Black does not immediately commit to a plan with either ...g7-g6 and ...♗g7 or ...e7-e6 and ...d7-d5. Instead he waits with an early ...d7-d6 in order to see how White will deploy his forces. This can be a slightly frustrating strategy for White to meet. If Black is not committed to a kingside fianchetto then developing the light-squared bishop with ♗c4 loses its point. Furthermore the ♗b5 strategy lacks bite when the threat to double Black's pawns can be met with ...♗d7.

Having said that, Black must be careful not to delay his development for too long or White may quickly open up the centre and put his advantage in mobility to good use. An early d2-d4 by White or, in some circumstances, e4-e5, can prove most awkward.

Games 38-39 see Black adopting a 'Scheveningen' set-up with his pieces, while in Games 40-41 he commits himself to the more risky ...♗g4. Games 42-47 see the sequence 2...d6 3 f4 g6 4 d4!?, while the offbeat, but by no means bad,

2...e6 3 f4 b6 is discussed in Game 48.

Game 38
Ochoa de Echaguen-J.Garcia
Spanish Championship 1991

1 e4 c5 2 ♘c3 ♘c6 3 f4 d6

The game Wahls-Kovalev, Hamburg 1993, was noteworthy. Black tried 3...a6 4 ♘f3 ♘d4!?

This is a new idea which he may have lifted from a modern line of the English Opening (1 c4 c5 2 ♘f3 ♘c6 3 ♘c3 ♘d4!?) 5 ♘xd4 cxd4 6 ♘e2 d5! 7 e5 (on 7 d3 Kovalev suggests either 7...♗g4 or

the more enterprising 7...♛b6!? 8 exd5 ♞f6!?) 7...♝g4 8 h3 ♝xe2 9 ♝xe2 e6 10 0-0 ♝c5 with equality. In Day-Ramesh, Yerevan Olympiad 1996, White played 5 d3, but that was obviously no challenge to Black and he rapidly equalised after 5...♞xf3+ 6 ♛xf3 d6 7 ♝e3 ♞f6.

The actual move order in the game was 2...d6 3 f4 ♞c6.

4 ♞f3

Set-ups with ♝c4 are rare when Black has not already committed himself to a king's fianchetto. The white bishop is often just asking for ...e7-e6 and ...d6-d5 to be played with gain of tempo. Ramos-Bouaziz from the same Olympiad went 4 ♝c4 ♞f6 5 d3 e6 6 ♝b3 a6 7 a3 d5 8 e5 ♞d7 9 ♞f3 ♝e7 10 0-0 b5 11 ♝a2 ♝b7 12 ♞e2 f6 with balanced prospects. Prates-Lima, Brazilian Championship 1995, varied with 6 ♞f3 ♝e7 7 e5 dxe5 8 ♞xe5 ♞d4 9 0-0 0-0 10 a4 b6 and was later drawn.

If White wishes to develop his king's bishop before his king's knight, it makes more sense for it to go to b5. In Epishin-Novikov, USSR Championship, St Petersburg 1990, chances were about level in the middlegame that commenced after 4 ♝b5 ♝d7 5 ♞f3 a6 6 ♝xc6 ♝xc6 7 0-0 e6 8 d3 ♞f6 9 ♛e1 ♝e7 10 b3 0-0 11 ♝b2. In De la Villa Garcia-Bouaziz, Szirak Interzonal 1987, White varied from Epishin's treatment with the less successful 10 e5 and after 10...♞d5 11 ♞e4 ♞b4!? 12 ♛f2 ♝xe4 13 dxe4 dxe5 14 fxe5 0-0 play was unclear but Black went on to win. White could not seem to figure out on which side of the board his strategy should be focused in Gurgenidze-Dvoiris, Kharkov 1985, where instead of 9 ♛e1 he played 9 ♞e2!? ♝e7

10 c4 ♛c7 11 ♛e1 ♞d7 12 ♜b1 0-0 13 ♞g3 ♜ae8!? 14 f5 d5 15 e5 f6! 16 ♞h5? ♞xe5 17 ♝h6 ♞xf3+ 18 ♜xf3 gxh6 19 ♞f4 ♝d6 and Black soon won.

4...♞f6

Thus Black presents the option of an Open Sicilian, probably some kind of Scheveningen, after 5 d4. Alternatively 4...e6 5 ♝b5 ♝d7 6 0-0 ♞ge7 would then take us into Kindermann-A.Petrosian, Dortmund open 1992, where opposite-side castling led to a complex middlegame after 7 d3 a6 8 ♝xc6 ♞xc6 9 ♛e1 ♛c7 10 ♝e3 0-0-0 11 a3 ♚b8 12 ♜b1 ♜c8 (an unusual shifting) 13 ♛f2 ♞e7 14 d4 cxd4 15 ♝xd4 f6 16 ♝b6 ♛c6. The other main alternative, 4...♝g4, is dealt with in Games 40 and 41.

5 ♝b5 ♝d7

The rarely seen 5...e6 is considered in the next main game.

6 0-0

Not the most critical line. It is unlikely that Black can demonstrate equality after 6 e5!, e.g. 6...dxe5 7 fxe5 ♞g4 8 ♛e2 and on 8...g6 9 d3 ♝g7 10 ♝f4 0-0 (or 10...♞d4 11 ♞xd4 cxd4 12 ♛xg4 dxc3 13 ♛xd7+ ♛xd7 14 ♝xd7+ ♚xd7 15 bxc3 with a clear extra pawn) 11 h3 ♞h6

12 ♗xc6 ♗xc6 13 g4 with the advantage because of the misplaced knight at h6. Alternatively 8...♘h6 9 ♘e4 e6 10 d4 was also better for White, who went on to win in Hector-Jislason, Reykjavik 1996.

6...e6 7 d3

White failed to prove any superiority after 7 e5 dxe5 8 fxe5 ♘d5 9 ♘e4 ♗e7 10 d3 0-0 11 ♗xc6 ♗xc6 12 a3 when chances were equal in Kurajica-Sigurjonsson, Wijk aan Zee 1977.

7...♗e7 8 e5 ♘d5

By comparison with the above-mentioned game Black might have made life simpler by first capturing on e5.

9 ♘xd5 exd5 10 exd6 ♗xd6 11 ♗xc6 ♗xc6 12 ♖e1+ ♗e7 13 ♕e2 ♔f8

Black has the bishop pair and a sound structure so the loss of castling rights may not prove that serious.

14 d4 cxd4 15 ♘xd4 ♗f6 16 ♗e3 g6 17 b4

Striving his utmost to do something tactically before Black completes his development, but naturally this thrust is very loosening.

17...♔g7 18 b5 ♗d7 19 ♕f3 ♖e8! 20 ♖ad1

On 20 ♕xd5 ♗xb5! is more than satisfactory.

20...♖e4 21 c4

see following diagram

In the same vein as his 17th move.

21...♕e7?

Miscalculating. 21...♕a5! looks right as 22 cxd5? loses to 22...♗xd4 23 ♗xd4+ ♖xd4 and e1 hangs.

22 cxd5 ♖e8? 23 ♘e6+

Of course.

23...♖xe6 24 dxe6 ♕xe6 25 f5 1-0

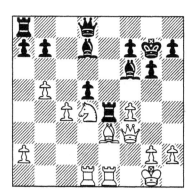

Game 39
Short-Azmaiparashvili
Yerevan Olympiad 1996

1 e4 c5

Zurab Azmaiparashvili varies from his habitual Modern Defence, in which he is one of the world's greatest experts. I can only ascribe his switch to the Sicilian to the vast amount of work on this opening that he must have done when acting as Kasparov's second.

2 ♘c3 d6 3 f4 ♘c6

The standard move. The alternatives are:

a) In King-Horvath, Germany 1995, Black did not pursue a classical scheme of development: 3...♘f6 4 ♘f3 ♗g4 5 h3 ♗xf3 6 ♕xf3 ♘fd7!? 7 d3 ♘c6 8 g4!? g6 9 h4 ♗g7 10 ♗h3 b5 11 0-0 b4 12 ♘d1 ♕c7 13 ♘e3 ♘b6 14 g5 h6 15 ♗g4 hxg5 16 hxg5 e6 and the game was later drawn in 41 moves.

b) In Keitlinghaus-Weber, Germany 1991, play seemed to be developing in a safe enough manner for Black until he let his guard slip: 3...e6 4 ♗b5+ ♗d7 5 a4 ♗e7 6 ♘f3 ♘f6 7 0-0 0-0 8 b3 ♘c6 9

♗b2 ♕c7 10 ♕e2 ♘d4 11 ♕d3 a6 12
♗xd7 ♘xf3+ 13 ♖xf3 ♘xd7 14 ♖h3
g6??

fxe5 ♘d5 10 ♘e4 h6 11 ♕e1 ♕b6 12 c4
♘db4 13 ♕e2 a6 14 ♗a4 ♕a5 15 ♗d1
♘d8 16 a3 ♘bc6 17 ♕f2 0-0 18 ♘f6+!

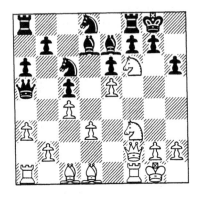

15 ♖xh7! ♘f6 (or 15...♔xh7 16 ♕h3+
and 17 ♘d5 decides) 16 ♖h3 and 1-0 in
39 moves.

In Conquest-Grünberg, Prague 1989,
White built up on the kingside and eventually broke through successfully after 4
♘f3 (instead of 4 ♗b5+) 4...♘f6 5
♗b5+ ♗d7 6 ♗xd7+ ♕xd7 7 d3 ♘c6 8
0-0 ♗e7 9 ♔h1 ♖c8 10 ♗e3 a6 11
♗g1!? 0-0 12 ♕d2 ♕c7 13 ♖ae1 b5 14
h3 ♘d7 15 ♘e2 ♖fe8 16 g4 ♕b7 17
♘g3 a5 18 ♕g2 a4 19 g5 and White
went on to win.

4 ♘f3 ♘f6 5 ♗b5 e6

A rarity.

6 ♗xc6+

Not missing his chance. In Ramik-
Mokry, Czech Championship 1994,
White held no advantage after 6 0-0 ♕c7
7 e5 ♘d7 8 d3 a6 9 ♗xc6 ♕xc6 10 ♕e2
d5 11 a4 b6 12 ♗d2 ♗b7. Mitkov-
Nalbandian, Cannes open 1995, varied
with 6...♗e7 when White turned his attentions not towards the creation of
weaknesses in the black queenside but
rather to a mating attack. This was quite
successful after 7 d3 ♗d7 8 e5 dxe5 9

Resigns!

6...bxc6 7 d3

On 7 e5 ♘d5 8 exd6 Black would
grab the f-pawn, but 8 ♘e2!? could be a
try for the advantage.

7...♘d7!

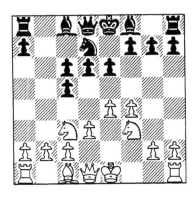

White was threatening to seize a big
strategical superiority with 8 e5.

8 0-0

Of course 8 e5 is met by 8...d5.

**8...♗e7 9 ♕e1 0-0 10 ♔h1 a5! 11
b3 ♘b6**

Intending to push on and swap the
isolated a-pawn.

12 a4 ♖a7!? 13 ♗d2 d5 14 ♘e2

♘d7

The a-pawn was attacked.

15 c4

It might have been better to have played 15 ♘g3 ♗a6 and only then 16 c4. Short follows the precepts of Aaron Nimzowitsch and the game comes to look very much like one of his.

15...♕b6 16 ♖b1 f5!

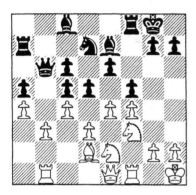

Azmai holds things up on the kingside.

17 ♘g3 ♘f6 18 h3

I am uncertain what the point of this move was. 18 ♘e5 directly looks better.

18...♗d8! 19 ♘e5 ♖e7 20 ♖f2 g6 21 ♖e2 ♖fe8

Azmai manoeuvres skilfully.

22 ♗c3 d4

A big decision. Black fixes the pawn structure but deprives the white bishop of its optimum diagonal. Superficially one might regard the black bishop pair as stifled here, but Azmaiparashvili shows that it has great latent potential.

23 ♗d2 ♘d7!?

Another important moment. White is granted the opportunity to exchange what ought to be Black's best minor piece, but after 24 ♘xd7 ♗xd7 the remaining knight is a long way from its

ideal outpost at e5 and Short would not be able to get it there without permitting Black to release all of the kinetic potential of his pieces with ...e6-e5.

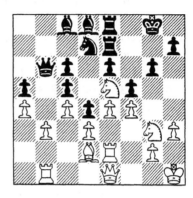

24 ♘f3

Accordingly this retreat.

24...♕c7 25 ♘f1 e5!?

Here we go. This was not strictly necessary and Azmai could have tacked around with, e.g. 25...♘f6, but he prefers a forcing sacrificial sequence to seize the initiative.

26 exf5 exf4 27 ♖xe7 ♖xe7 28 ♕c1 ♖e3!

The point of the breakout. Instead 28...gxf5?? would have been dreadful and 29 ♗xf4 ♕b7 30 ♗g5 wins on the spot.

29 fxg6 hxg6 30 ♗xe3 fxe3

The far-advanced connected passed pawn; the limited mobility of the rook; the vulnerability of the white king with a bishop pair gunning at it; the potential outposts around that king for the black knight; the general difficulty in undertaking anything active as White ... yes, this is a sound sacrifice!

31 ♕e1 ♔g7 32 g4 ♘f8 33 ♘g3 ♕f4 34 ♔g2 ♗c7 35 ♘e2 ♕d6 36 ♕h4

There is little to do. 36 ♕g3 ♕e7 37 ♕h4 ♕d6 38 ♘g3 ♘e6 would not have helped.

36...♘e6 37 ♖f1 ♗d7

Black could have forced matters with the line 37...♘f4+ 38 ♘xf4 ♕xf4 39 ♕e7+ ♔g8 40 ♕e8+ ♔g7 41 ♕xc8 ♕g3+ 42 ♔h1 ♕xh3+ 43 ♔g1 ♕g3+ 44 ♔h1 e2!? 45 ♕d7+ ♔h6 46 g5+ ♔h5 47 ♕h7+ ♔g4 48 ♕d7+ with a draw.

38 ♖h1 ♕f8 39 ♖f1 ♕d6 40 ♖h1 ♕f8

And they acknowledged the impasse.

41 ♖f1 ½-½

> *Game 40*
> **Varga-Hradeczky**
> *Budapest 1991*

---

1 e4 c5 2 ♘c3 ♘c6 3 f4 d6 4 ♘f3 ♗g4

Personally I don't like this much.

5 ♗b5!

Much more consequent than 5 h3 ♗xf3 6 ♕xf3 ♘d4!? 7 ♕d3!? a6 7 ♘e2 ♘c6!? 9 c3 e6 10 g3 ♘f6 11 ♗g2 d5 12 exd5 exd5 (Black has comfortable equality since White must lose further time to develop his queenside pieces and his bishops have limited scope) 13 0-0 ♗e7 14 ♕f3 0-0 15 d3 d4 16 c4 and a draw was agreed in Fahrner-Lendwai, Graz

1991.

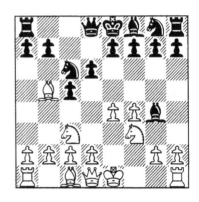

5...e6

5...♖c8, to avoid the doubled pawns, is considered in the next main game, along with Black's other alternatives.

6 ♗xc6+ bxc6 7 d3

White also won swiftly in Gavela-Ilic, Yugoslav Championship 1990, with 7 h3 ♗xf3 8 ♕xf3 ♕c7 9 0-0 ♘f6 10 d3 ♗e7 11 g4!? 0-0 12 g5 ♘d7 13 f5 exf5 14 exf5 f6 15 g6 ♖fe8 17 ♕h5 ♘f8 18 ♖f4 d5 19 gxh7+ ♘xh7 20 ♖g4 and 1-0 shortly afterwards.

7...♖b8

A vague sort of move. It would have been better to have got on with kingside development.

8 0-0 ♘e7 9 b3!? g6

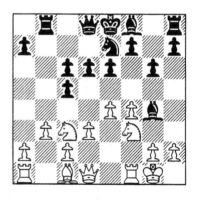

Black strives to avoid the impact of a disruptive e4-e5 advance when his knight is on f6, but whereas this worked well in the previous main game, here he cannot really prevent getting stuck with a chronically weakened pawn structure.

10 ♗b2 ♗g7 11 e5

Simple and crushingly effective.

11...d5 12 ♘a4 ♘f5 13 ♕e1

Already White is strategically winning.

13...h5 14 ♘xc5 ♗xf3 15 ♖xf3 g5 16 fxg5 ♕xg5 17 ♕f2 ♘h6?

18 ♖xf7!

An attractive kill.

18...♘xf7 19 ♘xe6 ♕g6 20 ♘xg7+ ♔d8

On 20...♕xg7 21 e6! is decisive.

21 ♕xa7 ♔c8 22 e6 1-0

Game 41
Plaskett-Kr.Georgiev
Aubervilliers (rapidplay) 1997

---

1 e4 c5 2 ♘c3 d6 3 f4 ♘c6 4 ♘f3 ♗g4 5 ♗b5 ♖c8?!

Thus he avoids the structural defect of doubled c-pawns, but presents a chance for a different type of advantage for White. Black has several other options here apart from 5...e6 (see the previous

game):

a) In Borgo-Marinelli, Italian Championship 1994, Black forced White's hand with 5...a6 and after 6 ♗xc6+ bxc6 7 0-0 ♘f6 8 d3 g6 9 ♕e1 ♗xf3 10 ♖xf3 ♗g7 he was a little worse.

b) Blatny proposes 5...g6 6 ♗xc6+ bxc6 7 0-0 ♗g7 8 h3 ♗xf3 9 ♕xf3 e6 10 d3 as offering equal chances, Black having saved a tempo there on the last example.

c) 5...♘f6 would have transposed to Bosboom-Hartoch, Dutch Championship 1993, where White castled, rather than taking on c6 straightaway. After 6...♘d7 7 ♗xc6 bxc6 8 ♕e1 e6 9 b3 ♗e7 10 ♗b2 ♗xf3 11 ♖xf3 ♕c7 12 ♘a4 ♗f6 13 ♗xf6 gxf6 14 ♕h4 0-0-0 15 ♖g3 White stood better, but Hartoch, once described by Botvinnik as 'the boy with gold in his fingers', went on to win.

d) Maybe 5...♕d7!? as in Timoseev-Dvoiris, USSR 1983, where chances were about even after 6 h3 ♗xf3 7 ♕xf3 a6 8 ♗xc6 ♕xc6 9 0-0 ♘f6 10 d3 e6 11 a4 ♗e7 12 a5 0-0-0.

6 d4!

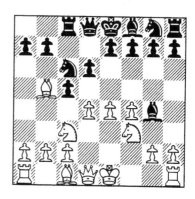

I do not think that Black can equalise now as he falls so far behind in development.

6...♗xf3

Perhaps 6...a6!?

7 gxf3 cxd4 8 ♕xd4 a6 9 ♗xc6+ ♖xc6 10 ♗e3 e6 11 0-0-0 ♕c7 12 ♖hg1 ♘f6 13 f5 ♘d7

Black is left with rather a grotty Open Sicilian position where he is behind in development and has difficulty getting his kingside pieces into play.

14 f4 ♖c4

For kicks, I sacrificed the queen.

15 fxe6!? fxe6

But he swiftly declined! Obviously White has huge compensation after 15...♖xd4 16 exd7+ but still I am sure that was the better option.

16 ♕d2?!

Better was 16 ♕d3.

16...♘f6 17 ♕d3

Notwithstanding the loss of time White still has an excellent attacking game.

17...g6 18 f5 ♖xc3

Really the only hope.

19 bxc3 d5 20 exd5 exf5 21 d6 ♕d7

see following diagram

Black had left himself with very little time and also I presumed that just about anything would do the job here.

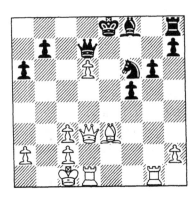

22 ♗d4?!

22 ♖ge1 was far stronger, e.g. 22...♗g7 23 ♗g5+ and Black can resign since 23...♘e4 is met with 24 ♖xe4+!

22...♗h6+!

Oops!

23 ♔b1 0-0

Still dead lost but now with a prayer.

24 ♗xf6 ♖xf6 25 ♖ge1 ♗f8 26 ♕c4+ ♔g7 27 ♕c7 ♖f7 28 ♕c5 ♖f6 29 ♖d5?

Hereabouts my brain went.

29...♗xd6 30 ♖ed1? ♗xc5 31 ♖xd7+ ♔h6 32 ♖xb7 f4

My absurd handling of things has given Black very real hopes of survival in the endgame.

33 ♔b2 f3 34 ♔b3 f2 35 ♖f1 ♗e3 36 ♔c4 g5 37 ♔d3 ♗c5 38 a4 ♖f3+ 39 ♔c4 ♗e3 40 a5 ♔g6

...and somewhere around here his flag fell.

> *Game 42*
> **Romanishin-Ilincic**
> *Lvov-Belgrade 1993*

1 e4 c5 2 ♘c3 d6 3 f4 g6 4 d4

This move gives the line its own status. Many other continuations would steer us towards already examined formations, or to a Closed Sicilian. The early development of the queen naturally grants Black the opportunity to gain time by kicking it around, but White hopes also to be successful in disrupting the opponent's development. Some intriguing gambit play has been tried by handlers of the white pieces in their search for long-term compensation, and the evidence points to this particular early recapture with the queen being a better try for the advantage than the line 1 e4 c5 2 f4 g6 3 d4 cxd4 4 ♕xd4 (see Chapter 8).

4...cxd4

4...♗g7 must be worth considering here, although the text has been almost always played at master level.

5 ♕xd4 ♘f6 6 e5 ♘c6

The usual move. 6...♘h5 is seen in Game 47.

7 ♗b5 dxe5

7...♘h5 is also popular – see Games 44 and 45, while 7...♘d7! (Game 46) has also been tried a couple of times recently.

8 ♕xd8+ ♔xd8 9 fxe5!?

Characteristically enterprising. Romanishin spurns the mundane 9 ♗xc6 and sacrifices a pawn for the initiative in a queenless middlegame. Another mode, 9 ♘f3, brought White nothing in Messa-Danner, Reggio Emilia 1983, after 9...♘d4 10 ♘xd4 exd4 11 ♘e2 ♗d7 12 ♗c4 ♖c8 13 b3 ♗g7 14 ♗b2 ♘g4 15 ♗xd4 ♗xd4 16 ♘xd4 ♘e3.

9...♘xe5

9...♘e8 is seen in the next main game.

10 ♗f4 ♘ed7

This looks like it results in congestion but after the more natural 10...♘c6 Black runs into bigger trouble as shown by Balashov-Piesena, Klaipeda 1977: 11 ♘f3 a6 12 0-0-0+ ♔e8 13 ♘e5! ♗g7 (or 13...axb5 14 ♘xb5 with advantage to White) 14 ♘xc6 ♗d7 15 ♘xe7 etc.

11 0-0-0 a6

In Van Wijgerden-Tatai, Amsterdam 1977, Black was unsuccessful with 11...♘h5 12 ♗e3 ♗g7 13 ♘f3 ♗xc3 (ridding himself of one of his best pieces does not look smart) 14 bxc3 ♔c7 15 ♖he1 a6 16 ♗c4 e6 17 ♘g5, when White's activity was too much to cope with and after 17...♘b6 18 ♗e2 f6 19 ♗xh5 fxg5 20 ♗d4 ♖f8 21 ♗e5+ ♔c6 22 ♗f3+ Black gave up the exchange with 22...♖xf3 but this was quite insufficient and he went on to lose.

12 ♗e2!?

Some earlier games had seen 12 ♗c4 but these had not resulted in any advantage for White, e.g. 12...e6 13 ♘f3 b5 14 ♗b3 ♗b7 15 ♘g5 ♚e8 16 ♖he1 ♘c5 17 ♗e5 ♗e7, as in Ghinda-Ribli, Warsaw Zonal 1979.

12...♚e8

12...♗g7 was Black's attempt to cope with the pressure in Romanishin-Ftacnik, Biel 1988. After 13 ♘f3 ♚e8 14 ♖he1 ♚f8 15 ♗c4 b5 16 ♗d5 ♖a7 17 ♘d4 ♗b7 18 ♗c6 e5!? 19 ♗xe5 ♗h6+ 20 ♚b1 ♘xe5 21 ♖xe5 ♗c8!? 22 ♘d5 ♘xd5 23 ♖e8+ ♚g7 24 ♖xh8 ♚xh8 25 ♗xd5 ♖d7 he ought to have been alright, but later on he defended inaccurately and lost.

13 ♗f3

Romanishin drew attention to another way forward with 13 ♘f3 b5 14 ♘e5 ♗b7 15 ♘xd7 ♘xd7 16 ♘d5 ♗xd5 17 ♖xd5 when the bishop pair, a development lead and the difficulties that Black will experience with his king now that castling rights have been forfeited (and not forgetting the a2-a4 lever) add up to very good compensation for White. He also observed that 16 ♘xb5 axb5 17 ♗xb5 ♗c8 18 a4 was a try for the advantage, but who knows whether he was being serious or not.

13...h5 14 ♘h3 ♗h6 15 ♘g5 e5

White would have maintained excellent positional compensation after 15...♘h7 16 h4 f6 17 ♘e6.

16 ♗d2 ♖b8 17 ♖hf1!

Keeping pressure on the weak spot at f7.

17...b5 18 ♗c6 ♚e7 19 ♗e3!

Better than 19 ♗xd7 ♗xd7 20 ♘xf7 ♗xd2+ 21 ♖xd2 ♚xf7 22 ♖xd7+ ♚e6 23 ♖a7 ♖a8 24 ♖g7 ♖hg8 with equality.

19...♖f8

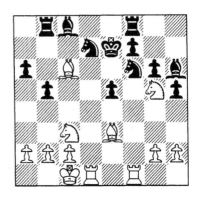

20 ♖xf6! ♚xf6 21 ♗xd7 ♗xg5

Or 21...♗xd7 22 ♘h7+ and wins (a typically original Romanishin tactic) or 21...♖d8 22 ♖f1+.

22 ♘e4+ ♚g7

Or 22...♚e7 23 ♗xg5+ f6 24 ♗e3 fxg5 25 ♗c5+ and wins.

23 ♗xg5 f6 24 ♗xc8 fxg5 25 ♗xa6

With a decisive advantage.

25...♖b6 26 ♖d7+ ♚h6 27 ♗b7 g4 28 ♗d5

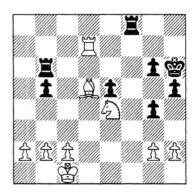

28...h4

On 28...♖f1+ there was one more moment of Romanishin magic awaiting Ilincic, viz. 29 ♚d2 ♖h1 30 ♗g8 g5 31 ♗h7 ♖xh2 32 ♗f5 ♖xg2+ 33 ♚e3 ♖g6 34 ♘f6! ♖g7 35 ♘g8+! ♖xg8 36 ♖h7 mate!

**29 ⏴f7 ⏶a6 30 c3 ⏶a4 31 b4 ⏶c8
32 ⏶d6 ⏴g7 33 ⏴xg6 ⏶xa2 34 ⏴f5
⏶ca8 35 ⏶d7+ ⏴f8 36 ⏶d2 ⏶8a3
37 ⏶c7 g3 38 hxg3 hxg3 39 ⏴b1
⏶a1 40 ⏴b2 ⏶a6 41 ⏶b3 ⏶1a3 42
⏶a5 1-0**

Wonderful creativity.

Game 43
Romanishin-Rashkovsky
USSR Championship 1976

**1 e4 c5 2 ⏶c3 d6 3 f4 g6 4 d4 cxd4
5 ⏴xd4 ⏶f6 6 e5 ⏶c6 7 ⏴b5 dxe5
8 ⏴xd8+ ⏴xd8 9 fxe5 ⏶e8**

This looks a bit wimpish, but he made it work.

**10 ⏴e3 ⏶c7 11 0-0-0+ ⏴e8 12 ⏶f3
⏴g7 13 ⏴a4 ⏴g4 14 ⏶d5 ⏶xd5 15
⏶xd5 a6 16 ⏶d4 ⏴d7 17 ⏶d1 ⏶xe5!**

If this were not a good move then Black would be in trouble but, fortunately, it is.

**18 ⏴xd7+ ⏶xd7 19 ⏶b5 axb5 20
⏶xd7 ⏴e5**

---
see following diagram

This piece will hold every aspect of Black's game together.

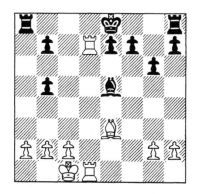

**21 h3 f5 22 ⏴g5 ⏴d6 23 ⏶xb7 h6
24 ⏴e3 f4 25 ⏴d4 ⏶f8 26 ⏶xb5**

Or 26 ⏴b1 ⏶f5.

**26...⏶xa2 27 ⏴b1 ⏶a4 28 b3 ⏶a6
29 ⏴g7 ⏶f5 30 ⏶dd5 ⏶f7 31 ⏴e5 f3
32 gxf3 ⏶xf3 33 ⏴xd6 ⏶xd6 34 h4
⏶h3 35 ⏶xd6 exd6**

This is yet another drawn rook ending.

**36 ⏶b4 ⏴d7 37 ⏶g4 h5 38 ⏶f4 ⏶g3
39 ⏴c1 g5 40 hxg5 ⏶xg5 41 ⏶f6 h4
42 ⏶h6 ⏶g4 ½-½**

Game 44
Romanishin-Portisch
Tilburg 1979

**1 e4 c5 2 ⏶c3 d6 3 f4 g6 4 d4 cxd4
5 ⏴xd4 ⏶f6 6 e5 ⏶c6 7 ⏴b5 ⏶h5 8
⏴e3**

White achieved no advantage with 8 e6 in Buturin-Novikov, Alushta 1992, after 8...⏴g7 9 ⏴xc6+ bxc6 10 exf7+ ⏴xf7 11 ⏴c4+ ⏴e6 12 ⏴xc6 ⏶c8 13 ⏴f3 ⏴xc3+ 14 bxc3 ⏶f6 because of the vulnerable c-pawns. Nor did the retrograde 8 ⏴d1 lead to anything in Gurgenidze-Georgadze, Tbilisi 1987, after 8...⏴h6!? 9 ⏴xc6+ bxc6 10 ⏴f3 dxe5 11 fxe5 ⏴xc1 12 ⏶xc1 0-0 13 ⏴e3 ⏴b6 14 ⏴xb6 axb6 15 ⏶f3 ⏴g4 with no problems for Black. 8 ♘f3 is the subject of the next main game.

8...♗g7 9 ♕d1

Threatening 10 g4. If 9 0-0-0 then 9...0-0 is unclear.

9...dxe5 10 ♕xd8+ ♔xd8 11 0-0-0+ ♗d7 12 fxe5 ♗xe5 13 ♘d5

13...♘g7

Also after 13...♘f6 14 ♘f3 White keeps up the pressure.

14 ♘f3 ♗d6 15 ♖he1 ♘e6 16 ♘g5!

In his own inimitable way Romanishin starts cooking up dangerous complications.

16...♘e5 17 ♘c3 f6 18 ♘ge4 ♗b4

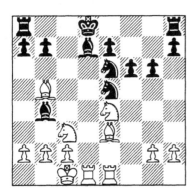

19 ♖xd7+! ♘xd7 20 ♖d1 ♘f8 21 ♗h6 a6

Or 21...♔c8 22 ♘d5 ♗d6 23 ♘xd6+

exd6 24 ♗g7 and wins.

22 ♗c4 ♗xc3 23 ♘xc3 ♖c8 24 ♗b3

Threatening 25 ♗g7.

24...e6 25 ♗xf8 ♖xf8 26 ♗xe6 ♖c7 27 ♘d5! ♘b8!

The best chance. On 27...♖c6 28 ♘f4 ♖c7 29 ♗xd7 ♖xd7 30 ♘e6+ ♔e7 31 ♖xd7+ ♔xe6 32 ♖xb7 wins trivially.

28 ♘xf6+ ♔e7 29 ♘d5+ ♔xe6 30 ♘xc7+ ♔e5 31 ♘d5 ♖f2 32 ♘e3 ♔f4

33 ♖d3?

The right way was 33 ♖e1 ♘c6 34 ♔d1 intending 35 ♖e2. Now Portisch's activity enables him to salvage a draw.

33...♘c6 34 ♔d1 ♔e4 35 ♔e1 ♖xc2! 36 ♖b3 ♖c5 37 ♘g4 ♔f4 38 ♘f2 ♖b5 39 ♖f3+ ♔g5 40 ♘d3 ½-½

Game 45
Christiansen-Ftacnik
Groningen 1991

1 e4 c5 2 ♘c3 d6 3 f4 g6 4 d4 cxd4 5 ♕xd4 ♘f6 6 e5 ♘c6 7 ♗b5 ♘h5 8 ♘f3

A novelty, but on the evidence of this game not one that gives Black too much trouble.

8...♗g7 9 0-0 0-0 10 ♗xc6 bxc6 11

♗e3 ♗g4 12 ♖ae1 ♕a5!

Highlighting the vulnerability of the e5-pawn.

13 ♗c1 ♖ad8 14 ♕e4

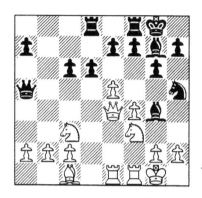

14...♕b6+

Christiansen preferred the idea of the immediate 14...d5 with ...f7-f6 to follow, but it seems to me that the text, although unproductive, does not spoil things too much.

15 ♔h1 d5 16 ♕d3 ♗c8

Better was 16...f6 17 ♗e3 ♕a5 (and not 17...♕xb2? 18 ♖b1 ♕a3 19 ♘xd5! winning).

17 ♘a4 ♕c7?

One backwards move too many. Now White establishes an advantage. 17...♕a5 18 ♕d4 f6 19 b3 was better.

18 ♘c5 ♗h6 19 ♘d4 ♘g7 20 ♖g1 f6 21 ♗d2 fxe5 22 fxe5 ♗xd2

Exchanging off a bad bishop, but unfortunately the other one is not much cop either.

23 ♕xd2 ♖f7 24 ♖gf1 ♖df8 25 ♖xf7 ♖xf7 26 ♔g1

White had more space, weak squares in the black camp to aim at and the superior minor piece.

26...♕b6 27 b4 ♘e6 28 ♘dxe6 ♗xe6 29 ♕d4 ♗f5 30 c3 a5

Black should have tried 30...♖f8.

31 ♘b3

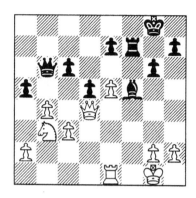

With the fall of the a5-pawn White's advantage reaches decisive proportions.

31...♕b5 32 ♘xa5 ♕a4 33 ♕d2 c5 34 ♘b3 cxb4 35 cxb4 ♕a7+

Presumably this was time shortage, since Black only helps the transfer of the knight to a better square. He should have played 35...♗e4 instead.

36 ♘c5 ♗e4 37 a4 ♖f5 38 ♕d4 ♖g5 39 g3 ♖f5 40 a5 ♖f3 41 ♖f1 ♖f5 42 ♖xf5 gxf5 43 ♕e3

The curtain could have come down here.

43...♕c7 44 ♕g5+ ♔h8 45 ♕h6 ♔g8 46 ♘e6 ♕a7+ 47 ♔f1 ♔f7 48 ♘g5+ ♔e8 49 ♕c6+ ♔f8 50 ♕e6 ♔g7 51 ♕f7+ ♔h6 52 ♘e6 1-0

Game 46
Plaskett-Relange
Hastings 1998/99

1 e4 c5 2 ♘c3 d6 3 f4 g6 4 d4 cxd4 5 ♕xd4 ♘f6 6 e5 ♘c6 7 ♗b5 ♘d7!

This improvement appears to give Black a comfortable game.

8 ♗xc6 bxc6 9 e6

Black meets 9 exd6 with 9...♘f6 and

will emerge with a good game as the white d-pawn is pinned.

9...♘f6 10 exf7+ ♔xf7

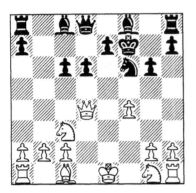

Although Black has had to move his king, he has the bishop pair and good central pawns which certainly compensate for the inconvenience. This position is similar to one which arises from the Austrian Attack against the Pirc Defence, viz. 1 e4 d6 2 d4 ♘f6 3 ♘c3 g6 4 f4 ♗g7 5 ♘f3 c5 6 e5 ♘g4 7 ♗b5+ ♗d7 8 e6 ♗xb5 9 exf7+ ♔d7 10 ♘xb5 ♕a5+ 11 ♘c3 cxd4 12 ♘xd4 ♗xd4 13 ♕xd4. Comparing the two positions, it would seem that the Sicilian Grand Prix Attack position is better for Black as he retains the useful light-squared bishop and does not have to worry about rounding up the rogue pawn on f7.

11 ♘f3

11 ♕c4+ ♗e6 12 ♕xc6 is a very dubious pawn grab. After 12...♖c8 13 ♕a4 ♕b6 14 ♘f3 h6 Black had plenty of compensation in Tanner-Behr, Germany 1987.

11...♕b6 12 ♕c4+ ♔e8 13 b3

This is too slow. A better plan for White is 13 ♗d2 ♕a6 (not 13...♕xb2 14 ♕xc6+ ♘d7 15 ♖b1 winning; however, 13...♗a6 looks fine) 14 ♕d4 ♖b8 15

0-0-0 ♕b6 16 b3 ♕xd4 17 ♘xd4 ♗d7 18 ♖he1 and the players had reached an equal endgame in Adams-Anand, Groningen 1997.

13...♘g4!

Suddenly White is in trouble. The threats against the dark squares are difficult to meet.

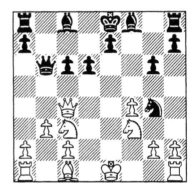

14 ♗d2 ♘e3 15 ♗xe3 ♕xe3+ 16 ♔d1 ♕b6 17 ♖e1 ♗g4 18 ♘a4 ♗xf3+ 19 gxf3

The doubled pawns on the open f-file mean that all endgames are horrible for White. This enables Black to gradually improve his position by constantly offering to exchange queens. In an attempt to retain the queens on the board, White is reduced to shuffling around planlessly and is unable to complete his development.

19...♕b5 20 ♕c3 ♖g8 21 ♕e3 ♖g7 22 ♘c3 ♕b6 23 ♕d3 d5 24 ♘a4 ♕b4

see following diagram

25 f5?

This is a blunder but the white position is riddled with holes and he will soon start to drop pawns.

25...gxf5 26 ♕xf5 ♕d4+ 0-1

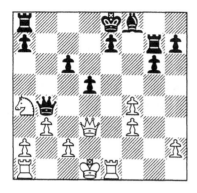

Game 47
Ermenkov-Paunovic
Hania open 1993

**1 e4 c5 2 ♘c3 d6 3 f4 g6 4 d4 cxd4
5 ♕xd4 ♘f6 6 e5 ♘h5 7 e6**

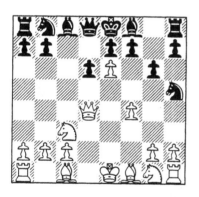

Flashy, but ultimately this does not yield any advantage. White should probably stick with 7 ♗b5+ ♘c6, transposing to Games 44 and 45.

**7...♗g7 8 exf7+ ♔xf7 9 ♗c4+ e6
10 ♕d3 ♖f8 11 ♘f3**

11 ♘e2, avoiding the need for g2-g3, was to be considered.

11...♔g8

Castling by hand, and incidentally threatening 12...f4.

12 g3 ♘c6 13 a3

Here was have reached a middlegame that is very similar to some Pirc Austrian Attacks and which ought to be fine for Black.

**13...♔h8 14 0-0 ♘f6 15 ♔g2 a6 16
♖e1 d5 17 ♗b3 b5!? 18 ♗e3**

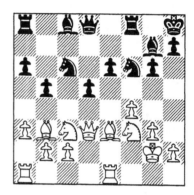

Black now had an extraordinary idea.
18...e5?!

Ten out of ten for imagination, but it doesn't work.

**19 fxe5 ♘g4 20 ♗c5 ♖xf3 21 ♕xf3
♘cxe5 22 ♕xd5 ♗d7**

Astonishingly cool, but not quite sound.

23 ♖ad1! ♗c6 24 ♕xc6!

The first principle of defence is the willingness to return any and all material gained. Ermenkov heads into a nice ending.

**24...♘xc6 25 ♖xd8+ ♖xd8 26 ♖d1
♘d4 27 ♖d3 ♗f6 28 h3 ♘xb3 29
♖xd8+ ♗xd8 30 cxb3 ♘h6**

see following diagram

No scope for flamboyance here: He's just in a lost ending.

**31 b4 ♗f6 32 ♔f3 ♘f7 33 ♔e3 ♘e5
34 b3 ♘c6 35 ♘d5 ♗b2 36 a4 h5
37 ♘c7 ♗e5 38 ♘xa6 bxa4 39 bxa4**

♗xg3 40 b5 ♘a5 41 ♘b4 g5 42 ♘c6 ♘xc6 43 bxc6 ♗c7 44 ♔d3 ♔g7 45 ♔c4 h4 46 ♔b5 g4 47 hxg4 h3 48 ♗g1 1-0

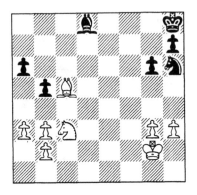

Game 48
Christiansen-Nunn
Wijk aan Zee 1982

1 e4 c5 2 ♘c3 e6 3 f4 b6!?

After 3...d5 White has the choice between 4 ♘f3 transposing to Chapter 7, Games 71-78 after 4...dxe4 5 ♘xe4, or 4 ♗b5+ ♗d7 5 ♗xd7+ ♕xd7 6 ♘f3 with an approximately equal position.

4 ♘f3 ♗b7 5 b3

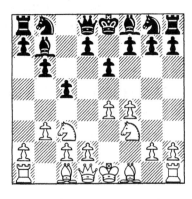

This does not really constitute picking

up the gauntlet that Black's third move threw down. 5 d4 cxd4 6 ♘xd4 has to be critical, reaching the sort of middlegames which Basman essayed in the seventies.

5...a6 6 ♕e2

Black was comfortably equal in Gomez-Nunn from the 1982 Marbella Zonal after 6 ♗e2 d5 7 exd5 exd5 8 d4 ♘f6 9 0-0 ♘c6 10 ♔h1 ♗e7 11 ♗b2 0-0.

6...♗e7 7 ♗b2 ♘f6 8 e5 ♘d5 9 g3 ♘xc3 10 ♗xc3 ♘c6

Black has no problems at all out of the opening.

11 ♗g2 b5!? 12 0-0 ♕b6 13 ♕f2 0-0 14 ♖ae1 ♖ac8 15 g4 ♘d4 16 ♘xd4 ♗xg2

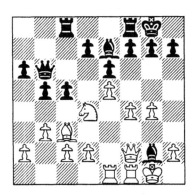

17 ♘f5

With characteristic ingenuity Christiansen tries to make something happen, but Nunn easily deals with it and the message of this game is that 5 b3 sets Black no serious problems.

17...exf5 18 ♕xg2 b4 19 ♗a1 fxg4 20 f5 c4+ 21 ♔h1 ♕c6 22 ♖e4 cxb3 23 cxb3 f6 24 ♖xg4 ♕xg2+ 25 ♖xg2 fxe5 26 ♗xe5 ♗f6 27 ♗d6 ♖fe8 28 ♗xb4 ♖c2 29 d3 ♖xg2 30 ♔xg2 ♖e2+ 31 ♖f2 ♖e3 ½-½

Summary

After 2 ♘c3 d6 3 f4 g6 White is probably best advised to head for the lines seen in the first two chapters as a quick d2-d4 just seems to be asking a little too much of the white position. Other Black tries in this chapter are playable but he must be careful not to fall too far behind in development while trying to adopt an unusual set-up.

1 e4 c5 2 ♘c3

2...♘c6

    2...d6 3 f4 g6 4 d4 cxd4 5 ♕xd4 ♘f6 6 e5 *(D)*

        6...♘c6 7 ♗b5

            7...dxe5 8 ♕xd8+ ♔xd8 9 fxe5 *(D)*

                9...♘xe5 – *Game 42*

                9...♘e8 – *Game 43*

            7...♘h5

                8 ♗e3 – *Game 44*

                8 ♘f3 – *Game 45*

            7...♘d7 – *Game 46*

        6...♘h5 – *Game 47*

    2...e6 3 f4 b6 – *Game 48*

3 f4 d6 4 ♘f3 ♘f6

    4...♗g4 5 ♗b5

        5...e6 – *Game 40*

        5...♖c8 – *Game 41*

5 ♗b5 *(D)* ♗d7

    5...e6 – *Game 39*

6 0-0 – *Game 38*

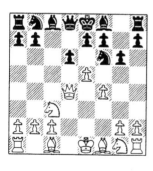

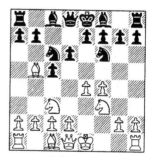

    6 e5   *9 fxe5*   *5 ♗b5*

CHAPTER FIVE

1 e4 c5 2 f4 d5 3 exd5 ♘f6

1 e4 c5 2 f4 d5 3 exd5 ♘f6

This gambit has become so popular and respected since Tal first deployed it in Game 50 (the current World Champion has also used it) that it is safe to say that it is the main reason for so many White players preferring to play 2 ♘c3 and then f2-f4 only on the third move.

Black's compensation takes the form of chances for an initiative, use of the excellent d4-square, maybe a backward d-pawn for White, and a general looseness of the white game plus a development lag which playing 2 f4 has created.

There are two ways of hanging on to the pawn: 4 c4 (Game 49) and 4 ♗b5+ (Games 50-58). Many players have often just handed the pawn back with 4 ♘c3 as in Game 59 or declined the gambit with 3 ♘c3 (Chapter 7).

Game 49
Rosich-Kasparov
Barcelona (simultaneous) 1988

---

1 e4 c5 2 f4 d5 3 exd5

In the game Hector-Yrjola, Gausdal

1987, we saw the one and only outing for 3 ♘f3!?, which actually led to a victory for the Swedish GM after 3...dxe4 4 ♘g5 ♘f6 5 ♗c4 e6 6 ♘c3 a6 7 a4 ♘c6 8 ♘gxe4 ♘xe4 9 ♘xe4 ♗e7 10 d3 0-0 11 0-0. Still, nobody has been moved to follow Jonny down that weird road.

3...♘f6 4 c4

Theory holds this move in low regard. 4 ♗b5+ (Games 50-58) is really the only try for an advantage against this gambit. Instead 4 ♗c4 ♘xd5 5 ♕h5 e6 gave White nothing in Lyons-Duncan, Dublin Zonal 1993, while 4 ♘c3 is Game 59.

4...e6 5 dxe6 ♗xe6

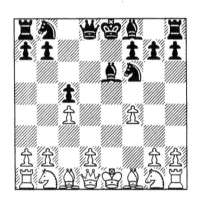

6 ♘f3 ♘c6 7 ♘c3

White was already worse after 7 d4?
♘xd4 8 ♘xd4 ♕xd4 9 ♕xd4 cxd4 in
Hodgson-Salov, Leningrad 1983. Nor
did White have a happy time of it in
Smolovic-Dobos, Budapest 1994, after 7
♗e2 ♗e7 8 0-0 0-0 9 d3

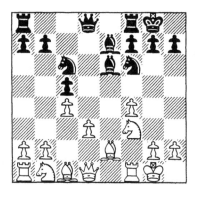

9...♕c7 10 ♘c3 ♖ad8 11 ♕b3 a6!? 12
♔h1 b5! 13 ♘e4 ♘xe4 14 dxe4 ♘d4 15
♘xd4 cxd4 16 f5 ♗xc4 17 ♗xc4 bxc4
18 ♕f3 f6 19 g4 d3 20 ♗d2 ♖b8 21 ♗c3
♗b4 22 ♗d4 ♖fd8 23 ♗e3 ♗c5 24 ♖f2
♗xe3 25 ♕xe3 ♕e5 26 ♖g1 ♖xb2 27
♖xb2 ♕xb2 28 g5 ♕d4 0-1.

7...♗d6

There is nothing wrong with the idea
of ...♗e7, ...0-0, ...♕c7 and ...♖ad8, as in
the previous note.

8 d4

Opening up the game avoids the
problems of a backward d-pawn, but
increases the scope of Black's pieces. 8
d3 was safer.

**8...cxd4 9 ♘xd4 0-0 10 ♘xe6 fxe6
11 ♗e3 ♕e7 12 ♕f3 ♗b4! 13 ♗e2
e5! 14 0-0-0**

If 14 0-0 simply 14...exf4 and there is
no satisfactory reply, e.g. 15 ♗xf4 ♘d4
wins a piece; 15 ♕xf4 ♗xc3 16 bxc3
♘d5 wins; or 15 ♘d5 ♘xd5 16 ♕xd5+

♔h8 and Black wins a bishop.

14...♗xc3 15 bxc3 exf4 16 ♗d4

On 16 ♗xf4 ♘e4 is very powerful.

**16...♖ae8 17 ♗xf6 ♖xf6 18 ♖d2
♔h8 19 ♖hd1 ♕a3+ 20 ♖b2 ♘e5**

Now the attack is unstoppable.

**21 ♕h3 f3! 22 gxf3 ♖b6 23 ♖dd2
♘d3+!**

24 ♗xd3 ♖e1+ 0-1

From these examples you will derive
an impression of how real Black's play is
for the gambitted pawn.

Game 50
Hartston-Tal
Tallinn 1979

---

1 e4 c5 2 f4 d5 3 exd5 ♘f6 4 ♗b5+

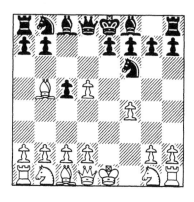

The only real test of Black's idea.

4...♗d7

For 4...♘bd7 see Game 58.

5 ♗xd7+

5 ♗c4 is awkward-looking and Black swiftly equalised in A.Bennett-Zimmer, New York open 1993, with 5...b5 6 ♗d3 c4 7 ♗e2 ♘xd5, and also in Gelashvili-Agnos, Greece 1996, after 5...♗g4 6 ♘f3 ♘xd5 7 ♘c3 e6 8 ♗b5+ ♘d7 9 h3 ♗xf3 10 ♕xf3 a6.

5...♕xd7

5...♘bxd7 did not work out so well for Black in Ostojic-Dam, Dieren 1989, after 6 c4 ♕c7 7 d3 e6 8 dxe6 fxe6 9 ♘c3 a6?! 10 ♘ge2!? ♗d6 11 0-0 0-0 12 h3 ♘h5 13 ♗e3 (returning the extra pawn to emerge with the better pawn structure) 13...♘xf4 14 ♕d2 ♘xe2+ 15 ♕xe2 ♘e5 16 ♘e4 and White stood better and went on to win.

6 c4 e6 7 ♕e2

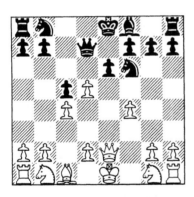

Making use of the pin to get in a constructive developing move. Two other moves have been tried here:

a) 7 ♘f3? gave White less than nothing in Bhend-King, Bern 1987, after 7...exd5 8 ♘e5 ♕c8 9 cxd5 ♗e7 10 ♘c3 0-0 11 d3 ♘a6 12 0-0 ♘c7 13 ♕f3 ♕d8 14 d6 ♗xd6 15 ♕xb7 ♗xe5 16 fxe5

♕d4+.

b) The immediate 7 dxe6 is rarely seen. Uusi-Karner, Estonia 1972, continued 7...♕xe6+ 8 ♕e2 ♕xe2+ 9 ♘xe2 ♘c6 10 ♘bc3 0-0-0 11 0-0 g6 13 b3 ♘b4 and Black had obvious compensation for the pawn.

7...♗d6

A far more common square for the bishop than e7 (see Game 57).

8 dxe6

Nowadays White usually delays this capture until after 8 d3 0-0 (Games 51-54) to remove the option of castling queenside with a quick ...♘c6 and ...0-0-0. The alternatives 8 ♘f3 and 8 f5 are considered in Games 55 and 56 respectively.

8...fxe6

Taking back with the queen also proved fine for Black in Poloch-Tischbierek, Leipzig 1984: 8...♕xe6 9 ♕xe6+ fxe6 10 ♘e2 (10 d3 0-0 transposes to Game 54, while Black varied by 10...♘c6 11 ♗d2 0-0-0 12 ♘e2 ♗c7 13 ♘c1 e5 14 0-0 exf4 15 ♗xf4 ♗xf4 16 ♖xf4 ♘b4 with equal chances in Pons-Moingt, Palma 1991) 10...♘c6 11 0-0 0-0-0 12 ♘bc3 ♘b4 13 b3 e5! 14 ♖b1 ♖he8 15 f5 e4 with advantage for Black.

9 d3 0-0

9...♘c6 10 ♘f3 0-0-0!? is a perhaps unjustly neglected alternative. In Antoshin-Oll, Berdiansk 1983, White won after 11 0-0 ♖he8 12 ♘e5?! ♗xe5 13 fxe5 ♕d4+ 14 ♗e3 ♕xe5 15 ♘c3 ♘d4 (perhaps 15...♘g4!?) 16 ♕d2 ♘f5 17 ♗f4 ♕d4+ 18 ♔h1 ♕xd3 19 ♕e1! e5 20 ♖d1 ♕xc4 21 ♖xd8+ ♖xd8 22 ♗xe5 ♘e3 23 ♖f4 ♕d3 24 ♖f3 ♘fg4 25 h3 ♘c2 and Black resigned, but the impression remains that the loss owed much to

Oll's over-ambition.

10 ♘f3

10 ♘h3 has the virtue of easing defence of the f4-pawn but the knight is far from optimally placed on the edge and the complications that developed after 10...e5 proved favourable for Black in Elmerenta-Rijhimaki, correspondence 1989-90: 11 0-0 ♘c6 12 ♘c3 ♖ae8 13 f5 ♘d4 14 ♕f2 e4!? 15 dxe4 ♗xh2+! 16 ♔h1 ♖xe4!? 17 ♗f4 ♖xf4! 18 ♘xf4 ♘g4 19 ♕h4 ♘xf5 0-1.

10...♘g4!?

Since this game this move has fallen into disuse due to preference for 10...♘c6 (Games 51-54).

11 ♘c3

Hartston returns the pawn hoping for some structural superiority, but Tal has active pieces.

11...♘c6 12 0-0 ♗xf4 13 ♕e4 ♕d4+!

From a clear blue sky.

14 ♕xd4

Not of course 14 ♘xd4?? ♗xh2+ 15 ♔h1 ♖xf1 mate!

14...cxd4 15 ♗xf4 dxc3 16 ♗d6 ♖fd8 17 c5 cxb2 18 ♖ab1 b6 19 ♖xb2 bxc5 20 ♗xc5 ♖xd3

Black's activity maintains the balance

even after a queen exchange.

21 h3 ♘f6 22 ♖c1 ♖ad8 23 ♔h2 e5 24 ♗f2 e4! 25 ♖xc6 exf3 26 ♗xa7 ♖d2 27 ♖cc2 ♖xc2 ½-½

Game 51
Short-Kasparov
Paris (rapidplay) 1990

1 e4 c5 2 f4 d5 3 exd5 ♘f6 4 ♗b5+ ♗d7 5 ♗xd7+ ♕xd7 6 c4 e6 7 ♕e2 ♗d6 8 d3 0-0 9 dxe6 fxe6 10 ♘f3 ♘c6 11 0-0

11 ♘c3 may transpose to the main game after 11...♖ae8 12 0-0, but 11...e5! is a very good option here, with the white king still in the centre, e.g. 12 f5 ♘d4! 13 ♘xd4 exd4 14 ♘e4 ♖ae8 15

0-0 ♘xe4 16 dxe4 ♖xf5 and Black was already slightly better in Poliakov-Nadyrhanov, Novorossijsk 1985.

11...♖ae8

The immediate 11...e5 is also possible here – see Game 53.

12 ♘c3

12 ♘e5? is to be avoided as Lev Psakhis convincingly demonstrated in his game as Black against Belotelov from the Biel open in 1995: 12...♗xe5 13 fxe5

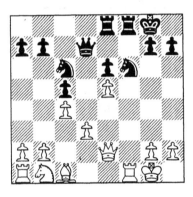

13...♘d4! (actually Black also succeeded in showing an advantage another way in Pirligras-Kapnisis, Baile Herculane 1994, with 13...♕d4+ 14 ♗e3 ♕xe5 15 h3 ♘d4 16 ♕d2 ♘c2! 17 ♕xc2 ♕xe3+ 18 ♕f2 ♕xd3 19 ♘c3 ♘e4! 20 ♕h4 ♕d4+ 21 ♔h2 ♕d6+ 22 ♔g1 ♕d4+ 23 ♔h2 ♘xc3 24 ♕xd4 cxd4 25 bxc3 ♖xf1 26 ♖xf1 dxc3, but Psakhis' move looks stronger still) 14 ♕d1 ♘g4! 15 ♕xg4 (15 ♖xf8+ ♖xf8 16 ♕xg4 ♘c2; 15 ♗f4 ♘c2! 16 ♕xc2 ♕d4+ 17 ♔h1 ♖xf4 18 ♘c3 ♘f2+ 19 ♖xf2 ♖xf2; or in this line 16 ♕xg4 ♕d4+ 17 ♔h1 ♘e3 18 ♕e2 ♘xf1 19 g3 g5 20 ♘c3 gxf4 21 ♖xf1 fxg3 all win) 15...♖xf1+ 16 ♔xf1 ♖f8+ 17 ♔g1 ♘c2 (White will not get enough for this exchange) 18 ♘c3 ♘xa1 19 ♘d5!? h5! 20 ♕h3 ♘c2 21 ♗g5 ♘d4

22 ♘e3 ♕f7 and White gave up.

12...e5 13 f5!?

Capturing on e5 would be asking for trouble.

13...♕xf5

The next game examines the more speculative 13...♘d4!?

14 ♗g5

A major parting of the ways. White can stop any ...e5-e4 break permanently with 14 ♘e4. The problem is that in the fixed pawn structure that arises after 14...♘xe4 15 ♕xe4 ♕xe4 16 dxe4 ♘d4

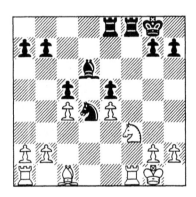

he will find it very difficult to show enough piece activity to demonstrate that Black, with his e- and c-pawns set on the same colour squares as his bishop, has anything more than a token inferiority.

Two examples bear this out:

a) Campora-P.Cramling, Seville open 1994, went (in fact White had developed his knight to d2 at move 12) 17 ♗d2 ♖f7 18 ♖f2 ♖ef8 19 ♖af1 h6 20 ♗e3 ♘c7 21 ♘d2 ♖xf2 22 ♖xf2 ♖xf2 23 ♔xf2 ♘e6 24 ♘b3 b6 25 ♘c1 ♔f7 26 ♘d3 ♘d8 27 ♔f3 ♔e6 28 ♔g4 ♘f7 29 b3 g6 and drawn in 56 moves.

b) Neither could one of the greatest endgame exponents ever win from here in Larsen-P.Nielsen, Aars 1995: 17 ♖f2 ♘xf3+ 18 ♖xf3 ♖xf3 19 gxf3 ♗e7 20 ♔f2 ♖d8 21 ♗e3 ♔f7 22 ♔e2 b6 23 ♖g1 ♖d6!? 24 ♗d2 ♖g6 (correctly judging that the pure bishop ending is drawn because White cannot penetrate with his king) 25 ♖g4 ♖xg4 26 fxg4 ♔e6 27 a3 a6 28 ♔d3 ♔d6 and drawn in 49 moves.

14...e4

This is certainly superior now to 14...♘d4, when after 15 ♘xd4 ♕xg5 16 ♘f5 ♗c7 17 ♘e4 ♘xe4 18 ♕xe4 White's minor piece is the better by far.

15 dxe4 ♘xe4 16 ♖ae1! ♘f6

16...♘xg5? 17 ♕xe8 wins for White.

17 ♕d1 ♖xe1 18 ♖xe1 ♘d4 19 ♗xf6 ♘xf3+ 20 ♕xf3 ♕xf3 21 gxf3 ♖xf6 22 ♖e8+ ♖f8 23 ♖e6 ♖d8 24 ♔g2 ♔f7

There is not a lot happening in this endgame but, remarkably, Short manages to win it!

25 ♖e4 g6 26 b3 ♗f8 27 ♘d5 b5

It would probably have been better not to go active. The consequences of this bid for play are more problematic for Kasparov than his opponent.

28 ♖f4+ ♔g7 29 ♔h3 bxc4 30 bxc4 ♖b8 31 ♖f6! ♖b7 32 ♖a6

Tying him down.

32...♔f7 33 f4 ♗g7 34 ♔g4 ♗d4 35 h4 ♔g7 36 h5 ♖b2

Trying to do something active before Short plays the advance f4-f5 and breaks over the fifth-rank boundary with his king.

37 ♖xa7+ ♔h6 38 hxg6 hxg6 39 ♘e7!

Short has created a mate threat out of nowhere!

39...♔g7

Forced.

40 ♘f5+ ♔f6 41 ♖a6+ ♔f7 42 ♘d6+ ♔e7 43 a4 ♖a2 44 ♔f3 ♔e6 45 ♘e4+ ♔e7 46 a5

This pawn is a winner.

46...♖a4 47 ♖xg6 ♖xa5 48 ♘d6 ♗f6 49 ♔e4 ♖a6 50 ♘b5 ♔f7 51 ♔f5 ♖c6 52 ♘c3 1-0

Game 52
L.Evans-King
London 1988

1 e4 c5 2 f4 d5 3 exd5 ♘f6 4 ♗b5+
♗d7 5 ♗xd7+ ♕xd7 6 c4 e6 7 ♕e2
♗d6 8 d3 0-0 9 dxe6 fxe6 10 ♘f3
♘c6 11 0-0 ♖ae8 12 ♘c3 e5 13 f5
♘d4!?

14 ♕d2?!

This does not work out well. Others:

a) 14 ♘xd4 exd4 15 ♘e4 ♘xe4 16 dxe4 ♖xf5 is very good for Black.

b) 14 ♕d1 looks right, when the game Bangiev-Lau, German Championship 1994, continued 14...♘xf5 (White has everything covered after 14...e4 15 dxe4 ♘xe4 16 ♘xd4 cxd4 17 ♘xe4 dxe4, as in the recent game Djurhuus-Dannevig, Norwegian Championship 1999) 15 ♗g5!? ♘g4 16 ♕d2!? h6 17 h3 ♘g3 18 ♖fe1 hxg5 19 hxg4 and White's superiority on the light squares plus the clear handicap of Black's bishop against the white knight gave him a big plus. After 19...♖f4 20 ♘xg5 ♖xg4 21 ♘ge4 ♘f5 22 ♘d5 he went on to win.

c) White also gained the advantage with 14 ♕e1!? ♘xf5 15 ♘g5 ♗b8 16

♘ge4 in Dorfman-Cifuentes, Platja D'Aro Barcino 1994, although that game ended in a draw.

14...♕xf5 15 b3 e4!

Winning. The black men pour down the open lines and White is overrun.

16 dxe4 ♘xe4 17 ♘xe4 ♖xe4

Aiming for the seventh rank.

18 ♕g5 ♘xf3+ 19 gxf3 ♖e2 0-1

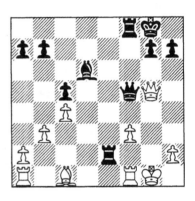

Game 53
Campora-Shirov
Buenos Aires 1993

1 e4 c5 2 f4 d5 3 exd5 ♘f6 4 ♗b5+
♗d7 5 ♗xd7+ ♕xd7 6 c4 e6 7 ♕e2
♗d6 8 dxe6 fxe6 9 d3 ♘c6 10 ♘f3
0-0 11 0-0 e5!?

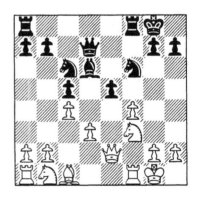

A move earlier than normal. Shirov rarely hangs around.

12 f5

Taking the pawn runs into obvious problems because of ...♖ae8, so Campora opts for the attempt at positional advantage through returning the pawn.

12...♘d4!? 13 ♘xd4

This leads nowhere special for White, but on 13 ♕d1 Black could speculate with 13...e4!? 14 ♘xd4 cxd4 15 dxe4 ♕c7!? 16 g3 ♗xg3 17 hxg3 ♕xg3+ 18 ♔h1 ♕h3+ with a draw.

13...exd4

Thus the white knight becomes deprived of its best square at c3.

14 ♗g5 ♖ae8 15 ♕f3 ♕c7 16 g3

On 16 h3 g6!? 17 ♗xf6 ♖xf6 18 ♕d5+ ♔g7 19 ♘d2 ♖e5 Black has counterplay, but simply 17 ♘d2 might be a better try.

16...♘d7 17 ♘d2 ♘e5 18 ♕d5+ ♘f7 19 ♗f4

This copes satisfactorily with Black's activity but proves inadequate as a winning attempt.

19...♗xf4 20 ♖xf4 ♖e5 21 ♕g2 ♖e3 22 ♘f1! ♖e5 ½-½

Not 22...♖xd3? 23 ♕e2. However, with Black avoiding this trap, there is little for either side to play for.

> ### Game 54
> ### Sveshnikov-Aseev
> *Kemerovo 1995*

1 e4 c5 2 f4

Evgeny Sveshnikov used always to meet the Sicilian with 2 c3, but he is diversifying as he gets older.

2...d5 3 exd5 ♘f6 4 ♗b5+ ♗d7 5 ♗xd7+ ♕xd7 6 c4 e6 7 ♕e2 ♗d6 8 d3 0-0 9 dxe6!? ♕xe6!?

This was actually the first time that a grandmaster had recaptured thus in this precise position, with the bishop already committed to d6.

10 ♕xe6 fxe6 11 ♘f3

If White plays slowly then Black can comfortably equalise with natural moves, e.g. 11 ♘c3 ♘c6 12 ♘ge2 ♖ad8 13 a3 (this precaution turns out to grant Black the time to make his way to equality) 13...♗c7 14 ♗e3 ♖xd3 15 ♗xc5 ♖f7 16 0-0?! (16 ♖d1 was a better try) 16...♘d7 17 ♗f2 ♗xf4 and a draw was agreed in Zollbrecht-Raedecker, German Bundesliga 1989.

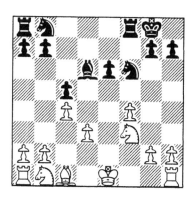

11...♘fd7!?

Aiming to hit the f4-pawn as fast as possible. The slower 11...♘c6 was tried in Keprt-Hajek, Czechoslovakia 1989, which continued 12 a3?! ♘h5 13 ♘c3 ♗xf4 14 0-0 ♖ad8 15 ♘e4 b6 16 ♘f2 ♘e5 17 ♘g5 ♘xd3 18 ♘xe6 ♘xc1 19 ♖axc1 ♗xc1 20 ♘xd8 ♗e3 21 ♘e6 ♖f6 22 ♘c7 ♘f4 23 ♘d5 ♘xd5 24 cxd5 ♔f7 25 g3 ♖xf2 26 ♖xf2+ ♔e7 27 ♔f1 ♗xf2 28 ♔xf2 ♔d6 and Black soon won. Naturally White's 12th move was not the most testing. He fared better in Campora-Zsu.Polgar, Biel 1987, with 12 ♘c3 ♖ad8 13 0-0 ♗c7 14 ♘g5 ♘d4 15 ♗e3 ♖fe8 16 ♗xd4 cxd4 17 ♘ce4 ♘g4 18 ♘c5 and the rampant white knights caused decisive problems after 18...e5 19 ♘ge6 ♖c8 20 f5.

12 0-0!?

A familiar notion: the pawn is returned in the hope of obtaining positional pluses.

12...♗xf4 13 ♗xf4 ♖xf4 14 ♖e1 ♖f6 15 d4 ♘c6 16 dxc5 ♘xc5 17 ♘c3

Black has fully equalised.

17...♘d3!?

Getting ideas.

18 ♖e2 ♖af8 19 ♖d1 ♘f4 20 ♖e3 ♘h3+!? 21 gxh3 ♖xf3 22 ♖xe6 ♖xh3 23 ♘d5 ♖h4 24 ♘e3 ♘d4

Aseev works up a dangerous initiative.

25 ♖e7 ♘f3+ 26 ♔g2 ♖xh2+ 27

♔g3 ♖h6! 28 ♖d5 ♖g6+ 29 ♔f2 ♘d4+ 30 ♔e1

30...♖e6

Black might have tried 30...♘c6!? 31 ♖xb7 ♖e6 32 ♖d3 ♖f3!? 33 ♔d2 ♖h3 34 b4 h5 with tense complications. Now the struggle fizzles out.

31 ♖dd7! ♖xe3+ 32 ♖xe3 ♘c2+ 33 ♔e2 ♘xe3 34 ♔xe3 ♖f7 35 ♖d8+ ♖f8 36 ♖d7 ♖f7 37 ♖d8+ ½-½

Game 55
Campora-Perez Pardo
Ceuta 1992

---

1 e4 c5 2 f4 d5 3 exd5 ♘f6 4 ♗b5+ ♗d7 5 ♗xd7+ ♕xd7 6 c4 e6 7 ♕e2 ♗d6 8 ♘f3

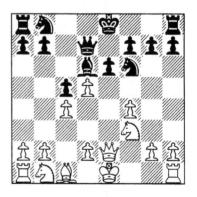

Campora has shown a liking for returning the pawn in this fashion, but it
does not look like it causes Black many
serious difficulties.

8...♗xf4 9 0-0 0-0 10 dxe6 fxe6

Another one of Campora's opponents, E.Ragozin, took back with the
queen at the Biel open in 1992, when
10...♕xe6 11 ♕xe6 fxe6 12 d4 ♗xc1 13
♖xc1 ♘c6 14 dxc5 ♘e4 led to a similar
middlegame to the previous main game.
This may be Black's simplest continuation here.

11 ♘c3 ♘c6 12 d3 ♗xc1

The game Sulskis-Fedorov, Minsk
1996, was far more exciting: 12...♘d4 13
♘xd4 ♕xd4+ 14 ♔h1

14...♗xh2! 15 ♕xe6+ (after 15 ♔xh2?
♕h4+ 16 ♔g1 ♘g4 White has no adequate defence) 15...♔h8 16 ♗e3 ♕xd3!
17 ♖ad1 (17 ♔xh2 ♕xe3) 17...♕g6 (now
protecting the bishop because of
18...♘g4+ and the win of the queen) 18
♗xc5 ♖fe8 19 ♕f5 ♕h6 20 ♕h3 ♕xh3
21 gxh3 ♗e5 22 ♗d4 ♔g8 and drawn at
move 41.

**13 ♖axc1 ♘d4 14 ♘xd4 ♕xd4+ 15
♔h1 ♘g4!?**

Such a move usually indicates that
Black is fishing around.

**16 ♕xe6+ ♔h8 17 ♘e4 ♕xd3 18
♖fe1 ♘f2+**

Black does not look too pressured
here, but he was lax over the next few
moves and Campora successfully
grabbed a pawn and steered towards a
won ending.

**19 ♘xf2 ♖xf2 20 ♕e8+ ♖f8 21 ♕e7
♖f2?! 22 ♕xc5 ♕d2 23 ♖f1 ♖xf1+
24 ♖xf1 h6 25 ♕f2 ♖d8 26 h3 ♕b4
27 b3 a5 28 ♕g3 ♕d6 29 ♕xd6
♖xd6**

**30 ♖f5 b6 31 a4 ♔h7 32 ♔g1 ♔g6
33 ♖b5 ♖f6 34 c5 bxc5 35 ♖xc5
♖f5**

White is winning of course, but this
hastens the end.

36 ♖xf5 ♔xf5 37 ♔f2 1-0

Game 56
Hajek-Salai
Czech Championship 1992

---

1 e4 c5 2 f4 d5 3 exd5 ♘f6 4 ♗b5+
♗d7 5 ♗xd7+ ♕xd7 6 c4 e6 7 ♕e2
♗d6 8 f5!?

Another approach entirely. White guarantees the win of a second pawn, however temporary, by keeping the queens on, but he abandons all hope of catching up in development.

8...0-0

Even very early on in chess there are still new ideas awaiting birth. Tischbierek's 8...♘a6!?, never yet played, is one.

9 fxe6 fxe6 10 dxe6

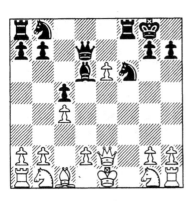

At least four different squares have been tried for the black queen, and maybe it is just a matter of time until someone goes to c6 with it!?

10...♕c8

Nobody is yet certain where the best place is for this piece. The game move intends to round up the e-pawn with 10...♖e8 and 11..♖xe6, but the following alternatives have also been tried:

a) In Hebden-Davies, Nottingham 1983, Black played 10...♕e8 and after 11 ♘f3 ♕h5 12 ♘c3 (12 0-0?? ♗xh2+ wins, while in Hajek-Bazant, Czech Team Championship 1992, White tried 12 e7 but gained no advantage after 12...♗g3+ 13 ♔d1 ♖e8 14 ♕e6+ ♔h8 15 ♕h3 ♕xh3 16 gxh3 ♗c7 17 d3 ♖xe7 18 ♘c3 ♘c6 19 ♗g5 ♘b4 20 a3 ♘xd3) 12...♘c6 13 d3 ♖ae8 14 ♗d2 ♗g3+ 15 ♔d1 and now the game would have been unclear after 15...♘g4 16 ♘e4 ♗c7.

b) In Moyano-Verat, Palma 1991, Black also worked up good counterplay with 10...♕e7 after 11 ♘f3 ♘c6 12 0-0 ♖ae8 13 ♖e1 ♘g4 14 h3 ♘ge5 15 ♘xe5 ♕xe6.

c) 10...♕c7 11 ♘f3 ♘c6 12 ♘c3 makes sense too, as in several games from the late eighties and early nineties:

c1) 12...♘d4 13 ♘xd4 cxd4 14 ♘b5 ♕b6 15 ♘xd6 ♕xd6 16 d3 ♖ae8 17 0-0 ♖xe6 18 ♕f3 ♕b6 19 ♗g5! and Black had lost the opening battle in Chernov-Giurimia, Bucharest 1991.

c2) 12...♖ae8 13 d3 (this permits an outbreak of tactics, but perhaps White feared an improvement on the earlier game Chernov-Eidelson, Kishinev 1989, which went 13 ♘b5 ♕e7 14 0-0 ♕xe6? 15 ♕xe6 ♖xe6 16 ♘g5! ♖e5 17 ♘xd6 ♖xg5 18 d4 with a clear advantage to

White; 14...a6 looks more to the point)
13...♘d4 14 ♘xd4 cxd4 15 ♘b5 ♗b4+

16 ♗d2 (in Maier-Kunze, Munich open 1992, White played 16 ♔d1, but this is unconvincing as the position after 16...♕b6 17 ♗f4 ♖xe6 18 ♕f3 ♖fe8 19 a3 ♖e1+ 20 ♖xe1 ♖xe1+ 21 ♔c2 ♖xa1 22 axb4 ought to have been very pleasant for Black, though he later blundered and lost) 16...♗xd2+ 17 ♔xd2 (here too the king is a bit insecure, and Black cleverly exploits this) 17...♕b6 18 ♕e5 ♖xe6 19 ♕xd4 ♘e4+! 20 ♔c1 ♘f2! 21 ♕xb6 axb6 22 ♔d2 (hanging on to the exchange with 22 ♖g1 would have led to a position that is almost certainly indefensible after 22...♖e2 23 ♘c3 ♘xd3+ 24 ♔d1 ♖xb2) 22...♘xh1 23 ♖xh1 ♖f2+ 24 ♔c3 ♖ee2 (ultimately the rooks will prove too strong) 25 ♘d4 ♖xb2 26 ♖e1 ♖xa2 27 ♖e7 ♖f7 28 ♖e8+ ♖f8 29 ♖e7 ♖xg2 30 ♖xb7 ♖g6 31 ♘c2 h5 32 h4 ♖f4 33 ♘e3 ♖xh4 34 ♘f5 ♖hg4 35 ♘e7+ ♔h7 36 ♘xg6 ♖xg6 0-1 Chernov-Bouaziz, Bucharest 1992.

11 ♘f3 ♖e8 12 0-0 ♖xe6 13 ♕d1

White also achieved nothing in Antoshin-Karpeshov, Berdyansk 1985, with 13 ♕f2 ♘c6 14 d3 ♘b4! 15 ♘c3 ♘xd3.

13...♘c6 14 ♘c3 ♕e8

Off to her most active spot.
15 d3 ♕h5

16 g3 h6 17 ♘b5 ♖d8 18 ♘h4 ♕xd1 19 ♖xd1 ♗b8

Black's activity is sufficient to hold the balance.

20 ♘f5 ♘g4 21 h3 ♘ge5 22 ♗f4 ♖f8 23 ♗xe5 ♗xe5 24 d4 ♖xf5 25 dxe5 ♘xe5 26 ♖d8+ ♔h7 27 ♘d6 ♖f3 28 ♔g2 ♖d3 29 ♘xb7 ♖xd8 30 ♘xd8 ♖d6 31 ♘b7 ♖d2+ 32 ♔f1 ♘xc4 33 ♘xc5 ♖xb2 34 ♘e4 ♘e3+ 35 ♔g1 ♘c2 36 ♖d1 ♖xa2 37 ♖d7

A situation of dynamic equality has been reached.

37...♔g8 38 ♘c5 ♘e3 39 g4 ♖g2+ 40 ♔h1 ♖g3 41 ♘e6 ½-½

Game 57
Hodgson-Mestel
Bath Zonal 1987

1 e4 c5 2 f4 d5 3 exd5 ♘f6 4 ♗b5+ ♗d7 5 ♗xd7+ ♕xd7 6 c4 e6 7 ♕e2 ♗e7!?

An unusual alternative to the normal 7...♗d6.

8 dxe6 ♕xe6!?

A fundamental decision. Black opts to get the queens off. In Beck-Orlowski,

German Bundesliga 1996, he preferred 8...fxe6 and after 9 ♘f3 ♘c6 10 ♘e5!? ♕d6 11 ♘xc6 ♕xc6 12 0-0 0-0-0 13 ♘c3 White held the advantage and went on to win.

9 ♕xe6 fxe6 10 ♘f3 ♘c6 11 0-0 ♖d8

Black was less successful in obtaining counterplay with 11...♘b4 in Sveshnikov-Rechel, Anapa 1991, when after 12 ♘c3 ♘d7 13 a3 ♘c6 14 d3 0-0 15 ♗e3 ♗f6 16 ♘e4 White was clearly on top.

12 ♘c3 0-0

Black has enough compensation due to his active play and White's problems in completing his development.

13 b3 ♘g4 14 ♘e2 ♗f6 15 ♖b1 e5

16 h3 ♘h6 17 fxe5 ♘xe5 18 ♘xe5 ♗xe5 19 ♖xf8+ ♔xf8 20 b4

With some ingenuity White has made progress in getting his game together.

20...cxb4 21 ♖xb4 b6 22 ♖b5 ♘f7

Bringing it back towards the scene of the fight.

23 a4 ♗f6 24 a5 ♘d6 25 ♗a3 ♔e8 26 ♗xd6 ♖xd6 27 axb6 axb6

You might regard this as the end of the beginning.

28 ♔f1 ♖xd2 29 ♖xb6

White's advantage is not enough for victory because of the reduced material and also the fact that the extra c-pawn is not sufficiently remote from those on the kingside.

29...♖c2 30 ♖e6+ ♔d7 31 ♖e4 ♔d6 32 ♘f4 ♖d2 33 ♘d5 ♗d4??

A howler.

34 ♔e1 1-0

Winning at least the exchange.

Game 58
Hodgson-Yrjola
Tallinn 1987

---

1 e4 c5 2 f4 d5 3 exd5 ♘f6 4 ♗b5+ ♘bd7

Quite another gambit, and in practice

a perhaps unfairly neglected alternative. There are far fewer practical examples of 4...♘bd7 than 4...♗d7, no doubt because the later has enjoyed such good results.

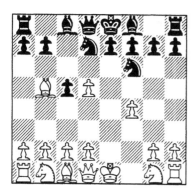

5 c4 a6 6 ♗a4

The capture with 6 ♗xd7+ ♗xd7 also grants Black fair compensation:

a) 7 d4 cxd4 8 ♕xd4 e6 9 ♘c3 ♖c8 10 ♗e3 ♗c5 11 ♕d3 ♗xe3 12 ♕xe3 0-0 13 ♘ge2 exd5 14 cxd5 ♖e8 15 ♕f2 ♘g4 16 ♕d4 ♘e3 and the black initiative became irresistible in Khalikian-Vitolins, Yerevan 1981. The finish was 17 ♖c1 ♖c4 18 ♕a7 ♗g4 19 ♔f2 ♗xe2 20 ♘xe2 ♘g4+ 21 ♔f3 ♕xd5+ 22 ♔xg4 ♕xg2+ 23 ♘g3 h5+ 0-1. Rather a characteristic game from the Latvian Vitolins. He has seconded Tal, and indeed I would not be surprised to learn that 3...♘f6 was his idea in the first place.

b) In Lau-Schmittdiel, Bad Endbach 1995, White tried 7 ♘c3 (7 ♘f3 is also met by 7...e6) instead and after 7...e6 8 ♕e2 ♗d6!? (7...♗e7, to meet 8 dxe6 with 8...♗xe6, looks more natural, as in the game Lazzeri-Yermolinsky, Alexandria open 1996) 9 dxe6 fxe6 10 d3 the game was obscure.

6...b5

Necessary to bust out.

7 cxb5

7...♘xd5

Watson-Razuvaev, London Lloyds Bank 1983, took a different turn with 7...♘b6!? 8 bxa6+ ♘xa4 9 ♕xa4+ ♗d7 10 ♕c4 e6 11 ♘c3 ♗d6 (Razuvaev proposed 11...exd5 12 ♘xd5 ♘xd5 13 ♕xd5 ♖xa6 14 ♘f3 ♖e6+ as an interesting alternative) 12 dxe6 ♗xe6 13 ♕b5+ ♘d7 14 ♘f3 and the scene is quite unclear although Black later won. Nobody seems to have tried 7...axb5.

8 ♘f3

Lyubisavljevic-D.Lazic, Yugoslav Team Championship 1992, saw instead 8 bxa6 ♖xa6!? (perhaps 8...♘b4!?) 9 ♘e2 e6 10 0-0 ♗e7 11 ♘bc3 0-0 12 ♗b5 ♖a7 and White went on to win.

8...g6!? 9 ♘c3 ♘5b6 10 d4 ♘xa4 11 ♕xa4 ♗g7 12 ♗e3

A better continuation was 12 dxc5 ♘xc5 13 ♕c4 ♘d3+ 14 ♔e2 ♘xc1+ 15 ♖axc1, when the situation is still unclear. **12...♘b6 13 ♕a5 0-0 14 0-0-0 axb5 15 ♕xb5 ♗a6**

see following diagram

Black has fearsome compensation due to threats against both white king and queen.

16 ♕xc5 ♘c4 17 ♖he1 ♕b8 18 b3?

A blunder in a difficult situation.

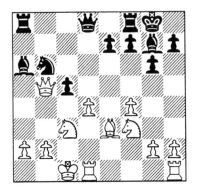

18...♖c8 19 ♕xc8+ ♗xc8 0-1

White's resignation was perhaps a little premature, although he is certainly lost after 20 bxc4 ♕b4.

The theory of 4...♘bd7 is still too fluid for definite conclusions to be drawn as yet.

Game 59
Plaskett-Filipowicz
Banja Luka 1985

1 e4 c5 2 f4

The previous occasion on which I had faced this opponent was four years earlier where I played 2 ♘f3 and a standard Open Sicilian arose. On that occasion I was unable to convert a technical advantage into a win, due to a blunder at move 104! I was therefore keen to see if I could wrap things up more quickly second time around.

2...d5 3 exd5 ♘f6 4 ♘c3

Hurrying to be the next one to offer a gambit.

4...♘xd5 5 ♘f3!?

The alternatives are:

a) 5 ♗b5+ brought White nothing in I.Rodriguez-Galarza, Spanish Junior Championship 1992, after 5...♗d7 6 ♗c4 ♗c6 7 ♘f3 ♘xc3 8 bxc3 b5 9 ♗e2 ♘d7.

b) The simplifying 5 ♘xd5 ♕xd5 6 ♕f3, as seen in the recent game Hort-P.Cramling, Veterans-Women 1998, should be nothing for White after 6...e6.

5...♘c6

It is by no means out of the question to grab on f4 with 5...♘xf4. One line then is 6 d4 cxd4? 7 ♗xf4 bxc3 8 ♕xd8+ ♔xd8 9 0-0-0+ and Black cannot avoid loss of a piece. That, however, is not entirely forced!

After 5...e6 I threw a great deal of material at my opponent in Plaskett-Yrjola, Sochi 1984, and was still unable to beat him: 6 ♘e5!? ♘d7 7 ♗b5 ♗d6 8 0-0 0-0 9 ♗xd7 ♗xd7 10 ♕e2 ♕c7 11 d3 ♘e7 12 ♘e4!? ♗xe5 13 fxe5 ♕xe5 14 ♗f4 ♕xb2 15 ♖ab1 ♕d4+ 16 ♗e3 ♕d5 17 c4 ♕c6 18 ♖f6!? b6 19 ♕h5!? ♘f5 20 ♗h6!?

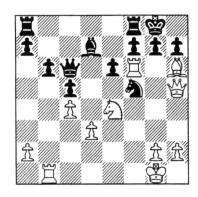

(as I made this move Tal wandered away shaking his head incredulously and muttering something to Psakhis) 20...♕c7 21 ♖xf5 exf5 22 ♗xg7 ♔xg7 23 ♕g5+ ♔h8 24 ♕f6+ ♔g8 ½-½. Was it all sound? Perhaps not 100%!

6 ♗b5 ♘xc3 7 bxc3 ♗d7 8 0-0 g6 9 ♕e2 ♗g7 10 ♗a3 b6 11 d4

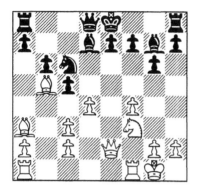

11...cxd4

After this Black is struggling. It would have been better to have let the c5-pawn go, as in certain lines of the Exchange Grünfeld.

12 ♖fe1 ♗f6 13 ♗xc6!? ♗xc6 14 ♘e5 ♗d7 15 ♖ad1 0-0 16 ♖xd4 ♕c8

An ingenious attempt to get out of the pin. Now after 17 ♖xd7 ♗xe5 Black defends, but White can do better.

17 ♗xe7! ♗xe7 18 ♘xd7 ♖e8 19 ♕f3

White's pieces are dominating their black counterparts, so, not surprisingly, he is able to generate a menacing initiative.

19...♗h4 20 ♖e5 ♔g7 21 f5 ♖xe5 22 f6+ ♔g8 23 ♘xe5 ♗g5 24 h4 ♗h6 25 ♕d5 ♕e8 26 ♘xf7! ♕e3+ 27 ♔h1 1-0

Summary

2...d5 3 exd5 ♘f6 is, frankly, a bit of a nuisance for White. It is difficult to see how he can hope to gain the advantage here and, if he accepts Black's gambit, he is often struggling. The best move may well be the simple 4 ♘c3 which at least keeps the position balanced.

1 e4 c5 2 f4 d5 3 exd5 ♘f6

4 ♗b5+ *(D)*
    4 c4 – *Game 49*
    4 ♘c3 – *Game 59*
4...♗d7
    4...♘bd7 – *Game 58*
5 ♗xd7+ ♕xd7 6 c4 e6 7 ♕e2 *(D)* **♗d6**
    7...♗e7 – *Game 57*
8 d3
    8 ♘f3 – *Game 55*
    8 f5 – *Game 56*
8...0-0 9 dxe6 fxe6
    9...♕xe6 – *Game 54*
10 ♘f3 ♘c6
    10...♘g4 – *Game 50*
11 0-0 *(D)* **♖ae8**
    11...e5 – *Game 53*
12 ♘c3 e5 13 f5 ♕xf5
    13...♘d4 – *Game 52*
14 ♗g5 – *Game 51*

    4 ♗b5+   *7 ♕e2*   *11 0-0*

CHAPTER SIX

1 e4 c5 2 f4 d5
3 exd5 ♕xd5

1 e4 c5 2 f4 d5 3 exd5 ♕xd5

Whereas many responses to 2 f4 offer the chance of transposition back into Open Sicilians, with 2...d5 3 exd5 ♕xd5 Black takes play into a quite independent line. The drawback is that after 4 ♘c3 he must lose time by moving his queen once more. Notwithstanding this some of the best players in the world believe in Black's game, indeed Yasser Seirawan expressed the opinion that following 4 ♘c3 ♕d6 the position is already favourable for Black! This is a little subjective, but Yasser likes to take gambitted pawns and therefore presumably regards the one on f4 as under threat. Many White aggressors would happily shed it in return for the further gains of time and the open f-file – GM Hickl is one of them.

The comparison with the Centre-Counter Defence is natural (indeed I suspect that it was the thought that f2-f4 is not entirely apposite in that opening that led people to think of the queen retreat). Since he is here denied access to a5 Black must post the queen elsewhere. The line of the Centre-Counter with 1 e4 d5 2 exd5 ♕xd5 3 ♘c3 ♕d8 was quite respected until Fischer crushed Robatsch with 4 d4 g6 5 ♗f4! ♗g7 6 ♕d2!, and then it was abandoned.

Some squares other than d8 have been tried for the queen retreat, e.g. d6 or f5, but the theoretical status of those moves is not as good. Portisch tries a disruptive check in Game 67, an idea akin to the line of the English Opening 1 c4 e5 2 ♘c3 e5 3 d4 exd4 4 ♕xd4 ♘c6 5 ♕e3+.

Frankly I am rather suspicious of the whole concept of 3...♕xd5, as it seems to cede valuable time in a system where White is looking to attack anyway.

After 4 ♘c3 ♕d8 5 ♘f3 Black opts for the immediate fianchetto with 5...g6 in Games 60-62, while plans based on the more solid 5...e6 are examined in Games 63-66. Finally, alternatives to 4...♕d8 are seen in Games 67-70.

Game 60
Westerinen-Plaskett
Brighton 1983

1 e4 c5 2 f4 d5

My only venture with this move.

3 exd5 ♕xd5 4 ♘c3 ♕d8

The usual retreat. 4...♕e6+ is considered in Game 67 and 4...♕d6+ in Games 68-70.

5 ♘f3 g6

5...♘f6 is the subject of Game 63 and 5...e6 in Games 64-66.

6 d4

The alternative 6 ♘e5 is seen in the next two main games.

6...♗g7

6...cxd4 7 ♕xd4 ♕xd4 8 ♘xd4 ♗g7 9 ♗e3 was also slightly better for White in Westerinen-Kudrin, Gausdal 1982.

7 ♗e3 cxd4 8 ♗xd4!

In Westerinen-Kiefer, German Bundesliga 1982, White had tried 8 ♘xd4 but only managed a draw after 8...a6 9 ♕d2 ♘f6 10 0-0-0 ♘g4 11 ♗g1 0-0 12 h3 ♘f6 13 g4 ♘bd7 14 ♗g2 e5 15 ♘b3 ♕c7. This time he unleashes a good and surprising new idea.

8...♘f6

An innocent enough move, or so I thought!

9 ♗xf6!

Thus White seizes a big lead in development and Black is struggling to equalise.

9...♗xf6 10 ♕xd8+ ♔xd8 11 0-0-0+ ♗d7 12 ♘e4 ♔c7 13 ♘xf6 exf6 14 ♗c4 ♖f8 15 ♘d4 a6 16 ♖he1

How does Black complete his development? I had to give him the seventh rank, a bind and, in view of my doubled f-pawns, a nominal pawn majority.

16...♘c6 17 ♘xc6 ♗xc6 18 ♖e7+ ♔b6 19 g3 ♖ae8 20 ♖de1 ♔c5 21 ♗b3!

And not 21 ♗xf7? ♖xe7 22 ♖xe7 ♔d6 23 ♖e6+ ♔d7 and wins.

21...a5 22 ♖xe8 ♗xe8

The pure bishop ending would have been an even tougher prospect for a salvage operation.

23 a3 ♔d6 24 ♔d2 ♗b5 25 ♖e3 g5

Trying to play as actively as possible.

26 c4 ♗c6 27 ♔c3 gxf4 28 gxf4 ♖g8 29 ♖g3 ♖e8 30 ♗c2 ♖e7?!

I remember having had rather a gloomy time of it up to here and I was not feeling too optimistic about my objective chances of making a draw, but, still, 30...h5 was more demanding of White. He should now just have grabbed on h7, but instead, in an attempt to finesse, Heikki lets me off the hook.

31 ♖d3+?! ♔c7 32 ♖h3 ♗e4!

Black scrambles into a drawn rook ending.

33 ♗xe4 ♖xe4 34 ♖xh7 ♖xf4 35 ♖xf7+ ♔c6 36 b4 axb4+ 37 axb4 b5 38 cxb5+ ♔xb5 39 ♖b7+ ♔c6 40 ♖h7 ♖f3+ 41 ♔c4 ♖f4+ 42 ♔c3 ♖f3+ 43 ♔b2 f5 44 ♔c2 ♔b5 ½-½

Game 61
Hebden-Kudrin
Hastings 1983/84

---

1 e4 c5 2 f4 d5 3 exd5 ♕xd5 4 ♘c3 ♕d8 5 ♘f3 g6 6 ♘e5!?

The early ♘e5 is one of the most frequent, and to my mind most logical attempts to achieve the advantage out of this opening.

6...♗g7

The alternative 6...♘f6 is seen in the next game.

7 ♗b5+

On 7 ♗c4 there is the intriguing possibility of 7...♗xe5 8 fxe5 ♕d4!, though 7 ♕f3 must also come into serious consideration.

7...♘d7

Four months earlier Kudrin had played 7...♗d7 against Hodgson in the Benedictine International in Manchester and play took a strange turn: 8 ♕f3 ♕c8 9 ♕d5 e6 10 ♕d6 a6 11 ♗xd7+ ♘xd7 12 ♘e4 with a useful advantage for White.

8 d4 cxd4 9 ♕xd4 ♘f6

Black will be hampered by the imposing placement of White's pieces. Were he here to try to gain some freedom of movement by 9...a6 10 ♗a4 b5 then 11 ♕e4!? is an interesting attempt to keep the edge.

10 ♗e3 0-0 11 0-0-0 ♕a5 12 h3!

see following diagram

An intriguing approach. In thematic fashion Hebden gives up a pawn on e5 for the initiative. Analysis confirms that the idea was a very good one.

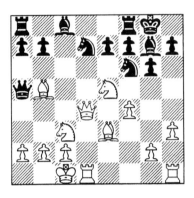

12...⧖xe5 13 fxe5 ⧖e8

Dreadfully retrograde, but after the more active 13...⧖h5 White's extra mobility translates itself into advantageous variations such as 14 g4 ⧖g3 (or 14...a6 15 gxh5 axb5 16 h6! ⧙h8 17 ⧖d5) 15 ⧘hg1 a6 16 ⧙c4 ⧙xe5 17 ⧔d3 and the stranded knight is a big problem, or even after the queen exchange 15...⧔xb5 16 ⧖xb5 ⧖e2+ 17 ⧔b1 ⧖xd4 18 ⧙xd4 ⧙d7 19 ⧖c7 ⧘ac8 20 ⧖d5 ⧘fe8 21 ⧙xa7 etc.

14 ⧙g5 a6 15 ⧙c4 ⧙xe5 16 ⧔e3

White has monster compensation.

16...⧖d6 17 ⧘d5! ⧔b4

Black still suffers after 17...⧖xc4 18 ⧘xa5 ⧖xe3 19 ⧘e5, e.g. 19...⧖xg2 20 ⧘e2 f6 21 ⧙h6 ⧖h4 22 ⧘xe7! ⧘d8 23 ⧖e4 and the attack triumphs.

18 ⧙b3

Threatening a2-a3 to trap the queen.

18...⧙xc3 19 bxc3 ⧔a3+ 20 ⧔b1 ⧙e6

see following diagram

21 ⧘hd1! ⧘ac8

Even grabbing the exchange does not help because of the rampant activity of the remaining white attackers. For example, 21...⧙xd5 22 ⧘xd5 and now:

22...⧖f5 23 ⧘xf5 gxf5 24 ⧙xe7 and 25 ⧔g5+; 22...⧘ae8 23 ⧔e5! f6 24 ⧔e6+ ⧔h8 25 ⧙c1 with an overwhelming initiative; or 22...⧘fe8 23 ⧔f3! and there is no defence, e.g. 23...⧖b5 24 ⧘xb5 axb5 25 ⧔xf7+ ⧔h8 26 ⧔f6+. Nothing else will save him either. On 21...⧖f5 comes 22 ⧘xf5 ⧙xf5 23 ⧙h6 ⧘fd8 24 ⧘d4 and wins, or 21...⧖b5 22 ⧙h6 ⧙xd5 23 ⧘xd5 ⧔a5 24 ⧔e5 ⧔xc3 25 ⧘xb5 ⧔xe5 26 ⧘xe5 and the ending is won.

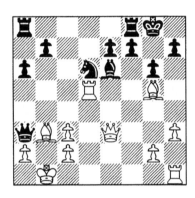

22 ⧘xd6! ⧙xb3 23 axb3 f6 24 ⧙h6 exd6 25 ⧔e6+ ⧔h8 26 ⧔e7 1-0

A blistering attack and a fine example of sacrificing to sustain the initiative.

Game 62
Hebden-Kindermann
Biel 1983

---

1 e4 c5 2 f4 d5 3 exd5 ⧔xd5 4 ⧖c3 ⧔d8 5 ⧖f3 ⧖f6 6 ⧖e5 g6

6...e6 is the subject of the next main game.

7 ⧙c4

A very different deployment, but one that has not scored well against Black's fianchetto. Stefan Kindermann proceeds to render it quite ineffectual.

7...e6 8 d3

White also obtained no advantage with 8 ♕f3 in R.Smith-Hjartarson, Lucerne Olympiad 1982, after 8...♗g7 9 0-0 0-0 10 d3 ♘fd7!? 11 ♘e4 ♕c7.

8...♘bd7 9 ♕e2 ♕e7!

To avoid a sacrifice at f7. The black kingside is now very bomb resistant and so Hebden turns his attention to other areas of the board, though without much success. The impression is that Black has already equalised.

10 a4 ♗g7 11 0-0 0-0 12 a5 ♘e8 13 ♗d2 ♘d6 14 ♖ae1

All the white pieces are now present and correct, but what's his plan?

14...♘f5

It is a feature of the geometry of the chessboard that a transfer of a knight to the square immediately in front of it needs at least three moves, but since White has no effective policy to pursue Black can afford to take time out to bring his king knight to the excellent f5-square.

15 ♘b5?!

This doesn't do much either.

15...a6 16 ♘a3 ♘xe5! 17 fxe5 ♗d7!
18 ♘b1 ♗c6 19 ♘c3 ♘d4 20 ♕d1 ♕c7

Rounding up the weakling on e5.

White has only one active move.

21 ♖f6

On 21 ♗f4 Black just takes the a-pawn, so Hebden sticks the rook in. I find this sally very hard to believe, but things certainly hotted up over the next few moves.

21...♗xf6 22 exf6 ♕d8 23 ♖f1 ♘f5 24 ♘e2 ♕xf6!

Kindermann decides to sort things out by heading into a situation where he has rook and two pawns for two minor pieces.

25 g4 ♖fe8 26 gxf5 exf5 27 ♘g3 ♖e7 28 ♕g4

A most Hebdenesque move!

28...♖e4! 29 ♘xe4?

This is unsound. He had to go back.

29...♛d4+ 30 ♖f2 fxg4 31 ♗xf7+
♚f8 32 ♗c4+ ♚e8 33 c3 ♛e5 34
♗f4 ♛g7 35 ♘xc5 ♗f3!

A good blocker.

**36 ♖f1 ♛e7 37 ♘e6 ♚d7 38 ♖e1
♖e8 39 ♖e5 ♚c8**

Black has consolidated and his
substantial material advantage must tell
in the end.

**40 ♗g5 ♛d7 41 d4 ♛a4 42 ♗f1
♛a1 43 c4 ♛xb2 44 ♗f6 ♛a3 45
♗h4 ♛d6 46 c5 ♛c6 47 ♗c4 ♛a4
48 ♗f1 ♛a2 0-1**

That time it was Mark who got blis-
tered.

Game 63
Campora-Smirin
Villarrobledo (rapidplay) 1998

**1 e4 c5 2 f4 d5 3 exd5 ♛xd5 4 ♘c3
♛d8 5 ♘f3 ♘f6 6 ♘e5 e6 7 ♛f3
♗e7 8 b3**

White places his queen's bishop on an
active diagonal and prepares to tuck his
king away safely on the queen's wing
behind the fianchettoed bishop.

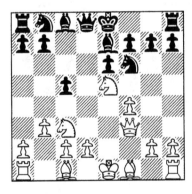

8...0-0

This looks very natural but 8...♘fd7 is
possibly better and generated comfort-

able play for Black in the following two
examples:

a) 9 ♗b5 0-0 10 ♘xd7 ♘xd7 11 ♗b2
a6 12 ♗d3 ♖b8 13 ♛h3 f5 and Black
stood well in Barle-Browne, Lone Pine
1979. If White castles queenside then
Black has swift counterplay with ...b7-b5
and ...c5-c4.

b) 9 ♗b2 tries to avoid wasting time
with the light-squared bishop, but Black
still gains good play, e.g. 9...♘xe5 10
fxe5 ♘c6 11 ♗b5 (ideally, White would
prefer to avoid this move but he must
defend his e-pawn and the options to do
this are limited – 11 ♘e4 ♘d4 gives
Black active play and 11 ♛g3 ♗h4 is a
bit sad) 11...♗d7 12 0-0 0-0 13 ♘e4
(White is trying to make something of
his attacking formation but his position
does not really have enough momentum)
13...♘xe5 14 ♗xe5 ♗xb5 15 c4 ♗d7 16
♛g3 f6 17 ♗c7 ♛c8 18 ♖ae1 e5 and
White had nothing for his pawn in Lang-
ner-Babula, Czechia 1996.

9 ♗b2

Due to Black's slight hesitancy on
move eight, White now has the attacking
formation he wants and can maintain
control of the centre while developing
his kingside initiative.

9...♘fd7

This creates the possibility of ...f7-f5,
to fight for space on the kingside.
9...♘bd7 is dangerous for Black, e.g. 10
0-0-0 ♛c7 (or 10...♘xe5 11 fxe5 ♘d7 12
♘e4 ♛c7 13 ♛g3 b6 14 ♗d3 ♗b7 15
♘d6 ♗c6 16 ♖df1 and White had a
pleasant position in Bangiev-Wittmann,
correspondence 1985) 11 ♖e1 a6 12 g4
b5! (this is a good move from Black who
is anxious to create queenside counterplay as quickly as possible; note that 13

♕xa8 fails to 13...♗b7 14 ♕a7 ♖a8 and the white queen is trapped) 13 ♗g2 ♘b6 14 g5 ♘fd5 15 ♕g3 ♗b7 16 ♗e4 (White probably saw that this would force a draw against his powerful opponent) 16...♘xc3 17 ♗xh7+ ♔xh7 18 ♕h3+ ♔g8 19 g6 fxg6 20 ♕xe6+ ♔h7 21 ♕h3+ ♔g8 22 ♕e6+ ♔h7 23 ♕h3+ ♔g8 ½-½ Hennings-Polugayevsky, Kislovodsk 1972.

10 0-0-0

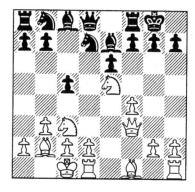

10...♘xe5

This is a mistake after which White's attack plays itself. The whole point of retreating the king's knight is to fight back with 10...f5!, after which White's chances of a successful attack on the kingside are much reduced. However, White has an alternative plan to play in the centre, i.e. 11 ♘xd7 ♗xd7 12 d4 cxd4 13 ♘b5 ♗c6 14 ♕e2 ♗e4 15 ♘xd4 ♕b6 16 ♕b5 ♕c7 17 ♕e5 ♕xe5 18 fxe5 with a small plus for White in the game Sveshnikov-Kovalevskaya, Oviedo (rapidplay) 1992.

11 fxe5 ♘c6 12 ♘e4 ♔h8 13 ♔b1 ♗d7 14 h4 ♘d4 15 ♕g4 ♗c6 16 ♗d3 ♕d5 17 ♖de1 f5

Black gets the right idea at last but it is a little late.

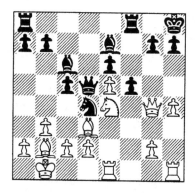

18 exf6 gxf6 19 ♘g5!

An attractive piece sacrifice which opens up the a1-h8 diagonal and the h-file.

19...fxg5 20 hxg5 ♕xg5 21 ♕xe6 1-0

A slightly surprising conclusion to the game as 21 ♗xd4+ would have forced a trivial mate, e.g. 21...cxd4 22 ♖xh7+ ♔g8 23 ♕xe6+ etc.

Game 64
Sax-Popovic
Zagreb 1985

---

1 e4 c5 2 f4 d5 3 exd5 ♕xd5 4 ♘c3 ♕d8 5 ♘f3 e6

Black managed to equalise in Wong-Suba, Lucerne Olympiad 1982, after 5...a6!? 6 g3 g6 7 ♗g2 ♗g7 8 0-0 ♘f6 10 d3 ♘c6, but 6 ♘e5, 6 ♗c4 or 6 d4, as in Kurajica-Sax, Vincovci 1976, must be more testing.

6 d4

6 ♗b5+ led to an extraordinary example of castling by hand in Bilek-Portisch, Hungarian Team Championship 1993, after 6...♗d7 7 ♕e2 ♘e7 8 b3 ♘f5 9 ♗d3 ♕e7!? 10 ♗b2 ♘c6 11 ♘b5!? ♔d8!? (remarkable!) 12 a4 a6 13 ♘a3 f6

14 ♘c4 ♔c7 15 0-0 ♖e8 16 ♕f2 ♕d8 17 ♖ad1 ♔b8 and drawn in 25 moves. 6 b3 (Game 65) and 6 ♘e5 (Game 66) are more dangerous lines, with White frequently aiming to get a swift attack going as in the previous main game.

6...♘f6 7 ♗e3 cxd4 8 ♕xd4 ♕xd4 9 ♘xd4 a6 10 ♗e2 ♗b4 11 ♗f3 0-0 12 0-0-0 ♗xc3

Popovic heads for equality.

13 bxc3 ♘d5 14 ♖d3 ♘xe3 15 ♖xe3 ♘d7 16 ♖d1 ♖a7

Black experiences some difficulty in mobilising fully, but the essential soundness of his structure means that White is never likely to be able to exploit that.

17 c4 g6 18 ♖a3 ♘c5 19 ♘b3 b6 20 ♖d6 ♘d7 21 ♗c6 ♘b8!

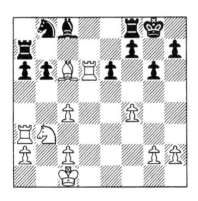

A defensive contortion of which the maestro Ulf Andersson would be proud!

22 ♗f3 ♘d7 23 ♗c6 ♘b8 ½-½

Game 65
Sveshnikov-Aseev
St Petersburg Zonal 1993

---

1 e4 c5 2 f4 d5 3 exd5 ♕xd5 4 ♘c3 ♕d8 5 ♘f3 e6 6 b3!? ♘f6 7 ♗b2

The bishop's birth. Later Sveshnikov will bury and then resurrect it.

7...♗e7 8 ♘e5 ♘bd7 9 ♕f3 a6!? 10 0-0-0 ♖b8

10...♖a7!? is an idea, intending ...b7-b5, ...♖c7 and ...♗b7, but Aseev's continuation seems simpler and better.

11 g4 b5 12 ♗g2 ♗b7 13 ♕e2 ♘xe5 14 ♗xb7

14...♖xb7?!

Passing over the chance to play 14...♘d3+ when White's best line would be 15 ♕xd3 ♕xd3 16 ♗c6+ ♕d7 with equality. I can only assume that Aseev saw no reason to fear the middlegame, but it soon starts to look as though the white offensive is the more powerful, and also that he can organise an unusual yet effective defensive formation.

15 fxe5 ♘d5 16 ♘e4 c4 17 ♖df1

Taking the pawn would expose his king to terrible dangers.

17...0-0 18 ♔b1 cxb3 19 axb3 ♕a5 20 c3!

Just about forced, but the play is still obscure.

20...♕d8 21 h4

Here we go.

21...a5 22 g5 a4 23 ♘f6+

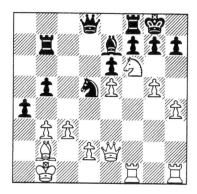

23...gxf6 24 gxf6 Bxf6 25 exf6 ♔h8 26 ♖hg1 ♖g8 27 b4

Certainly not the way that you are taught to arrange pawns around a dark-squared bishop, but White is doing well enough in other sectors to hold the balance.

27...♖b8 28 ♖g5 ♖xg5 29 hxg5 ♕g8

Wisely seeking an exchange of queens.

30 ♕h5 ♕g6+ 31 ♕xg6 hxg6 32 ♔c2 ♔g8 33 ♖f3 ♖c8 34 ♔d1 ♖c4 35 ♖g3 ♖h4 36 ♖g2 ♔f8 37 ♔c2 ♔e8 38 ♗c1 ♔d7 39 d3 ♖h1 40 ♗d2 1-0

see following diagram

Black lost on time, although he is no worse here.

A middlegame with some quite unusual themes. Aseev's systematic development of his queenside, notably gaining

time as he fianchettoed his queen bishop through the attack on the white queen, seemed quite satisfactory.

Game 66
Tkachiev-Portisch
Tilburg (2nd rapidplay game) 1994

1 e4 c5 2 f4 d5 3 exd5 ♕xd5 4 ♘c3 ♕d8 5 ♘f3 e6 6 ♘e5 a6

6...♘f6 would transpose to Game 63.

7 ♕f3

From here the queen also creates some problems for Black in developing the queenside. Portisch produces an interesting solution.

7...♘f6 8 b3 ♖a7!?

Another new move in the opening

from Lajos; he's always hatching them out. The idea has been seen before though, for example, in Turcan-M.Horvath, Slovak Championship 1994: 1 e4 c5 2 ♘c3 d6 3 ♘f3 ♘f6 4 e5 dxe5 5 ♘xe5 e6 6 f4 ♗e7 7 b3 0-0 8 ♗b2 a6 9 ♕f3 ♖a7 and the game was eventually drawn.

9 ♗b2 b5 10 ♗d3

10 0-0-0 is a consistent follow-up, but Tkachiev's straightforward development scheme also proves to be extremely strong.

10...♖c7 11 0-0 ♗b7 12 ♕g3 ♗d6 13 ♖ae1 ♘bd7

Castling had its risks. On 13...0-0 14 ♗xb5! is surprisingly hard to deal with, e.g. 14...axb5 15 ♘xb5 with dangerous threats.

14 ♕xg7 ♖f8

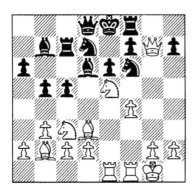

15 ♘e4??

Letting him right off the hook. 15 ♘xd7! and then capturing on h7 next move was one simple way to show a clear advantage. Despite the result of this game Portisch probably went back to his opening ideas drawing board.

15...♘xe4 16 ♗xe4 ♗xe4 17 ♖xe4 ♘xe5 18 fxe5 f5

Ouch!

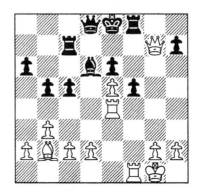

19 ♕h6 fxe4 20 ♕xe6+ ♗e7 21 ♖xf8+ ♔xf8 22 ♕f5+ ♔g8 23 ♕g4+ ♔h8 24 e6+ ♗f6 25 ♕g5 ♗d4+ 26 ♗xd4+ ♕xd4+ 27 ♔h1 ♖g7

This will do, but there might well be a stronger move!

28 e7 ♕a1 mate

Game 67
Tkachiev-Portisch
Tilburg (1st rapidplay game) 1994

---

1 e4 c5 2 f4 d5 3 exd5 ♕xd5 4 ♘c3 ♕e6+!? 5 ♗e2 ♘c6!?

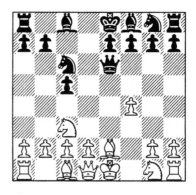

A novelty. 5...♘f6 6 ♘f3 g6 was known, but the position of the black queen is a little awkward.

6 ♘f3 ♘d4!?

A strange idea. Portisch seeks simplification, but it does not seem totally correct because he loses a fair amount of time.

7 ♘xd4

7 ♘e5, avoiding exchanges, is also interesting.

7...cxd4 8 ♘b5 ♕b6 9 c3 dxc3

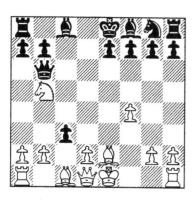

10 dxc3

A major decision. 10 bxc3 also looks likely to prove a little better for White after, e.g. 10...e6 (or 10...♘f6 11 d4 a6!?) 11 d4 ♘f6 12 0-0 ♗e7 13 c4 a6 14 ♘c3.

10...♗d7

10...♘f6 11 ♗e3!

11 a4

And here too he had the exciting move 11 ♗e3!, e.g. 11...♕xe3 12 ♘c7+ ♔d8 13 ♘xa8 and the complications are favourable for White. With only twenty minutes for the whole contest Tkachiev declines to plunge in, but that was the game's truly critical moment.

11...a6 12 ♘a3 ♗e6 13 ♘c4 ♕c7 14 ♘e5 ♘f6 15 a5

Fixing a strategical plus on the queenside, but Black is not too troubled.

15...g6 16 ♕a4+ ♘d7 17 ♗e3 ♗g7 18 ♘f3 0-0 19 ♖d1 ♘f6 20 0-0 ♘d5 21 ♗c1 ♖ad8 22 ♔h1 ♗d7 23 ♕c4

♕xc4 24 ♗xc4 ♗b5!?

24...♗c6 would also suffice for equality.

25 ♗xb5 axb5 26 ♘e5 e6 27 ♗d2 ♖a8 28 ♘d3 ♖fc8 29 ♖a1 ♖c6 30 g3 ♗f8 31 ♖fc1 f6 32 ♔g1 ♔f7

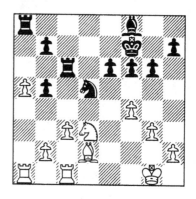

Nobody stands better.

33 ♔f1 ♖d8 34 ♔e2 h6 35 ♖f1 ♖a6 36 ♘c1 b4 37 c4 ♘c7 38 ♘b3 ♖c6 39 ♖ac1 ♘a6 40 ♗e3 ♖dc8 41 ♖fd1 ♔e8 42 ♗b6 ♗e7 43 ♖d4+ ♘c5 44 ♘xc5 ♗xc5 45 ♗xc5 ♖xc5 46 ♖d6 ♖8c6 47 ♖cd1 ♖xd6 48 ♖xd6

George Botterill once explained to me that it is because the other pieces have such great 'exchange-off' potential that rook endings are so common. Here is another.

48...♖xc4 49 ♖xe6+ ♔f7 50 ♖b6 ♖c2+ 51 ♔d3 ♖xb2 52 ♖xb7+ ♔e6 53 a6 ♖a2 54 a7 ½-½

Game 68
Hickl-Rajkovic
Altensteig 1990

---

1 e4 c5 2 f4 d5 3 exd5 ♕xd5 4 ♘c3 ♕d6

Why not stop here, a sensible enough square, rather than going all the way home? The problem is that sometimes the queen becomes a target to help White gain time.

5 ♘f3

5 ♗b5+ ♘c6 6 ♕f3?! brought White nothing in Popov-Afek, Paris open 1992, after 6...♘f6 7 ♘ge2 ♗d7 8 d3 a6 9 ♗xc6 ♗xc6 10 ♕f2 g6.

5...♘f6

If 5...♕xf4 then 6 d4 ♕d6 7 ♘b5 with excellent play, while after 5...♘c6 White can play 6 ♗b5 with the idea of 7 ♘e5.

6 d4

The critical test. 6 ♗c4 is the subject of Game 70.

6...cxd4 7 ♕xd4

7 ♘b5!? looks a fair try for the advantage, e.g. 7...♕d8 8 ♕xd4 ♗d7 9 ♕e5 ♗xb5 10 ♕xb5+ ♕d7 11 ♘e5 ♕xb5 12 ♗xb5+ ♘fd7 13 ♗e3 and White held a promising initiative in Campora-Komljenovic, Seville open 1999.

7...♕e6+!? 8 ♕e3 ♘c6 9 ♗b5 a6 10 ♗a4 b5 11 ♗b3 ♕xe3+ 12 ♗xe3 e6 13 0-0-0 ♘g4 14 ♗g1 ♘a5

see following diagram

Black has more or less equalised via normal Sicilian means. Hickl now speculates a pawn in a try for advantage.

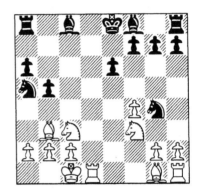

15 f5!? ♘xb3+ 16 axb3 exf5 17 ♘d5 ♗d6 18 h3 ♘h6 19 ♘b6 ♗f4+ 20 ♔b1 ♖b8 21 ♗c5 ♗g3 22 ♖d2 f6 23 ♖e2+ ♔f7 24 ♖e7+ ♔g6

Black has not been too disturbed by White's initiative, and he still has his extra pawn.

25 ♖d1 ♘f7 26 b4 ♖d8 27 ♘d4 ♘e5!

Rajkovic allows White a combinational possibility, but reasons that his activity in the resultant ending will suffice to hold the balance.

28 ♘xc8 ♖bxc8

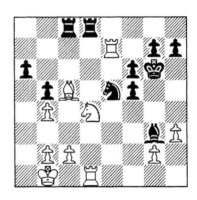

29 ♖xg7+! ♔xg7 30 ♘e6+ ♔g6 31 ♘xd8 f4 32 b3 h5! 33 ♘e6 h4

Although Black's kingside pawns are fractured they still constitute a majority and White must keep an eye on that zone for possible breakthroughs.

34 ♘d4 ♖e8 35 ♖d2 ♘f7 36 ♔b2 ♘e5 37 c3 ♗e1 38 ♖e2 ♗g3 39 ♔c2 ♖c8 40 ♘f3 ♔f5 41 ♘d4+ ♔g6 42 ♘f3 ♔f5 43 ♘d4+ ½-½

Calling it a day as nobody is getting anywhere.

Game 69
Sveshnikov-Sax
Ljubljana 1994

1 e4 c5 2 f4 d5 3 exd5 ♕xd5 4 ♘c3 ♕d6 5 ♘f3 ♘f6 6 d4 e6 7 ♗e3! ♘g4

Or 7...cxd4 8 ♘xd4 and White follows up with something like ♕f3 and 0-0-0, when Black loses further time due to the placing of his queen.

8 ♕e2! ♘xe3 9 ♕xe3 cxd4 10 ♘xd4 ♕b6 11 0-0-0

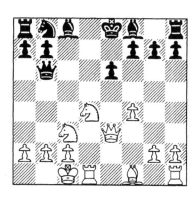

White has had to cede the bishop pair, but his great lead in development is the crucial factor and Black is never going to equalise from here. Indeed, he may already be lost.

11...♗e7 12 ♗b5+ ♗d7

Or 12...♘c6 13 ♖he1 and Black cannot castle without losing a pawn.

13 ♗xd7+ ♘xd7 14 ♖he1 0-0-0

When such a natural move as 14...0-0 is impossible, as here, because of 15 ♘xe6! ♕xe3+ 16 ♖xe3 fxe6 17 ♖xd7 then it is a sure sign that all is far from well.

15 ♘d5 exd5

Instead 15...♕c5 16 ♘xe7+ ♕xe7 17 ♘f5 ♕f8 18 ♘d6+ ♔b8 19 ♕e4 ♘c5 20 ♕e5 ♘d7 21 ♘xf7+! ♘xe5 22 ♖xd8+ ♕xd8 23 ♘xd8 is an attractive winning line.

16 ♕xe7

16...♖he8

There is no satisfactory solution. If 16...♕f6 17 ♘b5 ♔b8 18 ♕d6+ ♕xd6 19 ♘xd6 ♖hf8 20 ♖e7 wins.

17 ♕xe8 ♖xe8 18 ♖xe8+ ♔c7 19 g3 ♕c5 20 ♖e3 ♘b6 21 b3 ♕a3+ 22 ♔b1 ♔d7

22...a6 is probably better, but ultimately the rooks must triumph over the queen in such an open position.

23 ♖ed3 ♕c5 24 ♘f5 ♕f2 25 ♖1d2 ♕g1+ 26 ♔b2 g6 27 ♘e3 ♔e6 28 ♖e2! 1-0

see following diagram

Black resigned, because despite the reduced material his queen has been trapped.

Game 70
Fredericks-Altman
New York 1961

1 e4 c5 2 f4 d5 3 exd5 ♕xd5 4 ♘c3 ♕d6 5 ♘f3 ♘f6 6 ♗c4 ♘c6 7 0-0 g6

8 d3 ♘a5 9 ♘b5 ♕b6 10 ♖e1 ♘xc4 11 dxc4 ♗e6 12 ♘g5 ♖d8 13 ♘xe6! ♖xd1 14 ♘bc7+ ♔d7 15 ♖xd1+ ♔c6 16 ♘a8 ♕a6 17 ♘d8 mate(!)

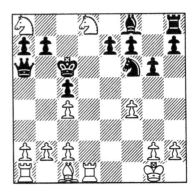

Perhaps not the most theoretically significant game in this book, but I could not resist its inclusion!

Summary

There is no really good reason for Black to play 3...♕xd5 as the lines in the previous chapter are so acceptable for him. These games therefore have mainly historical interest but a number of them demonstrate how quickly White can whip up a powerful attack against passive play from Black.

1 e4 c5 2 f4 d5 3 exd5 ♕xd5 4 ♘c3

4...♕d8
    4...♕e6+ – *Game 67*
    4...♕d6 5 ♘f3 ♘f6 *(D)*
        6 d4
            6...cxd4 – *Game 68*
            6...e6 – *Game 69*
        6 ♗c4 – *Game 70*

5 ♘f3 *(D)* ♘f6

    5...g6
        6 d4 – *Game 60*
        6 ♘e5
            6...♗g7 – *Game 61*
            6...♘f6 – *Game 62*
    5...e6
        6 d4 – *Game 64*
        6 b3 – *Game 65*
        6 ♘e5 – *Game 66*

6 ♘e5 *(D)* – Game 63

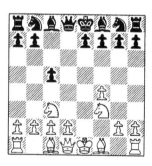
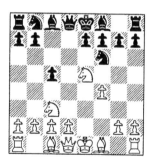

    5...♘f6   *5 ♘f3*   *6 ♘e5*

CHAPTER SEVEN

1 e4 c5 2 f4 d5 3 ♘c3

---

1 e4 c5 2 f4 d5 3 ♘c3

Rumour has it that Grandmaster Mark Hebden is said to have thought of this move (not his profoundest idea) whilst engaged in an inglorious activity. Due to its supposed provenance it acquired the soubriquet of the 'toilet' variation.

Obviously 3 ♘c3 cannot constitute any test of the gambit's worth because Black has several highly rational and satisfactory replies. 3...e6 takes us into Chapter 3; 3...♘f6 into the miscellany of Chapter 8. 3...d4 is quite sound but not often played. You may then retreat with equal logic to b1 or e2, the latter having been more popular. I am unaware of any game with 4 ♗b5+, except Tseleng-Battikhi, Moscow Olympiad 1994, which continued 4...♘c6 5 ♘ce2 ♘f6 6 d3?? ♛a5+ and Black found the extra bishop useful.

The great majority of players have chosen 3...dxe4 4 ♘xe4. The astute amongst you may notice that this position could be obtained after the initial four moves of Chapter 6, after 4...♛d8, were White moved to play 5 ♘e4 – a

sort of 'outside toilet'. Nobody has yet constructed one.

Game 71
Plaskett-Howell
British Championship, Brighton 1984

1 e4 c5 2 f4 d5 3 ♘c3 dxe4
3...d4 is far less well explored.

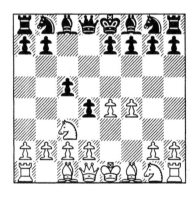

After 4 ♘ce2 (Hebden has also experimented with 4 ♘b1!?) 4...♘c6 White should not commit his knight to g3 too early or he may run into an assault by the black h-pawn, e.g. 5 ♘g3?! ♘f6 6 ♗c4 h5 7 ♛e2 h4 8 ♘f1 ♗g4 9 ♘f3 h3 and

---

Black was already doing very well in Reefschläger-Glek, Willingen 1999. 5 ۾f3 ۾f6 6 d3 is preferable, with a very complex game in prospect.

4 ۾xe4 e6

The usual move. Black's alternatives here are discussed in Games 79 and 80.

5 ۾f3 ♗e7

This move order grants White the chance to open up the centre, so perhaps the 5...۾f6 (Games 73 and 74) or 5...۾c6 (Games 75-78) are better. At the Hastings tournament of 1992/93 I disputed many blitz games with GM Ilya Gurevich in this line, in which he constantly deployed his king knight to f5 with 5...۾h6!?

Bojan Kurajica also played that against William Watson in Amsterdam 1985 and the game continued 6 d4 (I doubt that this is the best) 6...cxd4 7 ♕xd4 ♕c7 8 ♗d2 ۾c6 9 ♕c3 ۾f5 10 0-0-0 ♗b4 11 ♕d3 0-0 12 c3 ♗e7 13 g4 ۾d6 14 ۾xd6 ♕xd6 15 ♕xd6 ♗xd6 16 ♗e3 and a draw was agreed.

6 ♗c4

Mitkov-Stamenkovic, Yugoslav Team Championship 1990, varied with 6 ♗b5+ ♗d7 7 ♕e2 ♗xb5 8 ♕xb5+ ♕d7 9 ♕e2!? ۾c6 10 ۾e5 ۾xe5 11 fxe5 ۾h6

and was then agreed drawn. However, a serious improvement was introduced in Adams-Lautier, Tilburg 1997, where White played 6 d4! cxd4 7 ♕xd4 ♕xd4 8 ۾xd4, and after 8...a6 Adams recommends 9 g3! ۾f6 10 bg2 ۾bd7 11 ♗d2 with a clear plus.

6...۾f6 7 ♕e2 ۾c6 8 c3!?

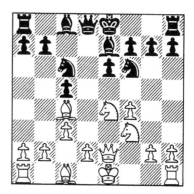

Not a developing move but one that takes the important d4-square away from Black.

8...0-0 9 0-0 b6 10 d3 ♗b7

Black did not fare well either in Reefschläger-Kurz, Germany 1988, with 10...۾xe4 after 11 dxe4 ♗b7 12 ♗d2 ♕c7 13 e5 ♖ad8 14 ♖ae1 ♖d7 when White started operations similar to those in my game with 15 f5, and the attack actually caused Black to resign six moves later.

11 ۾g3 ♗d6 12 ♗d2 ♕c7

Something is not quite right with this formation for Black. He adopts a stance that is too passive and drifts into a middlegame where he is reduced to a spectator regarding a nasty offensive. Maybe he would have done better to have chased White's bishop with 12...۾a5!?

13 ۾g5 ۾e7 14 ۾5e4! ۾xe4 15 dxe4

From here on in it is a very easy attack to play as White. Black must constantly worry over the advance of the f- or e-pawns.

15...♘g6 16 ♘h5 ♔h8 17 ♖ae1 ♖ad8 18 ♗c1

Tucking it out of harm's way. It will be just as effective one square further back.

18...♖d7 19 e5!

Enough of preparing.

19...♗e7 20 f5 exf5

21 ♖xf5?

21 ♗xf7! won on the spot. Fortunately White keeps a dangerous attack even after the gaffe.

21...♗d5

Naturally Black trades off the bishop before it can do any damage.

22 ♗xd5 ♖xd5 23 ♕g4 ♕d7 24 ♖ef1 ♔g8

see following diagram

25 ♘xg7!

Having missed an easy win at move 21, I try a far more iffy way to the full point.

25...♔xg7 26 ♕h5

Threatening to check on h6, take on f8 and then on f7.

26...♔g8 27 ♗h6 ♕e6 28 ♗xf8 ♘xf8 29 c4!

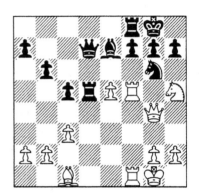

An important intermezzo. The black rook is shunted to a less effective square before White captures the pawn and so White will keep the e5-pawn.

29...♖d4 30 ♖xf7 ♕g6?

A blunder in time pressure.

31 ♕f3 ♘e6 32 ♖xe7 ♖f4 33 ♖xe6 1-0

Game 72
Minasian-Chekhov
Moscow 1992

1 e4 c5 2 ♘c3 e6

Via a transpositional move order we will reach the same position at move 6 as in the previous example.

3 f4 d5 4 ♘f3 dxe4 5 ♘xe4 ♗e7 6 ♗c4 ♘f6

In another Minasian game from the same year, versus Kharlov in a Moscow rapidplay tournament, Black was more successful with a different kingside development: 6...♘c6 7 d3 ♘h6!? 8 ♘e5 ♗d7 9 ♘xd7 ♕xd7 10 ♗e3 ♘f5 11 ♗f2 ♘a5 12 ♗b3 b6 13 0-0 0-0 14 ♕e2 ♖fd8 15 ♖ad1 h6 16 c3 ♘xb3 17 axb3 ♕b5 18 ♕c2 ♖d7 19 g4 ♘d6 20 ♘xd6 ♖xd6 21

♗g3 ♖ad8 and Black won in the end.

7 d3 0-0 8 0-0 ♘c6 9 a4

To preserve his bishop from the knight's attentions. In Coklin-Tratar, Ljubljana open 1993, Black nabbed it after 9 ♔h1 ♘a5 and went on to win after 10 ♕e1 ♘xc4 11 dxc4 b6 12 ♗d2 ♗b7 13 ♘g3 ♘d7.

9...b6

Passing over the last chance to trade queens, but Chekhov must have been happy enough with the result of the opening.

10 ♗d2 ♗b7 11 ♔h1 ♘d4 12 ♘xd4 cxd4 13 ♕e2 ♕d7 14 ♖f3 ♖fc8 15 ♖h3

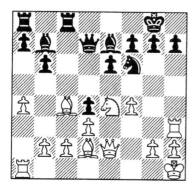

15...♗d5?

There had to be some mileage in the exchange sacrifice 15...♘xe4 16 dxe4 ♖xc4!? 17 ♕xe4 ♗xe4 when the white attack has evaporated and Black keeps the bishop pair, a sound formation and the threat of 18...♖c8. With the text he quite misjudges both the power of the attack and the significance of his own counterplay down the c-file.

16 ♗xd5 exd5 17 ♘xf6+ ♗xf6 18 ♕h5 h6 19 f5

With crude and extremely powerful threats.

19...♕c6 20 g4!

Minasian gives up his queenside. He won't be needing it.

20...♕xc2 21 ♗xh6 ♕xb2 22 ♖g1 gxh6 23 ♕xh6 ♗g7 24 ♕h7+ ♔f8 25 f6! ♗xf6 26 ♖f3 ♗g7 27 ♖xf7+!

Effectively crashing through the last defences.

27...♔xf7 28 ♖f1+ 1-0

Black resigned, for he will be mated very quickly.

Game 73
Hebden-King
British Championship, Brighton 1984

---

1 e4 c5 2 f4 d5 3 ♘c3 dxe4 4 ♘xe4 e6 5 ♘f3 ♘f6 6 ♘f2

A couple of other moves have proved popular here. 6 ♗b5+ is considered in the next main game, while 6 ♘xf6+ ♕xf6 7 ♘e5 led to an extraordinary contest in Wahls-Lutz, Germany 1994, 7...♕xf4! 8 ♗b5+ ♗d7 9 ♕e2 ♗xb5 10 ♕xb5+ ♘c6! 11 ♕xb7 (otherwise he remains a pawn down) 11...♕xe5+ 12 ♔d1 ♕h5+ 13 ♔e1 ♕e5+ 14 ♔d1 ♕h5+ 15 ♔e1 ♕h4+! 16 ♔f1 ♕f4+ 17 ♔g1 ♕d4+ 18 ♔f1 ♕f4+ 19 ♔g1 ♕d4+ 20 ♔f1

20...♕d7! 21 ♕xa8+ ♔e7 22 b4 (this rescue attempt is not good enough) 22...cxb4! 23 ♗a3 g6 24 ♗xb4+ ♘xb4 25 ♕e4 ♕xd2 26 ♖b1 ♔f6 0-1.

6...♘c6 7 b3 ♗d6 8 ♘d3

Hebden likes this deployment of the knight, but I am not sure that I do.

8...♘d5

Hebden-Leontxo Garcia, Lewisham 1984, continued instead 8...♕c7 9 g3 0-0 (Black forced the pace in Reefschläger-Hellers, Bad Wörishofen 1991, with 9...e5 but after 10 fxe5 ♘xe5 11 ♘fxe5 ♗xe5 12 ♕e2 0-0 13 ♘xe5 ♖e8 14 ♗b2 ♘g4 15 ♗g2 ♘xe5 16 0-0 f6 17 ♕b5 all that resulted was a small plus for White) 10 ♗b2 ♘d7 11 ♗h3!? b6 12 0-0 ♗a6 13 c4 ♗b7 14 ♕e2 ♖fe8 15 ♘g5 ♘d4

16 ♗xd4 cxd4 17 ♗g2 when White was slightly better. King's move does not gain him any time since White was going to play g2-g3 anyway.

9 g3 b6 10 ♗b2 0-0 11 ♗g2 ♗b7 12 0-0 ♕c7 13 ♘g5 ♘d4 14 c4 ♘e7 15 ♗xb7 ♕xb7 16 ♗xd4 cxd4 17 ♕f3

White hopes that the black bishop will be a little hindered in this queenless middlegame, but objectively I doubt that there is much wrong with either side's position. Note how the d3-knight has ended up playing the role of a blockader.

17...♕xf3 18 ♘xf3

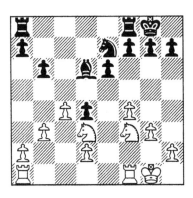

18...♘c6 19 ♖fe1 a5 20 a3 ♖fd8 21 ♔f1 ♖ab8 22 ♖eb1 ♖a8 23 ♘fe1 f6 24 ♘c2 e5

I am not sure that this was the right plan; the pawns get fixed on inappropriate coloured squares for Black's bishop. **25 fxe5 fxe5 26 ♖e1 ♖f8+ 27 ♔g2 ♖ae8 28 ♘f2**

see following diagram

A good knight versus bad bishop scenario, and a lovely blockading square at e4 for it too.

28...♗c7 29 d3 b5

Black panics and gives up a pawn in

pursuit of counterplay, but he never gets enough.

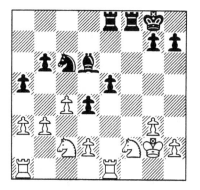

30 cxb5 ♘e7 31 ♘e4 ♘d5 32 a4 ♗d8 33 ♘d6 ♖e6 34 ♘c4 ♖fe8 35 ♖f1 ♗f6 36 ♖ae1 ♘c3 37 ♘xa5 e4 38 ♘c4 exd3 39 ♖xe6 ♖xe6 40 ♘b4 ♖e2+ 41 ♖f2 ♘e4 42 ♖xe2 dxe2 43 ♘d3 ♘c5 44 ♘cb2 ♘xb3 45 ♔f2 ♘a5 46 ♔xe2 ♔f7 47 ♘f4 ♔e7 48 ♔d3 ♔d7 49 ♘d5 1-0

Game 74
Lau-Armas
Wijk aan Zee 1989

---

1 e4 c5 2 f4 d5 3 ♘c3 dxe4 4 ♘xe4 e6 5 ♘f3 ♘f6 6 ♗b5+!? ♗d7 7 ♗xd7+ ♘bxd7 8 ♕e2 ♗e7 9 d3 ♕c7

In Motwani-King, Dublin 1991, Black just safely castled here: 9...0-0 10 0-0 b5 11 ♗d2 ♕c7 12 ♖ae1 c4 with a perfectly satisfactory position. Armas never quite gets around to it.

10 0-0 h6?! 11 ♗d2 ♘xe4 12 dxe4 g5?!

All rather unclassical and unwise.

13 ♗c3 f6 14 f5 e5 15 ♖ad1 c4 16 a4 ♗b4

This is an indication that his earlier poor strategy has produced a lack of natural good moves.

17 ♗xb4 ♕b6+

18 ♘d4!

I bet that Black was not expecting this one!

18...♕xb4

If 18...exd4 then 19 ♕xc4 leads to a decisive advantage for White.

19 ♘b5

The weaknesses and disruption in the black camp now mean that his cause is hopeless. On 19...0-0-0 20 ♘d6+ and 21 ♘f7 wins.

19...♔e7 20 ♖d6 ♘c5 21 ♕h5 ♖ad8 22 ♖xf6!

A nice tactic.

22...♖hf8 23 ♖xf8 ♖xf8 24 ♕xh6 ♘d7 25 ♕e6+ ♔d8 26 ♖d1 ♕c5+

27 ⚔h1 ♛c6 28 ♖d6 1-0

Game 75
Hebden-Mestel
British Championship, Southampton 1986

---

1 e4 c5 2 f4 d5 3 ♘c3 dxe4 4 ♘xe4 e6 5 ♘f3 ♘c6 6 g3

Hebden steers towards his favoured double fianchetto formation. This interpretation varies markedly from the attacking stances involving the development of the king's bishop along the f1-a6 diagonal. For 6 ♗b5 see Game 78.

6...♘f6

6...♗e7 7 ♗g2 ♘f6 8 ♘f2 transposes to the next main game, while 6...f5 is considered in Game 77.

7 ♘f2

In the game G.Giorgadze-Kouatly, Manila Olympiad 1992, White chose the possibly more natural course of taking on f6 and after 7...♛xf6 8 ♗g2 Black also opted to fianchetto. The continuation 9 0-0 ♗g7 10 d3 0-0 11 c3 ♛e7 12 ♗e3 ♖d8 13 ♛e2 ♗d7 was equal.

7...g6!?

Mestel rarely squanders an opportunity, as Black, to fianchetto his king's bishop. The routine 7...♗e7 8 ♗g2 is the

subject of the next main game (by transposition).

8 ♗g2

If he is aiming for a double fianchetto then this is already an inaccuracy and 8 b3 was to be preferred.

8...♗g7 9 0-0 0-0 10 ♘d3?!

Here this just doesn't fit at all, and Mestel swiftly exploits the misplacement. 10 d3 was a much better set-up.

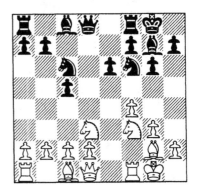

10...♘g4! 11 ♘xc5

Now White soon goes down the tubes, but how else was he to develop? On 11 h3 c4 is very nasty.

11...♛b6 12 d4 ♘xd4 13 ♘xd4 ♛xc5 14 ♛xg4 e5! 15 ♛f3 e4! 16 ♛xe4 ♗f5

Gaining all the time he can.

17 ♛xb7 ♗xd4+ 18 ⚔h1 ♛xc2 19 ♛b3 ♖ac8!

Even after the exchange of queens White has no chance because of the total domination of the black pieces in contrast to White's unmoved queenside.

20 ♛xc2 ♖xc2

---

see following diagram

---

21 ♖e1 ♖b8 22 ♗d5 ♖d8 23 ♗b3 ♖f2 24 h4 ♗g4 25 ♗d1 ♗xd1 26 ♖xd1 ♖e8 27 ♖xd4 ♖e1 mate

---

Sloppy handling of the opening was routed by Mestel.

1 e4 c5 2 f4 d5 3 ♘c3 dxe4 4 ♘xe4 e6 5 ♘f3 ♘c6 6 g3 ♗e7 7 ♗g2 ♘f6 8 ♘f2 ♕c7

Black challenged on the a1-h8 diagonal in Hebden-A.Rodriguez, Malaga 1987, with 8...0-0 9 b3 ♘d5. After 10 ♗b2 ♗f6 11 ♘e5 ♘xe5 12 fxe5 ♗e7 13 ♘e4 ♗d7 14 c4 ♘b4 15 0-0 ♗c6 16 a3 ♗xe4 17 ♗xe4 ♘c6 18 ♗c3 g6 19 ♕g4 ♕c7 20 ♖ae1 White had the bishop pair and attacking chances.

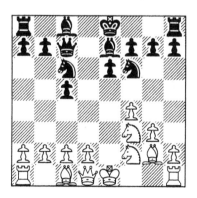

9 0-0 0-0 10 b3 b6 11 ♗b2 ♗b7

In Nunn-Kouatly, Brussels 1985, Black went a little further with 11...♗a6 12 c4 ♖ad8 13 ♕e2 ♖d7 14 ♖ad1 ♗b7 15 ♗h3 ♖ad8. Neither side is doing much here and after 16 d3 h6 17 ♗g2 a6 18 ♕e3 ♘b4 19 g4 ♘c2 20 ♕e2 they called a truce.

12 c4 ♖ad8

12...♖fd8 13 ♕e2 ♘e8 would have taken us into Dolezal-Ricardi, Acasusso Valle open 1994, when after 14 ♘g4 ♘d6 15 ♘e3 ♗f8 16 ♖ad1 ♘b4 17 a3 ♘c6 18 d3 a6 19 ♘d2 b5 not too much was happening, but Black managed to win later on.

13 ♕e2 a6 14 ♘d3

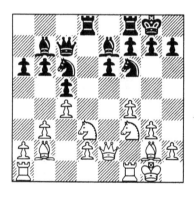

Off to e5.

14...♘e8 15 ♘de5 ♗f6 16 ♖ad1 ♘d6 17 g4 ♖fe8 18 h4

Black is not up to much, so why not grab some space?

18...♗e7 19 h5 ♗f8 20 h6 f6 21 ♘xc6 ♗xc6 22 ♘h2 ♗xg2 23 ♕xg2 ♕b7 24 ♖fe1 ♕xg2+ 25 ♔xg2

Black has no serious headaches here.

25...b5

This weakens, albeit almost imperceptibly, the c5-pawn, whilst not achieving much else for Black.

26 d3 ♔f7 27 hxg7 ♗xg7 28 ♘f3 h5
29 g5 ♘f5 30 ♔f2 h4 31 gxf6 ♗xf6
32 ♗xf6 ♔xf6 33 ♖e5 bxc4 34 bxc4
♖c8 35 ♘g5

The consequences of Black's 25th move tell against him now that the position has opened up. Hebden takes a nice pawn and realises the advantage.

35...♖c6 36 ♘e4+ ♔f7 37 ♘xc5
♖b8 38 ♘xe6! ♖b2+ 39 ♔f3 ♖xe6
40 ♖xf5+ ♔g6 41 ♖g5+ ♔f6 42 ♖h1
♖be2 43 ♖e5 ♖6xe5 44 fxe5+ ♖xe5
45 ♖xh4 ♖a5 46 ♖h2 ♔e6 47 ♔e4
♔d6 48 d4 ♖a4 49 ♖h6+ ♔c7 50
♖h7+ ♔c6 51 ♖h6+ ♔c7 52 ♔d5
♖xa2 53 ♖h7+ ♔b8 54 ♔c5 ♖b2 55
d5 a5 56 d6 1-0

Game 77
Hebden-C.Hansen
Malmo 1987

---

1 e4 c5 2 f4 d5 3 ♘c3 dxe4 4 ♘xe4
e6 5 ♘f3 ♘c6 6 g3 f5!?

The only game I know of where this move was played.

7 ♘f2 ♗d6 8 b3 ♘h6

I am uncertain why Black developed the knight here. If his aim was to support ...e6-e5 then it did not work out and he soon comes to rue passing over the usual squares for it.

9 ♗b2 0-0 10 ♗g2 ♘f7 11 ♘d3

Once again Hebden swivels the knight to his favourite spot.

11...b6 12 ♘g5!? ♕d7

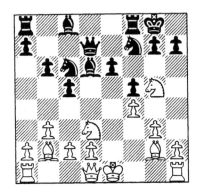

13 h4!? ♗a6 14 ♕h5

Very interesting play. White defers castling and prompts Black to post his king's knight awkwardly, since few people would wish to open the h-file when the white rook is still at h1.

14...♘h6 15 c4!

Keeping the bishop quiet.

15...b5 16 0-0!

Only now, after effective preparatory work, does White castle.

16...♖fe8 17 ♖fe1 bxc4

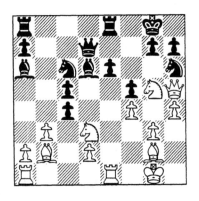

Now the roof caves in, but Black was stymied.

18 ♘xe6! ♖xe6 19 ♗d5 ♘d8 20 ♖xe6 ♘xe6 21 ♖e1 ♖e8 22 ♕xe8+! ♕xe8 23 ♖xe6 ♕f8 24 ♖xd6+ ♘f7 25 ♖xa6 cxd3 26 ♖xa7 1-0

One of Hebden's best games in the Grand Prix Attack.

Game 78
Horn-D.Cramling
Biel 1986

---

1 e4 c5 2 f4 d5 3 ♘c3 dxe4 4 ♘xe4 e6 5 ♘f3 ♘c6 6 ♗b5 ♗d7 7 0-0 ♘h6!?

Once again this intriguing stationing.

8 b3

8 ♕e2 would lead into Yudasin-Ulibin, Las Palmas 1993, where chances were equal after 8...a6 9 ♗xc6 ♗xc6 10 b3 ♘f5 11 ♗b2 ♗e7 12 ♘e5 ♖c8 13 d3 0-0 14 ♖ae1 ♘d4.

8...♗e7 9 ♗b2 ♘f5 10 ♕e2 0-0 11 ♔h1 a6 12 ♗xc6 ♗xc6 13 ♘e5 ♗e8!?

Hoarding his bishops.

14 ♕f2 ♖c8 15 a4?!

This only helps Black to weaken the white queenside foundations.

15...f6 16 ♘f3 c4! 17 ♘d4 ♘xd4 18 ♗xd4 cxb3 19 cxb3 e5! 20 ♗c5 ♗xc5 21 ♘xc5 ♕d5 22 b4 a5

The white position is creaking.

23 fxe5 axb4 24 d4 ♗c6 25 e6 b6 26 ♘d3 ♕xe6 27 ♘xb4 ♗e4 28 d5 ♕g4 29 ♕d2?

29...♖c4!

Winning.

30 ♖f2 ♖xb4 31 d6 ♖d4 0-1

Game 79
Popchev-Petrovic
Novi Sad 1986

---

1 e4 c5 2 f4 d5 3 ♘c3 dxe4 4 ♘xe4 ♕c7

Another idea here is 4...♘f6!?

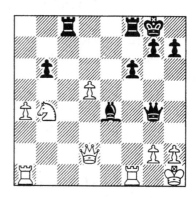

5 ♘xf6+ (turning it into something akin to the Modern Caro-Kann, i.e. 1 e4 c6 2 d4 d5 3 ♘c3 dxe4 4 ♘xe4 ♘f6 5 ♘xf6+ exf6; 5 ♘c5, grabbing the c5-pawn, would presumably be met by 5...e5, but White might then hang on to his pawn with 6 ♘d3!?) 5...exf6 6 ♗b5+ ♗d7 7 ♕e2+ ♗e7 8 ♗xd7+ ♕xd7 9 ♘f3 0-0 10 0-0 ♘c6 and a draw was agreed in Fries Nielsen-B.Kristensen, Danish Championship 1987.

5 g3 ♘f6

In Horn-Shabalov, Geneva open 1992, Black found himself minus a rook after 5...b6 6 ♗g2 ♗b7 7 ♕e2 g6?? 8 ♘d6+, but he still managed to draw the game!

6 ♘f2 g6 7 b3 ♗g7 8 ♗b2 ♘c6 9 ♘f3 0-0 10 ♕e2 ♗f5

A rare instance in this line of the black queen's bishop not being developed in a fianchetto.

11 ♗g2 ♖ad8 12 0-0 ♘d4

Taking the c-pawn on either of the two previous moves would only have resulted in the loss of the bishop after d2-d3.

13 ♘xd4 cxd4 14 ♖ac1 ♖fe8 15 ♘d3 h5 16 ♖fe1 ♘d7 17 ♕f3 ♘c5

½-½

Game 80
Ermenkov-Adorjan
Budapest Zonal 1993

1 e4 c5 2 f4 d5 3 ♘c3 dxe4 4 ♘xe4 ♕c7 5 ♘f3!? ♘f6

If Black takes on f4 then White has 5...♕xf4 6 ♘xc5 ♘f6 7 d4 ♕c7 8 ♘e5!? as a try for the advantage.

6 ♘xf6+

This move is rarely seen, but, as you might suspect, the more common 6 d3 offers White nothing after 6...♘bd7 7 g3 g6 8 ♗g2 ♗g7 9 0-0 0-0.

6...exf6

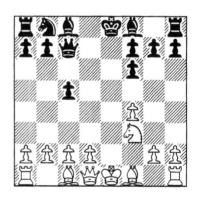

The other recapture, of course, was an option, with similar structure to a 4...♘f6

5 ∆xf6+ gxf6 Caro-Kann.

7 g3 ♗e7 8 ♗g2 0-0 9 0-0 ∆c6 10 b3 ♗g4 11 h3 ♗e6 12 d3 ♖fd8 13 ♗e3

Abandoning the fianchetto idea. On 13 ♗b2 a5 14 a4?! c4! is effective.

13...♖ac8 14 a4 b6 15 ♔h2 h6! 16 ♕e2 f5

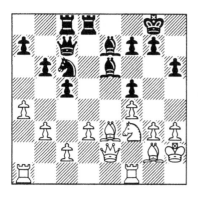

It looks as though there is little for either side to do, but Black first places his pieces as actively as possible and then starts to advance his queenside pawns. Gradually things will turn his way.

17 ♖ae1 ♗f6

Starting to make its presence felt.

18 ♕f2 ♖e8 19 ∆d2 ♗c3 20 ♖e2 ♖e7 21 ∆b1 ♗f6 22 ♖ee1 ♖ce8 23 ♗d2 ♕d7 24 ∆a3

Not 24 ∆c3? because of 24...∆b4 25 ♖c1 ♗xc3! 26 ♗xc3 ∆a2 winning.

24...∆d4

The black pieces become ever the more dominant.

25 ♗e3 ♗d5 26 ♗xd5 ♕xd5 27 ∆c4 ♖e6 28 ♗xd4

Removing the oppressive beast, but Adorjan now has the better minor piece and he works skilfully to exploit its superiority.

28...♗xd4 29 ♕d2 ♕c6 30 h4 a6!

Better than the precipitate 30...♗c3 when White can resist with 31 ♖xe6 ♕xe6 32 ♕g2 ♕e8 33 ♖f2 ♗d4 34 ♖d2 ♖e1 35 ♕f3, etc. Adorjan gains some queenside space, and also introduces the possibility of a minority attack to increase his advantage.

31 ♖xe6 ♕xe6 32 ♕g2 b5 33 axb5 axb5 34 ∆e5

Giving up a pawn in his attempts to resist the squeeze, but 34 ∆d2 was met by 34...♕e2 35 ∆f3 ♕xg2+ 36 ♔xg2 ♖e2+ 37 ♔h3 ♗c3 with total domination.

34...♗xe5 35 fxe5

The pure queen ending after 35 ♖e1 ♕d6 36 fxe5 ♖xe5 37 ♖xe5 ♕xe5 was also lost.

35...♕xe5 36 ♖f2 b4 37 ♕f3 g6 38 ♕f4 ♔g7 39 ♕xe5+ ♖xe5

Black now handles the technical phase accurately to bring home the full point.

40 ♔g2 g5 41 hxg5 hxg5 42 ♖d2 ♔g6 43 ♔f3 g4+ 44 ♔f4 ♖e1 45 ♖h2 f6 46 ♖f2 ♖g1 47 c3 bxc3 48 ♖c2 ♖f1+ 49 ♔e3 ♖f3+ 50 ♔e2 ♖xg3 51 ♖xc3 f4 52 ♖xc5 ♖g2+ 53 ♔f1 ♖b2 54 ♖b5 f3 55 ♖b8 ♔g5 0-1

A powerfully played game by Andras Adorjan.

Summary

3 ♘c3 is probably the most promising way to meet 2...d5. It does not feel as if this should be a dangerous position for Black but if he plays too quietly White can often start a dangerous attack. The best plans for Black are those which involve an early challenge to White's set-up, as White's development certainly lags in the early stages, thus 4...♕c7 looks quite promising.

1 e4 c5 2 f4 d5 3 ♘c3 dxe4 4 ♘xe4 *(D)*

4...e6
    4...♕c7
        5 g3 – *Game 79*
        5 ♘f3 – *Game 80*
5 ♘f3 ♘c6 *(D)*
    5...♗e7 6 ♗c4 ♘f6
        7 ♕e2 – *Game 71*
        7 d3 – *Game 72*
    5...♘f6
        6 ♘f2 – *Game 73*
        6 ♗b5+ – *Game 74*
6 g3
    6 ♗b5 – *Game 78*
6...♘f6
    6...♗e7 – *Game 76*
    6...f5 – *Game 77*
7 ♘f2 *(D)* – *Game 75*

4 ♘xe4

5...♘c6

7 ♘f2

CHAPTER EIGHT

1 e4 c5 2 f4:
Other Lines

---

1 e4 c5 2 f4

In this chapter we deal with other, more rare alternatives for Black.

Systems with ...♞c6, ...d7-d6, ...♞f6 and ...e7-e6 have been comparatively rare in practice, although all of Black's moves contribute to a logical development.

There have been surprisingly few games with 2...♞f6 3 ♞c3 d5, although this move order is probably alright provided that Black is prepared to defend one of the main lines of the Classical French, by transposition.

Although 1 e4 c5 2 ♞f3 b6!? has a poor reputation, grandmasters such as Larsen, Andersson, Miles, Nunn and Csom have all been prepared to play 2...b6 against the Grand Prix Attack.

In this chapter Games 81-82 see Black developing quietly with 2...♞c6 and 3...d6. Games 83-85 witness the immediate central counter with 2...e6 and 3...d5. 2...g6 is a natural try for Black and the attempt to force the pace with 3 d4 is seen in Games 86-89. Finally, two off-beat tries, 2...♞f6 and 2...b6 are seen in Games 90 and 91 respectively.

Game 81
King-Csom
Gausdal 1993

1 e4 c5 2 f4 d6 3 ♞f3 ♞c6 4 ♗b5 ♗d7 5 c4!?

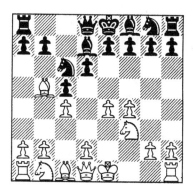

Erecting a Maroczy Bind as fast as possible. The delayed Maroczy of Sveshnikov-Poluljahov, Anapa 1991, was less of a success for White after 5 0-0 g6 6 c4 ♗g7 7 ♞c3 ♞h6!? (or 7...♞f6 8 d3 a6 9 ♗xc6 ♗xc6 10 ♗d2 b5 11 ♕e2 ♞d7 12 ♖ae1 0-0 and Black went on to win in West-Arakhamia, Sydney 1991) 8 d3 0-0 9 h3 f5!? 10 ♗e3 a6 11 ♗a4 ♖b8

---

12 e5!? dxe5 13 fxe5 ♘d4 14 ♗xd4 cxd4 15 ♗xd7 ♕xd7 16 ♕a4?? b5 17 cxb5 dxc3 0-1. Finally, 6 d3 ♗g7 7 c3 a6 8 ♗a4 ♘f6 9 ♗c2 e5 10 fxe5 dxe5 was equal in Horn-Gallagher, Zug 1991.

5...a6 6 ♗xc6 ♗xc6 7 ♘c3 e6 8 d4

8 0-0 would transpose to Campora-Novikov, Bern 1993, when after 8...♘f6 9 ♕e2 ♗e7 10 d3 0-0 11 h3 ♘d7 12 ♗e3 ♖e8 13 d4 cxd4 14 ♘xd4 ♖c8 chances were balanced.

8...cxd4 9 ♘xd4 ♖c8 10 ♕e2 ♗e7 11 0-0 ♘f6 12 ♔h1 0-0 13 b3 ♕b6 14 ♗b2!?

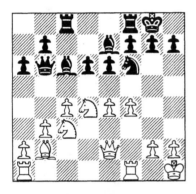

14...♕xd4!? 15 ♘d5 ♕xe4 16 ♘xe7+ ♔h8 17 ♕xe4 ♘xe4 18 ♘xc8 ♖xc8

With one pawn and a solid position for the exchange this is a resolution very much in the mode of Ulf Andersson and Black has comfortable equality.

19 ♔g1 ♔g8 20 ♖ad1 f6 21 ♖fe1 d5 22 f5 dxc4 23 fxe6 ♖e8 24 bxc4 ♖xe6 25 ♖e3 ½-½

> *Game 82*
> **Miles-Gligoric**
> *Tilburg 1977*

1 e4 c5 2 f4 ♘c6 3 ♘f3 ♘f6 4 ♘c3

d5 5 e5 d4 6 exf6 dxc3 7 fxg7 cxd2+ 8 ♕xd2

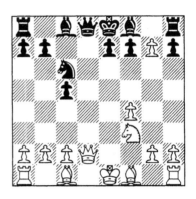

8...♗xg7?!

It is probably better to exchange queens first, in similar fashion to Game 90, so as to expedite development.

9 ♕xd8+ ♘xd8 10 ♗b5+ ♗d7 11 ♗xd7+ ♔xd7 12 c3 f5

Maybe eyeing the e4-square as an outpost for the knight.

13 ♗e3 ♔c6 14 0-0-0 ♘f7 15 ♖he1 ♖ad8

On 15...♘d6 16 ♗g1 ♘e4 White challenges the knight with 17 ♘d2 and keeps the edge, but the text affords Miles an even better opportunity which he does not pass over.

16 ♖xd8 ♖xd8

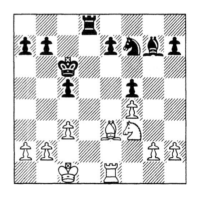

17 ♗xc5!? ♚xc5 18 ♖xe7 ♖f8 19 ♖xb7

White has three healthy pawns already and Gligoric cannot really prevent him taking a fourth, e.g. 19...a6 20 ♘h4! ♚c6 21 ♖a7 ♚b6 22 ♖e7. Accordingly he cedes the a-pawn in an attempt to liberate and co-ordinate his army.

19...♗f6 20 ♖xa7 ♚b6 21 ♖d7 ♚c6 22 ♖d2

The end of his escapade, and now four pawns for a bishop should suffice for victory.

22...♘d6 23 ♖e2 h5 24 h4 ♘e4 25 ♘g5 ♚d5 26 ♚c2 ♖a8 27 a3 ♘d6?

Probably underestimating the response. A far tougher defence was to return a piece for the three white queenside pawns by 27...♘xc3! 28 bxc3 ♖xa3 when the c-pawn will also fall and it is a moot point whether White retains enough to win.

28 ♖e6! ♗xg5 29 ♖e5+ ♚c6 30 hxg5 h4 31 ♚d3 ♖a4?

Another inaccuracy. 31...♖h8 was tougher. Miles now spots a clever way to make progress by getting the rooks off the board.

32 b4! ♖xa3 33 ♖a5

The rook exchange leads to a situation where the knight cannot cope with the far separated passed pawns.

33...♖xa5

33...♖b3? 34 ♚c2.

34 bxa5 ♘e4 35 ♚d4 ♚d6 36 a6 ♘c5 37 a7 ♘e6+ 38 ♚c4 ♘c7 39 g6 ♚e6 40 ♚c5

Now 40...♚f6 41 ♚c6 ♘a8 42 ♚b7 is decisive so Black resigned.

1-0

Game 83
Sax-Van der Wiel
Amsterdam 1983

1 e4 c5 2 f4 e6 3 ♘f3 d5

3...♘e7!? is a rarely tried move.

Hodgson-Plaskett, Lewisham 1982, continued 4 g3 d5 5 e5 ♘ec6 6 ♗g2 ♗e7 7 0-0 0-0 8 d3 b5 9 ♘c3 b4 10 ♘e2 ♘d7 11 ♗e3 a5 12 d4 ♗a6 13 ♖f2 ♕b6 14 dxc5 ♗xc5 15 ♘2d4 f6 16 exf6 ♘xf6 17 ♗h3 e5 18 fxe5 ♘e4 19 c3 bxc3 20 bxc3 ♘xc3 21 ♕b3 ♕xb3 22 axb3 ♘e2+ 23 ♖xe2 ♗xe2 and White resigned.

4 exd5

4 ♘c3 d4 5 ♘e2 ♗e7 6 ♘g3 a6 7 ♘e5 ♘d7 8 ♘xd7 ♗xd7 9 d3 ♕c7 10 ♗e2 f5 was comfortably equal for Black

in Lombardy-Larsen, Buenos Aires 1979, and he went on to draw. Larsen was probably not to happy with that result though, for he won the great majority of his games in that tournament to end up wining it by a three-point margin. The immediate 4 ♗b5+ is considered in the next main game.

4...exd5 5 ♗b5+ ♗d7 6 ♗xd7+

6 ♕e2+ ♕e7 7 ♘e5 has some similarities to lines of the Tarrasch French. Sikora Lerch-Jansa, Warsaw Zonal 1979, continued 7...♘c6 8 ♘c3 ♘f6 9 ♗xc6 ♗xc6 10 0-0 ♘d7 11 ♘xc6 ♕xe2 12 ♘xe2 bxc6 13 b3 ♘b6 14 ♗a3 and a draw was agreed.

6...♘xd7

6...♕xd7 is also playable, transposing to the next main game.

7 0-0 ♗d6 8 d4 ♘e7 9 ♘c3

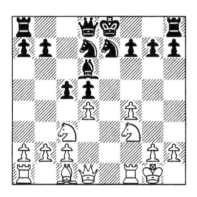

White also got nothing from the opening in Kurajica-Pritchett, London 1976, after 9 ♗e3 c4!? 10 ♘c3 0-0 11 g4 ♖e8 12 ♗d2 ♗b4 13 f5 ♗xc3 14 bxc3 ♘f6 15 ♘e5 ♘e4 16 ♖b1 ♘c6! and Black went on to win.

9...0-0 10 ♔h1 ♘f6 11 ♗e3 ♖c8 12 ♗g1 c4 13 ♘e5 ♗b4 14 ♘e2 ♘e4

Possession of this outpost grants Black a comfortable life.

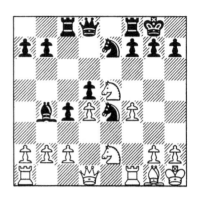

15 f5 f6 16 ♘g4 ♕d7 17 c3 ♗d6 18 ♘e3 g6 19 ♕c2 gxf5 20 g3 ♔h8 21 ♘g2 f4 22 ♘exf4 ♗xf4 23 ♘xf4 ♖ce8 ½-½

Game 84
Wahls-Lerner
Biel open 1994

---

1 e4 c5 2 f4 e6 3 ♘f3 d5 4 ♗b5+ ♗d7

After 4...♘c6 White has a choice between 5 ♘c3, transposing to Games 23-31, and the following alternatives:

a) 5 ♕e2!? was tried in Romero Holmes-Zso.Polgar, Leon 1989, with White establishing a large superiority after 5...d4?! 6 ♗xc6+ bxc6 7 d3 ♘f6 8 0-0 ♗e7 9 ♘bd2 0-0 10 ♘e5 ♕c7 11 ♘dc4 ♘e8 12 ♗d2 and going on to win.

b) Rather than just sit back and watch White set his doubled c-pawns in cement, Black enterprisingly gambitted, a strategy we have already seen reap spectacular rewards, in Westerinen-Abramovic, Moscow 1982, after 5 ♗xc6+ bxc6 6 d3 c4!? 7 dxc4 ♘f6. This proved marvellously successful, for after 8 exd5 cxd5 9 0-0 ♗c5+ 10 ♔h1 0-0 11 ♘e5 ♗a6 12 ♘d3 ♗b6 13 cxd5 ♕xd5

14 ♘c3 ♕f5 Black's active pieces meant that he was doing fine, and he topped things off beautifully after 15 a4 ♖fd8 16 ♘b5 ♖ac8 17 b3 ♘g4 18 ♗d2

with 18...♖xc2! Westerinen resigned, somewhat unsportingly, for 19 ♕xc2 is met by 19...♕h5 20 h3 ♕xh3+!! 21 gxh3 ♗b7+.

5 ♗xd7+ ♕xd7

This recapture permits White to subsequently play ♘e5 with tempo, but that is not such a problem. The clear impression from Games 38 and 39 is that these open e-file positions are not much to concern Black. The alternative recapture 5...♘xd7 is considered in the next game.

6 exd5 exd5 7 ♘e5 ♕c7 8 ♘c3 ♘f6 9 ♕f3

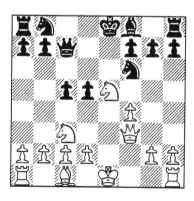

9...♘c6!

Black should give up the d-pawn as 10...♕d6 and 10...♕d8 are both met by the reply 11 ♕e2 ♗e7 12 ♕b5+ ♘bd7 13 ♕xb7.

10 ♘xd5 ♘xd5 11 ♕xd5 ♖d8 12 ♕e4 ♘xe5 13 fxe5 ♖d4 14 ♕e2 ♖d5 15 ♕b5+

In Westerinen-Nei, Espoo 1990, White castled and a draw was swiftly agreed after 15...♕xe5 16 ♕xe5 ♖xe5 17 b3 f6 etc.

15...♕d7 16 ♕xd7+ ♔xd7 17 0-0 ♔e6 18 b3 ♖xe5 19 ♗b2 ♖e2 20 ♖ad1

Varying from a game he had played in the Beijing open the previous year against Qi Jingxuan where he chose 20 ♖ae1. There too nobody's pulse was racing and the struggle came to a draw at move 40.

20...f6 21 ♖f4 ♔f7 22 ♔f1 ♖e8 23 d4 ♗d6 24 ♖f3 ♖d8 25 ♖fd3 ½-½

> *Game 85*
> **Balashov-Sveshnikov**
> *Leningrad 1977*

1 e4 c5 2 f4 e6 3 ♘f3 d5 4 ♗b5+ ♗d7 5 ♗xd7+ ♘xd7 6 d3 ♗d6

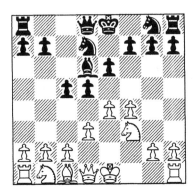

This development definitely looks just as natural as the fianchetto.

7 0-0 ♘e7 8 c4 0-0 9 ♘c3 ♗c7 10 ♕e2 dxc4

Some players have preferred to block the centre but I prefer Sveshnikov's treatment.

11 dxc4 ♗a5

An unusual posting.

12 ♘d1 ♘c6 13 ♘f2 ♕e7 14 ♗e3 ♖ad8 15 e5 f6 16 ♘e4 fxe5 17 ♘xe5 ♘cxe5 18 fxe5 ♖xf1+ 19 ♖xf1 ♖f8 20 ♖xf8+ ♕xf8 21 ♕g4 ♕e7 22 ♘g5 ♘f8

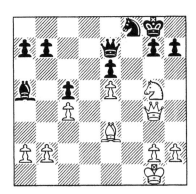

All of White's attempts are parried and Black holds equality.

23 h3 ♗c7 24 ♕e4 ♗d8 25 ♘f3 ♕c7 26 a3 ♗e7 27 h4 ♕b6 28 ♕c2

½-½

Game 86
Westerinen-Watson
Brighton 1983

---

1 e4 c5 2 f4 g6 3 d4 cxd4

3...d5 is the subject of Game 89. Nobody seems to have tried 3...♕a5+!? (which, I suppose, would constitute some species of Pterodactyl) although I should think it is worth a go.

4 ♕xd4 ♘f6 5 e5 ♘c6

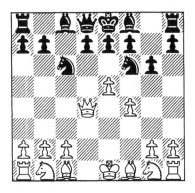

6 ♕d3

White was not very successful with 6 ♕d1 in Turcan-Mocalov, Sala open 1994, which concluded 6...♘h5 7 ♗e3 d6 8 exd6 ♗g7!? 9 ♘c3 exd6 10 ♘f3 0-0 11 ♕d2 ♕a5 12 ♗e2 d5! 13 0-0? d4 14 ♘xd4 ♘xd4 15 ♗xh5 gxh5 0-1. In Westerinen-Arnason, Brighton 1981, a complex situation arose after 7 ♗e2 (instead of 7 ♗e3) 7...d6 8 ♗xh5 ♗f5 9 ♕b3 gxh5 10 ♘f3 ♕d7 11 0-0 e6 12 ♘a3 0-0-0 13 ♗e3 dxe5 14 ♘b5. In Damljanovic-Arsovic, Belgrade 1995, Black played 6...♘e4 instead of 6...♘h5 and after 7 ♗e3 d5 8 ♗d3 ♕a5+ 9 c3 ♗g7 10 ♘f3 f6 11 exf6 ♘xf6 chances were equal.

6...♘g8

6...♘g4 is considered in Game 88.

7 ♗d2

In Hodgson-Ortega, Yerevan 1986, the more obvious 7 ♗e3 was tried. After 7...♗g7 8 ♘c3 Black gambitted with 8...d6 9 exd6 ♘f6 10 0-0-0 0-0 and this proved very effective indeed. Hodgson declined the opportunity of playing 11 dxe7 ♕xe7, when Black has good compensation, and instead continued 11 ♘f3 ♗f5 12 ♕d2 ♖c8 13 ♗c5 ♕a5!? 14 dxe7 ♖fe8 15 ♗a3 ♘b4 with an excellent attack which swiftly crashed through: 16 ♗xb4 ♕xb4 17 ♘d4 ♖xe7 18 a3 ♕b6 19 ♗b5 ♖ec7 20 ♖he1 ♖xc3!

21 bxc3 ♘e4 and White went under rapidly, in similar fashion to many a practitioner of the white side of the Yugoslav Attack against the Dragon.

7...♗g7 8 ♗c3

This does not seem a very natural posting to me.

8...d6 9 ♘f3 ♗f5

For 8...♘h6!? see the next main game.

10 ♕b5

This is not what I would call classical chess from White: the queen heads off to a very strange spot.

10...♕d7

In Horn-Züger, Biel 1986, Black retreated with 10...♗d7 and then followed it up with great imagination, 11 exd6 exd6 12 ♗d2 ♘ge7 13 0-0-0 0-0 14 ♕e2 ♗f5 15 h3 ♘b4 16 a3!? a5!?

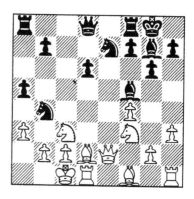

17 ♘e1 ♘ec6!? 18 ♗e3 ♕f6 19 ♘d3 ♘xd3+ 20 cxd3 and they agreed a draw!

11 ♘bd2 ♘h6

This piece is quite misplaced but most of the other features of the position are good for Black.

12 0-0-0 0-0 13 h3 dxe5 14 fxe5 ♕c7 15 g4 a6 16 ♕b3 ♗d7 17 ♘e4 b5!? 18 ♘c5 ♗c8

Temporarily back to base, but Watson has very definite plans of expansion.

19 ♗g2 b4! 20 ♘d4

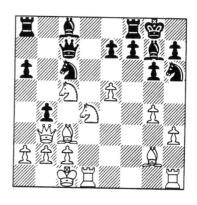

20...♘xe5!

Cutting loose.

21 ♗xa8 bxc3 22 ♕xc3 ♗xg4! 23 hxg4 ♖xa8 24 g5 ♘hg4 25 ♖he1 ♖c8 26 ♘e4 ♘c4 27 ♕g3 ♕xg3 28 ♘xg3 ♘f2

The activity of Watson's knights has proved too much and now he regains his slight material investment with a winning endgame.

29 c3 ♘xd1 30 ♖xd1 h6 31 gxh6 ♗xh6+ 32 ♔b1 ♖d8 33 ♖e1 e5 34 ♘c6 ♖e8 35 ♘e4 ♔g7 36 b3 ♘e3 37 ♘c5 ♖c8 38 c4 ♖xc6 39 ♘d7 ♖e6 0-1

A fine counter-attacking display from William Watson, reminiscent of many victories he has recorded on the black side of the Sicilian Dragon, Yugoslav Attack.

Game 87
Jacobs-Strauss
London Lloyds Bank 1984

---

1 e4 c5 2 f4 g6 3 d4 cxd4 4 ♕xd4 ♘f6 5 e5 ♘c6 6 ♕d3 ♘g8 7 ♗d2 ♗g7 8 ♘f3 d6 9 ♗c3 ♘h6!?

see following diagram

This gambit is not strictly necessary.

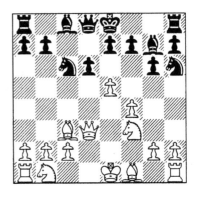

10 exd6

Hodgson-Mokry, Copenhagen 1985, instead saw 10 ♘bd2 0-0 11 0-0-0 dxe5 12 ♘xe5 ♘xe5 13 fxe5 ♕xd3 14 ♗xd3 ♘g4 15 ♖de1 ♘f2 16 ♖hf1 ♘xd3 17 cxd3 ♗e6 when Black was clearly better.

10...0-0 11 ♗xg7 ♔xg7 12 ♘c3 ♗f5

Mokry suggested 12...♘f5!?

13 ♕d2 ♕xd6 14 ♕xd6 exd6 15 0-0-0 ♘g4 16 ♖xd6 ♖ad8 17 ♖xd8 ♖xd8 18 ♗b5 ♘b4 19 ♘h4!

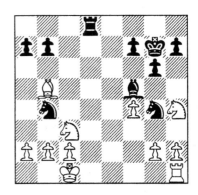

I suspect that Strauss had overlooked this move. Now Black is rather stretched to demonstrate that he has enough for the pawn, and he certainly possesses no chances of being better.

19...♗e6 20 a3 ♘d5 21 ♘xd5 ♖xd5 22 ♗c4 ♖d6 23 ♗e2 ♔f6 24 ♗xg4

♗xg4 25 h3 ♗e2 26 ♖e1 ♗b5 27
♖e3?!

Simply 27 ♘f3 was good.

**27...h6 28 ♘f3 ♗f1! 29 ♘e1 ♖d4
30 f5 gxf5 31 c3 ♖d6 32 ♔c2 ♖c6
33 ♔d2 ♖d6+ 34 ♔c2 ♖c6 35 ♔d2
♖d6+ ½-½**

Game 88
Westerinen-B.Kristensen
Esbjerg 1982

**1 e4 c5 2 f4 g6 3 d4 cxd4 4 ♕xd4
♘f6 5 e5 ♘c6 6 ♕d3 ♘g4!?**

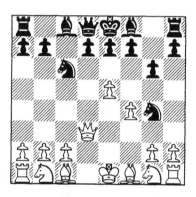

The main drawback of this line will be
the offside position of this piece when it
retreats to h6.

**7 h3 ♘h6 8 g4 ♗g7 9 ♘f3 0-0 10
♗g2 ♕b6 11 ♘c3 d6 12 ♘d5 ♕d8
13 0-0 ♗e6**

A complex setting with some similarities to certain lines of the Pirc Austrian
Attack has arisen. Due to that awkward
knight placing I would not imagine that
Black could be equal here.

**14 c4 ♖c8 15 ♗e3 dxe5 16 fxe5 f6
17 exf6 exf6**

So Black has relieved the cramp a little, but he still suffers from poor co-
ordination.

18 ♘d4!

This is very hard to meet. Kristensen
sheds a pawn, but it is a healthy one for
White to grab.

**18...♗d7 19 ♘xc6 ♗xc6 20 ♗xa7
♘f7 21 ♗d4 ♘e5 22 ♗xe5 fxe5 23
♖xf8+ ♗xf8 24 ♖f1 ♗c5+ 25 ♔h1
♔g7 26 b3 b6 27 ♕e2 ♗d4 28 ♘f6
♗xg2+ 29 ♕xg2 ♖c7 30 a4 ♖f7 31
♘e4 ♖xf1+ 32 ♕xf1**

They say that queen and knight co-
operate together better than queen and
bishop. Westerinen shows how.

**32...♕h4 33 ♔g2 h5 34 ♕e2 hxg4
35 hxg4 ♔f8 36 ♕f3+ ♔e7 37 ♕g3
♕h6 38 g5 ♕h5 39 ♕f3 ♕xf3+ 40
♔xf3**

Better king position, better pawn

structure and a good knight versus a bad bishop, plus the extra pawn, add up to a simple enough win.

40...♔e6 41 ♔g4 ♗e3 42 b4 ♗c1 43 b5 ♗a3 44 ♔f3 ♗e7 45 ♔e3 ♔d7 46 ♔d3 ♔c7 47 c5 ♗xc5 48 a5 ♗e7 49 a6 ♗d8 50 ♔c4 ♔b8 51 ♔d5 ♗c7 52 ♔e6 1-0

Game 89
Hodgson-Van der Wiel
Wijk aan Zee 1986

---

1 e4 c5 2 f4 g6 3 d4 d5!?

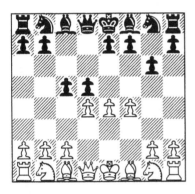

The first appearance of this move. Here too the same idea is known to the theory of the Modern Defence, e.g. 1 e4 g6 2 d4 ♗g7 3 f4 d5!?

4 exd5 ♕xd5 5 ♘c3!?

In Hebden-Simic, Montpellier 1988, a draw was agreed after 5 ♘f3 cxd4 6 ♕xd4 ♕xd4 7 ♘xd4 a6 8 ♘c3.

5...♕xd4 6 ♕f3!?

An interesting gambit. 6 ♕xd4 cxd4 7 ♘b5 ♘a6 was merely level.

6...♘f6 7 ♗e3 ♕b4?

7...♕d6 was a better route to equality, e.g. 8 ♗b5+ ♘bd7 9 ♖d1 ♕c7 10 ♗xc5 ♗g7.

8 ♗b5+ ♘fd7

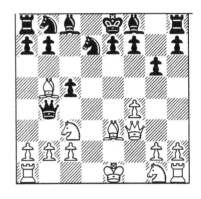

9 ♘ge2!

9 0-0-0 would have allowed more counterplay after 9...♗g7.

9...♗g7

There are mines all over the shop. If 9...a6 10 ♗d2! axb5 11 ♘d5 ♕a4 12 ♘ec3 ♕a5 13 ♘xb5 wins.

10 a3 ♕a5

Not 10...♕xb2? 11 ♔d2 and the lady is trapped, so Black must return the pawn.

11 ♗xc5 0-0 12 ♗b4 ♕d8 13 0-0-0

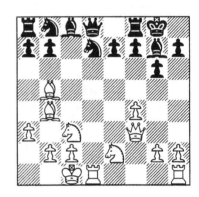

White emerges from the opening with the more imposingly placed pieces and a clear advantage.

13...a5 14 ♗c5 ♘a6 15 ♗f2 ♘c7 16 ♗xd7

Hodgson cashes in. Another good

resolution was 16 ♗b6 ♘xb6 17 ♖xd8.

16...♗xd7 17 ♕xb7 ♖b8 18 ♕a7 ♕c8 19 ♗d4 ♗c6 20 ♗xg7 ♔xg7 21 ♖hg1!

A move with both a defensive and an attacking aspect.

21...e6 22 ♕xa5 ♕b7 23 b3 ♘d5 24 f5!

Increasing his superiority.

24...♔g8

Or 24...gxf5 25 ♘xd5 ♗xd5 26 ♕c3+ ♔g8 (26...f6 27 g4) 27 ♘f4! ♖fc8 28 ♕g3+ ♔f8 29 ♘xd5 exd5 30 ♕d6+ ♔g8 31 ♖d3 and wins.

25 fxe6 fxe6 26 ♕c5 ♘xc3 27 ♘xc3 ♗xg2 28 ♕e3 ♕c6 29 ♔b2 ♖bc8

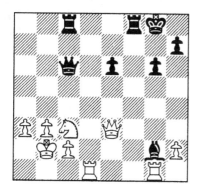

30 ♖d3??

One move chucks away all of the fruits of his labours. The most straightforward win was 30 ♖xg2! ♕xg2 31 ♕xe6+ ♔h8 32 ♕e5+ ♔g8 33 ♖d7 ♖f7 34 ♕e6 ♖cf8 35 ♘d5! and then to push the a-pawn.

30...♗f1!

If the d3-rook moves then 30...♖f3 will be most annoying, so White has to part with the exchange and he shortly afterwards abandons his attempts to win the game.

31 ♖xf1 ♖xf1 32 a4 ♖f7 ½-½

Game 90
Miles-Plachetka
Dubna 1976

1 e4 c5 2 f4 ♘f6 3 ♘c3 d5 4 e5

The most consequent move. White got nothing from 4 ♗b5+ in Maliutin-Mochalov, Minsk 1993, after 4...♗d7 5 ♗xd7+ ♕xd7 6 d3 dxe4 7 ♘xe4 ♘xe4 8 dxe4 ♕xd1+ 9 ♔xd1 ♘c6 10 ♘f3 0-0-0+, or from 4 exd5 ♘xd5 5 ♕f3?! ♘b4! 6 ♗b5+ ♗d7!? 7 ♕xb7 ♘8c6 in Rührig-Kraut, Germany 1989.

4...d4

This is perhaps already an inaccuracy. 4...♘g8 makes sense, as in Zinn-Ubilava, Tbilisi 1972, and 4...♘fd7 5 ♘xd5 ♘xe5 yields White nothing so his best is probably 5 ♘f3 ♘c6 6 d4 with transposition to a Classical French Defence.

5 exf6 dxc3 6 fxg7 cxd2+ 7 ♕xd2 ♕xd2+

In the game Plaskett-Gutman, Hastings 1984/85, 7...♗xg7 was played and White should then have sought a similar type of structural edge to that pursued in the stem games here by 8 ♕xd8+. Instead he kept queens on with 8 ♗d3 ♘c6 9 c3 ♕d5!? 10 ♕e2 ♗f5 11 ♗c4

♕e4 12 ♘f3 ♗h6 13 g3 0-0 14 ♔f2 and was only a little better.

8 ♗xd2 ♗xg7 9 0-0-0 ♗f5

Nor did Black equalise in Bisguier-Hartston, Hastings 1975/76, with 9...♘c6 10 ♗b5 ♗d7 11 ♗e3 b6 (in Kurzuev-Sveshnikov, Russian Championship 1998, Black tried to revive this line with 11...a6 12 ♗c4 ♘d4, but 13 ♗d5 looks like a good response) 12 ♘f3 ♘e5 13 ♗xd7+ ♘xd7 14 ♖he1. His problem is that the pawn structure has saddled him with three pawn islands to White's two, which is a small but significant disadvantage.

10 ♘e2 ♘c6 11 ♗e3 ♖c8?

Allowing a surprising tactical possibility to clinch White's superiority.

12 ♘g3 ♗g4 13 ♖d5!

Threatening the c-pawn and also to win a bishop with 14 ♖g5.

13...♗d4 14 ♗xd4 cxd4? 15 ♗b5

Now the d4-pawn is terribly vulnerable.

15...♗d7 16 ♘e4 ♖d8

see following diagram

17 ♗xc6!

This wins because 17...♗xc6 fails to 18 ♘f6+! gxf6 19 ♖e1+.

17...bxc6 18 ♖xd4 ♗f5 19 ♖a4 ♖d7 20 ♘g3 ♗e6 21 ♖d1 ♖c7 22 f5 ♗c8 23 ♖g4! e5? 24 ♘e4 ♔e7 25 f6+ ♔e6 26 h3 1-0

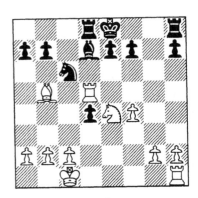

A surprisingly tactical victory in view of the simplified position that came from the opening and the structural nature of White's advantage.

Game 91
Kosten-Arakhamia
Aosta 1990

---

1 e4 c5 2 f4 b6 3 ♘c3

White obviously has a wide choice here:

a) One bizarre continuation is 3 ♗c4!? ♗b7 4 ♗d5!? ♘c6 5 d3 e6 6 ♗xc6 ♗xc6 7 c4 d5 8 ♕e2 dxe4 9 dxe4 ♕h4+ 10 g3 ♕e7 11 ♘c3 ♕b7 12 ♘h3 ♗e7 13 0-0 h5 14 f5 with obscure play in Westerinen-Csom Wiesbaden 1981.

b) White's restrained treatment in Suetin-Csom, Lenk 1993, gave him nothing after 3 ♘f3 ♗b7 4 d3 d5 5 exd5 ♕xd5 6 ♗e2 ♘c6 7 ♘c3 ♕d8 8 0-0 ♘f6.

c) Finally, 3 c4 aims to establish some sort of Maroczy Bind and led to a slight plus for White after 3...♘c6 4 ♘f3 g6 5

d4 cxd4 6 ♘xd4 ♗g7 7 ♘f3!? d6 8 ♗d3
♘f6 9 0-0 0-0 10 ♘c3 ♗b7 11 ♕e1 in
Larsen-Andersson, Geneva 1977.

3...♗b7 4 ♘f3

4 g3 is not very challenging and after
4...♘c6 5 ♗g2 g6 6 ♘h3 ♗g7 7 0-0 d6 8
d3 ♕d7 9 f5 ♘e5 Black was quite comfortable in Valkesalmi-Csom, Jarvenpaa
1985.

4...♘f6!?

5 e5 ♘d5 6 ♗c4 e6 7 0-0 ♗e7

Grabbing the f4-pawn would be crazy.
After 7...♘xf4? 8 d4 and ♘g5 to follow
Black would be crushed.

8 d4 0-0

If now 9 dxc5 Black has a variety of
acceptable responses, e.g. 9...♘xc3 10
bxc3 ♕c7. Kosten seeks a resolution of
the central tension and trusts that his
space advantage will be sufficient to con-
fer an edge.

9 ♘xd5 exd5 10 ♗d3 c4

To push the bishop from its most
menacing diagonal.

11 ♗e2 d6 12 c3

see following diagram

This looks sensible, but Arakhamia
swiftly gets her act together. I prefer 12
f5 when I doubt that Black is okay.

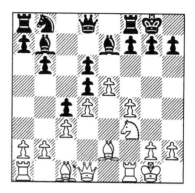

**12...dxe5 13 dxe5 ♗c5+ 14 ♘d4
♘c6 15 ♗e3 f6! 16 e6 f5!**

Now threatening to round it up.

17 g4

What else is there to do?

**17...♕d6 18 gxf5 ♗xd4! 19 ♗xd4
♖xf5 20 ♗g4 ♖xf4 21 ♕e2**

21...♘xd4?!

Not the most efficient. I prefer
21...♖af8 when White has some hopes of
showing compensation for the pawn but
Black is definitely on top.

22 cxd4 ♖e4 23 ♕g2

Intending 24 ♖f7.

**23...♖f8 24 ♖xf8+ ♔xf8 25 ♖f1+
♖f4 26 ♖e1**

It becomes apparent that the e6-pawn
constitutes a humungous asset.

26...♕e7 27 ♕g3 g5 28 h4! h6 29 hxg5 hxg5 30 ♖e5 ♗c6 31 ♗h5 ♖f6

She cannot keep him out any longer.

32 ♕xg5 ♗e8 33 ♖f5

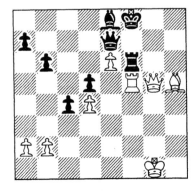

see following diagram

This is decisive. White exchanges down to a queen and pawn endgame where he has a huge passed pawn on e7.

33...♖xf5 34 ♕xf5+ ♔g7 35 ♗xe8 ♕xe8 36 ♕e5+ ♔h6 37 e7 ♔h7 38 ♕e6 ♔g7 39 ♔g2 1-0

The king is coming.

Summary

2...e6 and 3...d5 is a perfectly good way to meet 2 f4 and, if White tries to force the issue with 4 exd5 or 4 ♗b5+, Black appears to be fine. White's best may well be 4 ♘c3, probably transposing into lines from the previous chapter. 2...g6 is also quite reasonable and, as 3 d4 does not seem overly troubling for Black, White's best may well be to transpose into lines considered earlier in the book.

1 e4 c5 2 f4

2...♘c6

    2...e6 3 ♘f3 d5 *(D)*

        4 exd5 – *Game 83*

        4 ♗b5+ ♗d7 5 ♗xd7+

            5...♕xd7 – *Game 84*

            5...♘xd7 – *Game 85*

    2...g6 3 d4 *(D)*

        3...cxd4 4 ♕xd4 ♘f6 5 e5 ♘c6 6 ♕d3 *(D)*

            6...♘g8 7 ♗d2 ♗g7 8 ♗c3

                8...d6 – *Game 86*

                8...♘h6 – *Game 87*

            6...♘g4 – *Game 88*

        3...d5 – *Game 89*

    2...♘f6 – *Game 90*

    2...b6 – *Game 91*

3 ♘f3 d6

    3...♘f6 – *Game 82*

4 ♗b5 ♗d7 – *Game 81*

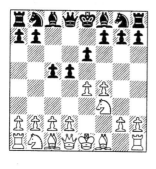

    3...d5   *3 d4*   *6 ♕d3*

INDEX OF COMPLETE GAMES